PRAYER

Previously Published Records of Building Bridges Seminars

The Road Ahead: A Christian–Muslim Dialogue,
Michael Ipgrave, Editor (London: Church House, 2002)

Scriptures in Dialogue: Christians and Muslims Studying the Bible and the Qur'ān Together,
Michael Ipgrave, Editor (London: Church House, 2004)

Bearing the Word: Prophecy in Biblical and Qur'ānic Perspective,
Michael Ipgrave, Editor (London: Church House, 2005)

Building a Better Bridge: Muslims, Christians and the Common Good,
Michael Ipgrave, Editor
(Washington, DC: Georgetown University Press, 2008)

Justice and Rights: Christian and Muslim Perspectives,
Michael Ipgrave, Editor
(Washington, DC: Georgetown University Press, 2009)

Humanity: Texts and Contexts: Christian and Muslim Perspectives,
Michael Ipgrave and David Marshall, Editors
(Washington, DC: Georgetown University Press, 2011)

Communicating the Word: Revelation, Translation, and Interpretation in Christianity and Islam,
David Marshall, Editor
(Washington, DC: Georgetown University Press, 2011)

Science and Religion: Christian and Muslim Perspectives,
David Marshall, Editor
(Washington, DC: Georgetown University Press, 2012)

Tradition and Modernity: Christian and Muslim Perspectives,
David Marshall, Editor
(Washington, DC: Georgetown University Press, 2012)

For further information about the Building Bridges process, please visit:
http://berkleycenter.georgetown.edu/resources/networks/building ebridges

PRAYER

Christian and Muslim Perspectives

A record of the tenth Building Bridges Seminar
Convened by the Archbishop of Canterbury
Georgetown University School of Foreign Service in Qatar
May 17–19, 2011

Edited by David Marshall
and Lucinda Mosher

Georgetown University Press
Washington, DC

Library of Congress Cataloging-in-Publication Data

Building Bridges Seminar (10th : 2011 : Qatar)
Prayer : Christian and Muslim perspectives : a record of the tenth Building Bridges Seminar, convened by the Archbishop of Canterbury, Georgetown University School of Foreign Service in Qatar 17–19 May 2011 / edited by David Marshall and Lucinda Mosher.
p. cm.
Includes bibliographical references and index.
SBN 978-1-58901-677-4 (pbk. : alk. paper)
1. Islam—Relations—Christianity—Congresses. 2. Christianity and other religions—Islam—Congresses. 3. Prayer—Christianity—Congresses. 4. Prayer—Islam—Congresses. I. Marshall, David. II. Mosher, Lucinda. III. Title.
BP172.B834 2011
248.3'2—dc23

2012049969

∞ This book is printed on acid-free paper meeting the requirements of the American National Standard for Permanence in Paper for Printed Library Materials.

15 14 13 9 8 7 6 5 4 3 2 First printing

Printed in the United States of America

Contents

Participants and Contributors

Muhammad Abdel Haleem
King Fahd Professor of Islamic Studies, School of Oriental and African Studies, University of London

Asma Afsaruddin
Professor of Islamic Studies, Department of Near Eastern Languages and Cultures, Indiana University

Akintunde Akinade
Visiting Professor of Theology, Georgetown University School of Foreign Service, Qatar

Seyed Amir Akrami
Researcher, Iranian Institute of Philosophy, Tehran

Rkia Elraoui Cornell
Senior Lecturer and Language Coordinator in Arabic, Department of Middle Eastern and South Asian Studies, Emory University, Atlanta, Georgia

Vincent J. Cornell
Asa Griggs Candler Professor of Arabic and Islamic Studies, Department of Middle Eastern and South Asian Studies, Emory University, Atlanta, Georgia

Caner Dagli
Assistant Professor of Religious Studies, College of the Holy Cross, Worcester, Massachusetts

Gavin D'Costa
Professor of Catholic Theology, University of Bristol, U.K.

Susan Eastman
Assistant Professor of the Practice of Bible and Christian Formation, Duke University, Durham, North Carolina

David Ford
Regius Professor of Divinity, University of Cambridge, U.K.

Lucy Gardner
Tutor in Christian Doctrine, St. Stephen's House, University of Oxford, U.K.

Timothy Gianotti
Noor Fellow in Islamic Studies, York University, Toronto, Canada

Toby Howarth
Secretary for Inter Religious Affairs, Church of England

Muhammad K. Khalifa
Professor of Comparative Religions, Faculty of Islamic Studies, Qatar Foundation

Daniel A. Madigan
Director of Graduate Studies, Department of Theology, Georgetown University, Washington, DC

Jane Dammen McAuliffe
President, Bryn Mawr College, Pennsylvania

Ibrahim Mogra
Chairman, Mosque and Community Affairs Committee, Muslim Council of Britain

M. M. Dheen Mohamed
Associate Dean for Academic Affairs, College of Sharia and Islamic Studies, Qatar University

Lucinda Mosher
Faculty Associate for Interfaith Studies, Hartford Seminary, Hartford, Connecticut

Michael Plekon
Professor of Sociology and Anthropology, Program in Religion and Culture, Baruch College of the City University of New York

Sajjad Rizvi
Associate Professor of Islamic Intellectual History, University of Exeter, U.K.

Philip Seddon
Formerly Tutor, Southern Theological and Educational Training Scheme, Salisbury, U.K.

Recep Şentürk
Director General and Dean of Graduate Studies, Alliance of Civilizations Institute, Fatih Sultan Mehmet Vakif Üniversitesi, Istanbul

Reza Shah-Kazemi
Research Associate, Institute of Ismaili Studies, London

Samy Shehata
Dean, Anglican Pro-Cathedral of St Mark, Alexandria, Egypt

Philip Sheldrake
Senior Research Fellow, Cambridge Theological Federation, U.K.

Mona Siddiqui
Professor of Islamic Studies and Public Understanding,
University of Glasgow, U.K.

Janet Soskice
Professor of Philosophical Theology, University of Cambridge, U.K.

Michael Welker
Professor of Systematic Theology, University of Heidelberg, Germany

Rowan Williams
Archbishop of Canterbury, Church of England

Timothy Wright
Abbot Emeritus, Ampleforth Abbey, U.K.

Jihad Youssef
Monk, Deir Mar Musa el-Habashi, Syria

Rkia Elraoui Cornell was prevented from attending the seminar, but her paper was presented at it on her behalf and is included in this volume. Vincent Cornell and Gavin D'Costa were also prevented from attending, but their brief contributions to the volume's concluding section, "Personal Reflections on Prayer," are included.

Introduction

DAVID MARSHALL

THIS VOLUME presents a record of the tenth Building Bridges seminar for Christian and Muslim scholars, on the theme of "Prayer," convened by the Archbishop of Canterbury, Dr. Rowan Williams, and held at the Georgetown University School of Foreign Service in Qatar, May 17–19, 2011.

Following an established pattern, after an opening day of public lectures, the second and third days were spent in private sessions. This volume follows the structure of the seminar closely. The preface draws on comments made by Rowan Williams in introducing the seminar. After reviewing the development of the Building Bridges process to this point, he cites George Herbert's description of prayer as "God's breath in man returning to its birth," which reminds us that we pray "because God breathes into us a capacity to be related to him, to serve and love him, to be united, as far as any creature can be, with his will, his purpose, his life." Prayer is also "about the way in which the self-giving outgoing of God becomes real in us and for us, so as to transform our own sense of ourselves, of what is possible for us, of what is owed to one another, of how we look at the world." The theme of prayer thus relates to all the other topics on which past Building Bridges seminars have focused, putting all those other discussions "into a new and greater context."

Part I ("Surveys") consists of revised versions of the first day's lectures, which were given in three pairs. Michael Plekon's emphasis is on "people who pray," rather than on an abstract theory of prayer; he selects four examples of Christians who "*became* what they prayed, *lived* their prayer," uniting love of God and love of neighbor. Plekon's essay is richly illustrated with quotations from his chosen examples: St. Seraphim of Sarov, Paul Evdokimov, Mother Maria Skobtsova, and Thomas Merton (whose correspondence with Abdul Aziz about Sufism is particularly noted). Foundational to Shah-Kazemi's essay on a Qur'ānic theology of prayer is the theme of the knowledge of God. Referring to the *ḥadīth qudsī* in which God says "I was a hidden treasure and I willed to be known," Shah-Kazemi argues that "worship becomes the primary means by which the divine purpose of creation is achieved, and by which knowledge of God . . . is attained." Furthermore, God "knows Himself through us in the very measure of our self-effacement [*fanāʾ*]." Other themes woven into his discussion are the vision of God, *dhikr* (the invocation of the name of God), the theurgic power of the name of God, gratitude, and loving emulation of the Prophet.

In the second pair of essays M. M. Dheen Mohamed and Philip Sheldrake address the practice of prayer in Christianity and Islam, respectively. Dheen Mohamed distinguishes between *ṣalāt*, *duʿāʾ* and *dhikr*, explaining the basis of each in the Qurʾān and ḥadīth and noting that *dhikr* is "the very purpose" of *ṣalāt* and is "in one sense the supreme form of prayer." After some discussion of Sufi approaches, the essay concludes with comments on the negative impact of modernity and puritanical reform movements on Muslim prayer, particularly in the author's native Sri Lanka. After introductory comments on the relationship between prayer and theology, Sheldrake, speaking out of the Western Catholic tradition, surveys six styles of prayer: common prayer, whether spontaneous or formalized in liturgical worship; *lectio divina*, the prayerful reading of scripture; unceasing prayer, as in the Jesus Prayer ("Lord Jesus Christ, Son of God, have mercy on me a sinner"); popular devotions, encompassing shrines, pilgrimages, outdoor dramas, and religious art; meditation, both in mediaeval and modern forms; and informal, conversational prayer. He offers a more extended account of one particular spiritual tradition, Ignatian prayer. Concluding comments touch on locations for prayer and the experience of men and women in prayer.

The third pair of essays offers a Muslim perspective on Christian prayer and, conversely, a Christian perspective on Muslim prayer. Caner Dagli suggests that the Qurʾān presents a "nuanced and complex" picture of Christianity; it generally "praises Christians in their devotion to God, while . . . condemning them for their theology." He discusses the Christian understanding of sacraments, arguing that there is perhaps more in common with the Muslim understanding of the five pillars than is usually imagined. Turning to the Lord's Prayer, Dagli focuses on how to understand "Father" and the relationship between the petition for forgiveness and Christian thought on atonement. The final section responds to the links between Christian prayer and Trinitarian theology. Daniel Madigan's essay contrasts the rich physical expressiveness of Islamic worship with a Christian tendency to let word eclipse gesture; he also compares Islam's sense of lay responsibility with the dependence of Catholic Christianity on priestly ministry. Madigan notes the "robust masculinity" and the naturally public nature of Muslim worship while also mentioning "the relegation of women to a position out of sight."

After touching on memory (*anamnesis*, *dhikr*) and on Muslims and Christians praying together, Madigan concludes with reflections on the essence of the Christian experience of prayer.

In the response that follows, Rowan Williams reflects on the lectures of the seminar's opening day and some of the discussion that the lectures generated. He identifies and comments on five key themes: friendship, knowledge, desire, protest, and unity (both the unity of God and our unity with God).

Part II records proceedings of the seminar's second day, when the focus was on scripture and prayer. Susan Eastman and Rkia Elraoui Cornell introduce key themes from the best-known prayers in the Bible and the Qur'ān: the Lord's Prayer and *al-Fātiḥa*. In a second pair of essays Philip Seddon and Asma Afsaruddin comment respectively on Romans chapter 8 and Qur'ān 3:190–94 and 29:45, among the best-known scriptural passages about prayer. These four essays each served as an introduction to an extended period of study in small groups of the scriptural texts in question.

Part III has the same structure as part II but with the focus now moving to how Christians and Muslim learn to pray. In the first pair of essays Lucy Gardner and Ibrahim Mogra reflect on how Christians and Muslims are taught to pray, with particular reference to childhood formation, while in the second pair Timothy Wright and Timothy Gianotti look at approaches to growing in prayer, and methods and disciplines adopted by those seeking to develop deeper lives of prayer.

The volume contains three more pieces. In "Conversations in Qatar" Lucinda Mosher draws on notes taken in the group discussions to offer an account of the main points emerging from them. In his afterword Rowan Williams offers brief concluding thoughts on the seminar as a whole. This is followed by a collection of personal reflections on prayer written by participants before the seminar and circulated within the seminar group.

This volume seeks to give some impression of the scope and depth of the conversations that unfolded over the days of this seminar, within an atmosphere of openness that had been encouraged by the circulation of the personal reflections just mentioned. As at all Building Bridges seminars, discussion moved naturally between commonalities and areas of difference, including differences not just between Islam and Christianity but also between different traditions within each faith. Joint Christian–Muslim prayer was not organized, but there were opportunities for Christians to attend Muslim devotions and vice versa, which greatly enriched discussions. As Rowan Williams had suggested at the seminar's launch, reflecting together on prayer led participants into many of the deepest questions in the two faiths; it was thus quite natural that the final plenary discussion yielded an extraordinarily long agenda for the continuing work of dialogue to which the Building Bridges process is committed.

Acknowledgments

Sincere thanks are due to His Highness Sheikh Hamad bin Khalifa Al-Thani, Amir of the State of Qatar, for the generous hospitality that made it possible for the tenth Building Bridges seminar to be held in Doha. The Georgetown University School of Foreign Service in Qatar was an excellent location for the seminar: many thanks are due to Mehran Kamrava (interim dean at the time), Maya Primorac, and all their colleagues who made us so welcome. As ever, thanks go to the president of Georgetown University, John J. DeGioia, for his continuing support for Building Bridges over many years and for making the publication of this volume possible. The seminar could not have happened without much hard work by members of the Archbishop's staff at Lambeth Palace: particular thanks to Guy Wilkinson, Toby Howarth, Clemmie Jones, and Tess Young. Thanks also, once again, to Richard Brown and the staff of Georgetown University Press.

Note on Translations of the Bible and the Qur'ān

When not indicated otherwise in the notes, the translations of the Qur'ān in this volume are either from M. A. S. Abdel Haleem, *The Qur'an: a New Translation* (Oxford: Oxford University Press, 2004) or are the author's own translation, and translations of the Bible are either from the New Revised Standard Version or are the author's own translation.

Preface

ROWAN WILLIAMS

In a sense it is true to say that Doha is the seedbed for the Building Bridges enterprise over the years. The success of the seminar held here in April 2003 encouraged all those who took part in it to believe that it was possible, desirable, and indeed necessary that the conversations we had begun should be continued. In the years that have passed since then the Building Bridges seminars have built up a very distinctive style, involving working together, studying sacred texts together, and above all learning to listen to one another speaking to God and also to watch one another speaking to God. It is a style that has been patient, affirming, and celebrating.

So Doha has a great deal to answer for, and we have a great deal for which to be grateful, particularly to His Highness the Amir. Without his invitation to Qatar in 2003, that first seminar would not have been what it was. And his generous invitation to return has at last borne fruit this year. It has been a great pleasure to be the recipients of his warm hospitality once again. It has also been extremely significant that, with the support of His Highness, recent years have seen such encouraging developments in inter faith understanding in this historic heartland of Islam. I refer especially to the fruitful work of the Doha International Center for Interfaith Dialogue. We can only applaud such initiatives and ask for God's blessings upon them.

Over the years we have also developed an enormous debt to Georgetown University, and this year we are delighted to be meeting at the splendid campus of the Georgetown School of Foreign Service in Qatar. Our warm thanks go to all those who have made this seminar possible here. We remain deeply grateful to the president of Georgetown University, John J. DeGioia, for the vision, enthusiasm, and generosity with which he has supported Building Bridges.

In these last eight years Building Bridges has established itself as a distinctive enterprise in inter religious conversation—even though it has never sought to be very large or particularly influential in the world's terms. We have thought it was worth talking to one another whether or not we got into the newspapers. Enough things get into the newspapers already, in all conscience, for us not to want to add too much extra, though it is often sad that the good news of something like Building Bridges does not get into the public press as much as we might wish. But we do it because it is worth it, because we love it, and because we love each other.

We love each other as communities. I believe that, in spite of all the rhetoric that sounds around the world, it remains true that in so many contexts around the globe Christian and Muslim communities are characterized locally by real mutual love, appreciation, and support. In the very difficult days in some countries in recent months, perhaps the most moving thing for many of us Christians has been to see the generous support of local Muslims who have stepped out, who have taken risks to defend their Christian neighbors in Pakistan, in Egypt, and in other places. The importance of this to us cannot easily be exaggerated. It is a sign of that same love and trust that we seek to build up in Building Bridges. We are able to do it with confidence because we know that in so many contexts that is the truth on the ground.

But we have also come to love one another within the context of the Building Bridges seminars. We have learned so gratefully from one another something of the things of God. We have learned to appreciate cultural and theological riches. We have simply learned to enjoy one another's company as human beings. For that, I thank God and I thank all the participants.

The life of an Archbishop has the occasional little trial or difficulty in it, and not every international visit immediately fills an Archbishop with enthusiasm and joy. Building Bridges, however, has not been one of those meetings that cast a cloud before them. On the contrary, each time I have emerged enriched and delighted by what we have shared. So for me, speaking personally, in recent years this has been a constant source of nourishment.

Over the years we have touched on a number of quite varied topics. We have looked at issues of public concern; we have looked at how we understand human nature, justice, poverty; we have tackled questions about religion and science, tradition and modernity; we have returned to classical theological themes such as prophecy. But, again and again, we come back to the experience and the challenge, when we meet, of seeing one another praying. So it seemed very natural that at some point we would have to address the question of what we understand by prayer.

It is sometimes said by Christians that Christian doctrine began quite simply through Christians reflecting on what happened when they prayed. I would be interested to hear what our Muslim friends have to say about that as a way into the subject. But to put things in this way is simply to illustrate the central significance of the question.

In the public lectures that open our seminar we shall be hearing not only from inside each tradition but also something about our perceptions of one another. Quite frequently, in inter faith encounter, one of the first challenges that has to be overcome is misperception, misreading. We regularly assume that we know better than the other what the other is really doing. And if there is one thing that inter faith dialogue is dedicated to overcoming, surely it is that assumption. So we shall be hearing about perspectives and understandings of one another today as well as hearing from the heart of each tradition.

There is a particular phrase used by George Herbert, the seventeenth-century priest and poet, that opens up immense horizons, which I hope will be in our minds this week. In his poem "Prayer (1)" Herbert describes prayer as "God's breath in man returning to its birth." This is a reminder that we pray because God gives us the grace to pray; we pray because God breathes into us a capacity to be related to him, to serve and love him, to be united, as far as any creature can be, with his will, his purpose, his life.

To speak about prayer is to speak about where and who we are, not simply to speak about an activity that begins and ends; it is certainly not simply to speak about a way in which human beings attempt to get in touch with a remote or distant God. Prayer is about the way in which a relationship is realized and sustained. Prayer is about the way in which the self-giving outgoing of God becomes real in us and for us, so as to transform our own sense of ourselves, of what is possible for us, of what is owed to one another, of how we look at the world. To learn to pray is to learn to inhabit the world in a particular way, and to see the world in a particular way.

So in reflecting as we do this week about prayer, we reflect not simply on one isolated subject in Christian or Muslim discourse. We reflect on what it is for a human creature to be related to the Creator. We reflect on what God expects from the human creation and what God has made possible. As we enter more deeply into that mystery, we enter more deeply, surely, into an understanding of all those other topics we have discussed such as justice, human nature, tradition and modernity, religion and science. We put all those discussions into a new and greater context. To pray, we believe, is to be in touch with our deepest nature and our truest destiny as human beings. Without being in touch in that way with what is most true in us, we shall not be able effectively to engage our world, to bring peace and reconciliation where it is needed, to bring justice in situations of oppression, and hope in situations of despair.

This week we are addressing some very fundamental questions. As we do so, we ask for your prayers that in the days ahead we may indeed be drawn deeper into the heart of our inspiration and our motivation as human beings seeking to serve our Creator.

Note

This preface brings together, in lightly edited form, comments made on two occasions on May 16 and 17, 2011, before the beginning of the seminar.

PART I

Surveys

Lived Prayer

Some Examples from the Christian Tradition

MICHAEL PLEKON

> Anthony called his two companions . . . and said to them, "Always breathe Christ."
>
> Athanasius of Alexandria[1]

The Long Search, a world religions documentary series, included an episode focused on Christianity in which the host, Ronald Eyre, asked a Benedictine monk, Father Miguel, "What is prayer?" They were at the monastery of Montserrat, surrounded by pilgrims lighting candles, attending the services, singing hymns, and kissing the image of the Virgin Mary long revered there. The pilgrims were also laughing, enjoying the sun and picnic lunches outside the monastery church. The host observed that it seemed like a summer day at the beach or in a park: what did all this have to do with prayer? The monk smiled at the question and said that there was no such thing as prayer, or for that matter, faith, hope, or love. These did not exist in the abstract, in theory, in definitions, although there were thousands of pages of efforts to describe and define prayer.

I very much agree with Father Miguel. As he went on to say, "There are only people who pray, have faith, hope, and love, and live accordingly." Since, in recent years, my writing has consisted of listening to the voices of individuals looking for God, trying to live holy lives, I will do the same here with some favorite persons of faith.[2] Of course, much has been said about prayer in more formal theology, from the scriptures through the teachers of the early church and the desert mothers and fathers and many other writers. The procession of writers marches through history—from Augustine to Basil the Great, from Benedict to Teresa of Avila, from Julian of Norwich to Newman. In the twentieth century the cloud of witnesses includes figures such as Charles de Foucauld, Simone Weil, Etty Hillesum, Dietrich Bonhoeffer, Anthony Bloom, Mother Teresa of Calcutta, and Henri Nouwen.[3]

There are so many voices to which we could listen, but here I will propose only a few, some of whom may be less known but all of them persons of faith who have spoken very powerfully about life with God and prayer, and who lived what they said, incarnated what they prayed. The first is St. Seraphim of Sarov (1759–1833), one of the most beloved of Russian saints, in many ways very much like Francis of Assisi, and of a similar stature. He is reported to have said,

> The true aim of our Christian life is the acquisition of the Holy Spirit. As for fasts, and vigils, and prayer, and almsgiving, and every good deed done because of Christ, they are only means of acquiring the Holy Spirit. . . . This Holy Spirit, the All-Powerful, is given to us . . . he takes up his abode in us and prepares in our souls and bodies a dwelling place for the Father. . . . Of course, every good deed done because of Christ gives us the grace of the Holy Spirit, but prayer gives it to us most of all, for it is always at hand, so to speak, as an instrument for acquiring the grace of the Spirit. For instance, you would like to go to church, but there is no church or the service is over; you would like to give alms to a beggar, but there isn't one, or you have nothing to give. . . . You would like to do some other good deed in Christ's name, but either you have not the strength or the opportunity is lacking. This certainly does not apply to prayer. Prayer is always possible for everyone, rich and poor, noble and humble, strong and weak, healthy and sick, righteous and sinful.[4]

What Seraphim says here has been cited numerous times because of the clarity and simplicity he brings not only to prayer but to living life in, with, and for God and our neighbor. While we cannot go into the details of Seraphim's biography, suffice it to say he practiced what he preached and became what he prayed. The words quoted here come from his well-known conversation with a friend, Motovilov, in a snowy forest. Seraphim was filled with joy and was radiant from within with a light that warmed and calmed.[5] But he told his friend that the same radiance was emanating from him too. It was of no significance that Seraphim was a monk and priest and his friend a layperson, for the Spirit dwells in us all. Every day of the year Seraphim would use the Easter greeting, "Christ is risen!" and would call every person he met "My joy." He also said, "Acquire peace within and a multitude of people around you will find their salvation in you."

Seraphim takes for granted that the whole point of our spiritual life is living in the Spirit of God. As he says often in the conversation, we are given the Spirit from the start, and as the Eastern Church prayer says, the Spirit "is everywhere, filling all things." We are always in the Spirit or, better, the Spirit and therefore the Father and Christ are in us, with us. Notice the ease with which the Spirit, Christ, and the Father are mentioned. The Spirit is given and makes his home in us; the Father thus dwells in us, and Christ is wherever the Father and the Spirit are. Father, Son, and Spirit are one and always present to us, prayer being our presence before God and God's being present to us. Or, following St. Paul, whom Seraphim cites frequently, he says: "The grace of the Holy Spirit, given at baptism in the name of the Father and of the Son and of the Holy Spirit, continues to shine in our heart as divine light in spite of our falls and the darkness of our soul. It is this grace that cries in us to the Father: 'Abba, Father!' and who reclothes the soul in the incorruptible garment woven for us by the Holy Spirit."[6]

If prayer is always possible for everyone, then prayer must be like our very breathing, it must be our living in and with and for God and our neighbor. Thus, whether we are praying in a church service or not, whether we are giving to those in need or not, prayer is always possible. There is no single reason for praying, any more than there is one reason for living. And if prayer is a way of life, is there anything that cannot be prayed about or prayed for except something evil? The seventh-century saint Isaac the Syrian says that prayer gives us "a merciful heart . . . the heart's burning for the sake of the entire creation, for men, for birds, for animals, for demons, and for every created thing; and by the recollection and sight of them the eyes of a merciful man pour forth abundant tears. From the strong and vehement mercy which grips his heart and from his great compassion, his heart is humbled and he cannot bear to hear or to see any injury or slight sorrow in creation."[7] Prayer puts us in communion not only with God but with all others, with all of God's children and all of God's creatures.

Perhaps it is a surprise that for these two spiritual fathers, one from more than a thousand years ago and the other from the recent past, the point of prayer is love—God's limitless, forgiving, wildly compassionate love is given to each of us.[8] And in turn, you and I are to love that way—as God loves. No mention of enemies or heretics, no anxiety over rules and law and rubrics—so very different from the practice of "religion" we often encounter, so open and free. Prayer always opens us up to God, to ourselves, and to others. It is a caricature to consider others or the world around us as distractions, intrusions of something profane into what is sacred. Prayer linked every one of the persons of prayer we are listening to here with many sisters and brothers, near and far away, with those in need, as well as those needing prayer because of their power.

Coming even closer to our time, we can listen to a lay theologian, a married man and father, who worked with the French Resistance to save people during the Second World War and later administered hostels for the homeless, the poor, and foreign students. Paul Evdokimov (1901–70), a Russian émigré who made his home in France, argued that in the context of the United Nations, the richer nations of the world should tax themselves so their impoverished sisters and brothers in the Third World could eat, work, and live. A teacher and writer unafraid to comment on global economics, he was uniquely able to write the following:

> A saint is not a superman, but one who discovers and lives his truth as a liturgical being. The best definition of a human being comes from the liturgy . . . "I will sing to the Lord as long as I live". . . . It is not enough to say prayers; one must become, be prayer, prayer incarnate. It is not enough to have moments of praise. All of life, each act, every gesture, even the smile of the human face, must become a hymn of adoration, an offering, a prayer. One should offer not what one has, but what one is.[9]

For Evdokimov, prayer is not only participation in the liturgy in church but a living out of that liturgy afterward, in all of one's everyday life. He sees liturgy as essential. It is like the embrace and kiss of the beloved, eating and conversing and being with the friend, the spouse, the lover, the beloved child. Evdokimov knew John Chrysostom's powerful statement that after celebrating the sacrament on the altar in church, we must continue to celebrate it in the heart of every sister or brother we meet. Just as the two great commandments bring together love of God and love of neighbor, so too the Eucharist, the heart of Christian worship, involves not only receiving the bread and cup of Christ's body and blood but venerating the neighbor in whom God dwells. As we shall see later, Mother Maria Skobtsova wrote eloquently on the indivisibility of these great loves.

Evdokimov follows the biblical vision in seeing prayer as cosmic, extending the presence and praise of God into all corners of life. Further, while prayer connects us with God and others, our prayer is the means by which God transforms us, mends that which is broken, heals that which is infirm, and makes of us an encounter with God for those around us.[10] This is indeed the universal teaching of the Christian tradition, whether in the Catholic, Orthodox, or Reformation churches, in the East or the West, or in the northern or southern hemispheres.

Our next example of lived prayer, Mother Maria Skobtsova (1891–1945), is a woman of our time. Poet, wife, mother, intellectual, and activist for the suffering, her personality and her work embody the diversity, the creativity, and the critical spirit of the modern and postmodern eras. Again, time prevents delving into her fascinating life, full of twists and turns almost worthy of dramatization. Swept up and almost executed twice in the Russian revolution, her exile landed her in Paris in the miseries of the Great Depression and then the Nazi occupation during the Second World War. The last years she spent as a professed nun, not cloistered but running a hostel for the poor, unemployed, and suffering. And when she, her chaplain, and staff attempted to hide and protect the targets of the Gestapo—Jewish people and others—they were arrested and died in concentration camps. She and three companions were formally recognized as saints in 2004.

A prolific writer despite her many responsibilities leading the hostels in Paris, Mother Maria took particular aim at the demands on the Christian tradition of life in the mid twentieth century. Like others in a renaissance of religious reflection in the Russian émigré communities in Paris, she understood the life of faith not as an escape but an engagement with all the wonders and horrors of her time. She often spoke of a believer being "Christified"—more than just christened into a religion but, following St. Paul's teaching, being transformed by Christ who lives within.[11] Here is an echo of the way in which the Father, the Son, and the Spirit are experienced as one, and the relationship that is prayer is with the Father, through the Son, and in the Spirit.[12]

Holiness is a gift from God, and being a saint is not some feat of heroic virtue. Rather, every person can sing to God in words but also in all the activities of everyday life, for example, by caring for a child or an elderly person, cooking, cleaning, producing goods, or providing services. Not only does one witness to or become an image of God by prayer and prayerful living, one also becomes a point of encounter. If God dwells in us, then through us God can listen to, touch, heal, and forgive those around us. Observing that during services the priest or deacon in the Eastern Church censes not just the altar and icons but also the faithful gathered in prayer, Mother Maria says this is because these women and men gathered in prayer as well as all the others they will encounter in loving service are "living icons of God."[13]

Well acquainted with the traditional piety of her Russian Orthodox Church, Mother Maria was critical of various forms of religiosity that were ends in themselves, whether ascetic, aesthetic, intellectual or national. Having argued in her essays for the impossibility of separating love of God and of the neighbor, she also rejected the division between liturgy and life, between prayer and action. She echoed Chrysostom's phrase by claiming that, from the start, Christians celebrated another liturgy "outside the temple or church building." As the following quotation makes clear, Christ's new commandment of love had to be the heart of all we do: for Mother Maria, prayer has as much to do with the neighbor—our sister or brother—as with God and with ourselves.

> The way to God lies through love of people. At the Last Judgment I shall not be asked whether I was successful in my ascetic exercises, nor how many bows and prostrations I made. Instead I shall be asked, Did I feed the hungry, clothe the naked, visit the sick and the prisoners. That is all I shall be asked. About every poor, hungry and imprisoned person the Savior says "I": "I was hungry and thirsty, I was sick and in prison." To think that he puts an equal sign between himself and anyone in need. . . . I always knew it, but now it has somehow penetrated to my sinews. It fills me with awe.[14]

Even closer to our time is the American Roman Catholic monk and writer Thomas Merton (1915–68). Few contemporary religious authors have as many works still in print almost a half century after their death as Merton.[15] Much like some of the other voices we have heard, Merton's life was a true journey—from a romantic, idealized view of monastic life in his first best seller, *The Seven Story Mountain*, to his later controversial stances in the civil rights, disarmament, and antiwar movements. He became a critic of the church's lethargy in the face of the late twentieth century's challenges. But he also abandoned his early idealizing of monastic life and became an important voice for renewal. He was able as a writer to talk about the spiritual life in general, and prayer in particular, in a most accessible way. Over his life he wrote a prodigious amount of essays, books, reviews, and poetry as well as maintaining a gigantic correspondence.

One of Merton's correspondents was Abdul Aziz, a civil servant in Karachi, Pakistan, whose dedication to Sufism became the bond between them. The scholar Louis Massignon gave Aziz Merton's name and address, and for eight years they exchanged letters and books. In response to Aziz's inquiry about his daily schedule and prayer—Merton was then living at his hermitage on the Gethsemani monastery property—Merton offered a rare glimpse of his own experience of prayer.

> Now you ask about my method of meditation. Strictly speaking I have a very simple way of prayer. It is centered entirely on attention to the presence of God and to His will and His love. That is to say that it is centered on faith by which alone we can know the presence of God. One might say this gives my meditation the character described by the Prophet as "being before God as if you saw Him." Yet it does not mean imagining anything or conceiving a precise image of God, for to my mind this would be a kind of idolatry. On the contrary, it is a matter of adoring Him as invisible and infinitely beyond our comprehension, and realizing Him as all.[16]

I am reminded here of the description of prayer given by Jean Vianney and others, that prayer is one's looking at God and God looking back, being with God. While the encounter of the nothingness that is not God in silence before God might sound like the most isolated, solitary of experiences, the many other comments in the Merton–Aziz letters argue otherwise. Sarah Coakley has recently written of the transformative power of her keeping silent in meditative prayer earlier in her life as well as of the central place of desire in prayer.[17]

Prayer can become one's habit, one's very way of going about the day and all its chores. Merton's way of prayer was certainly woven into a very full day—of liturgical celebration, his following of the hours or daily cycle of prayer both at the monastery and the hermitage, a great deal of reading and writing including letters, also meals and chores around the hermitage—not to mention sleep! He describes it in the following striking passage: "What I wear is pants. What I do is live. How I pray is breathe. Who said Zen? Wash out your mouth if you said Zen. If you see a meditation going by, shoot it. Who said 'Love?' Love is in the movies. The spiritual life is something people worry about when they are so busy with something else they think they ought to be spiritual. Spiritual life is guilt. Up here in the woods is seen the New Testament: that is to say, the wind comes through the trees and you breathe it."[18] One might be tempted to call this sarcastic, but given his profound experience in prayer and life in solitude with God, I insist that Merton's words are a very powerful witness to what prayer is in life. The sheer volume of Merton's published and unpublished writing, added to years of hard manual labor at the monastery, and to all kinds of translating and editing tasks given him by the abbot, not to mention his decades of teaching younger monks—all this gives evidence of his commitment to the Benedictine rule's ideal: *ora et labora*, a life of prayer and work. As with some true persons of prayer I know, the practice over time shapes the one who performs it. Or, to use Evdokimov's phrase again, Merton and these others *became* what they prayed, *lived* their prayer.

Prayer is at the center of who we are and what we do, not just an activity prescribed in liturgical services at certain times. If we do not live our prayer, we do not really pray. Rather than separating us from others, our prayer unites us with them as the sister and brother to be loved. Finally, it is not surprising that so much discussion of prayer is all about *us*—our difficulties, our distractions. What about God's place in it all? God's point of view? The scriptures present God speaking directly to us in so many places, but the essential message is the same: "Seek me and you will find me . . . come closer to me and I will come closer to you . . . come to me all you who labor and are weary and I will give you rest."[19] Put simply (if one can do this with God), God is "everywhere present, filling all things." In some of the most beautiful words he ever wrote, Merton imagines what is in the mind and heart of God. Although there is no explicit reference to prayer in this passage, I use it to close these reflections because Merton's compelling vision of the transforming love and mercy of God points us to that which underlies all our prayer, and makes it possible.

> The Voice of God is heard in Paradise:
>
> What was vile has become precious. What is now precious was never vile. I have always known the vile as precious: for what is vile I know not at all.
>
> What was cruel has become merciful. What is now merciful was never cruel. I have always overshadowed Jonas with My mercy, and cruelty I know not at all. Have you had sight of Me, Jonas My child? Mercy within mercy within mercy. I have forgiven the universe without end, because I have never known sin.
>
> What was poor has become infinite. What is infinite was never poor. I have always known poverty as infinite: riches I love not at all. Prisons within prisons within prisons. Do not lay up for yourselves ecstasies upon earth, where time and space corrupt, where the minutes break in and steal. No more lay hold on time, Jonas, My son, lest the rivers bear you away.
>
> What was fragile has become powerful. I loved what was most frail. I looked upon what was nothing. I touched what was without substance, and within what was not, I am.[20]

Notes

1. Athanasius, *The Life of Antony*, ed. Archibald Robertson, tr. H. Ellershaw. Nicene and Post-Nicene Fathers Series 2, vol. 4, eds. Philip Schaff and Henry Wace (Peabody, MA: Hendrickson Publishers, 1995), 91–92.
2. See my publications *Living Icons: Persons of Faith in the Eastern Church* (Notre Dame, IN: University of Notre Dame Press, 2002), *Hidden Holiness* (Notre Dame, IN: University of Notre Dame Press, 2009), and *Saints as They Really Are* (Notre Dame, IN: University of Notre Dame Press, 2012).
3. See two excellent series of publications: *Modern Spiritual Masters* (Maryknoll, NY: Orbis) and *Classics of Western Spirituality* (Mahwah, NJ: Paulist Press). For a historical overview, see Philip Zaleski and Carole Zaleski, *Prayer: A History* (Boston: Houghton Mifflin Harcourt, 2005).
4. Quoted in Valentine Zander, *St Seraphim of Sarov* (Crestwood, NY: St. Vladimir's Seminary Press, 1975), 85–86.
5. Ibid., 83–94. In the text of the "conversation with Motovilov," Seraphim several times insists that we are given the Holy Spirit at baptism and that the Spirit is always with us—what Christ meant by saying that "the kingdom of God is within you." Also see Ann Shukman, "'The Conversation between St Seraphim and Motovilov': The Author, the Texts and the Publishers," *Sobornost* 27, no. 1 (2005), 47–57.
6. Zander, *St Seraphim of Sarov*, 89.
7. *The Ascetical Homilies of Saint Isaac the Syrian* (Boston, MA: Holy Transfiguration Monastery, 1984), 344 (from homily 71).

8. See "God's Absurd Love and the Mystery of His Silence," in *In the World, of the Church: A Paul Evdokimov Reader*, trans. and ed. Michael Plekon and Alexis Vinogradov (Crestwood, NY: St. Vladimir's Seminary Press, 2001), 175–94.

9. Paul Evdokimov, *The Sacrament of Love*, trans. Anthony P. Gythiel and Victoria Steadman (Crestwood, NY: St. Vladimir's Seminary Press, 1985), 61–63. Also see Paul Evdokimov, *Ages of the Spiritual Life*, trans. and ed. Michael Plekon and Alexis Vinogradov (Crestwood, NY: St. Vladimir's Seminary Press, 1998, 2001).

10. In the Eastern Church administration of the sacraments—baptism, penance, Eucharist, ordination, marriage, anointing of the sick—the prayers speak of the healing that occurs within each of these actions.

11. For an anthology of her writings in translation, see Mother Maria Skobtsova, *Essential Writings*, trans. Richard Pevear and Larissa Volokhonsky (Maryknoll, NY: Orbis, 2003).

12. The sense of God in communion as Trinity mirrors the communion that we have in prayer with others. The famous icon of the Trinity by the Russian monk Andrei Rublev (c. 1360–c. 1430) expresses this by the openness of the circle of the angels to us who stand before them.

13. Skobtsova, *Essential Writings*, 80–81.

14. Quoted in Sergei Hackel, *Pearl of Great Price* (Crestwood, NY: St. Vladimir's Seminary Press, 1982), 29–30.

15. For a good biographical overview, see Jim Forest, *Living with Wisdom: A Life of Thomas Merton* (Maryknoll, NY: Orbis, 2008). The best biography in depth is Michael Mott, *The Seven Mountains of Thomas Merton* (Boston: Houghton Mifflin, 1984). Merton's own writings, many still in print, are too voluminous to be cited. They include volumes of journal entries, letters, notes, and drafts published after the embargo stipulated by his literary estate. Both Forest and Mott review most of the major writings, and the Thomas Merton Center at Bellarmine University is an excellent resource: www.merton.org.

16. Letter to Abdul Aziz, January 2, 1966, in Thomas Merton, *The Hidden Ground of Love: The Letters of Thomas Merton on Religious Experience and Social Concerns*, ed. William H. Shannon (New York: Farrar, Strauss and Giroux, 1985), 63–64. The passage continues: "My prayer tends very much to what you call *fana*. There is in my heart this great thirst to recognize totally the nothingness of all that is not God. My prayer is then a kind of praise rising up out of the center of Nothing and Silence. If I am still present 'myself' this I recognize as an obstacle. If He wills He can then make the Nothingness into a total clarity. If He does not will, then the Nothingness actually seems itself to be an object and remains an obstacle. Such is my ordinary way of prayer or meditation. It is not "thinking about" anything, but a direct seeking of the Face of the Invisible, which cannot be found unless we become lost in Him who is Invisible. I do not ordinarily write about such things and ask you therefore to be discreet about it."

17. Sarah Coakley, "How My Mind Has Changed: Prayer as Crucible," *Christian Century* 128, no. 6 (March 22, 2011), 32–40. For a discussion by St. Augustine on prayer as desire, see his exposition of "All my desire is before you" (Psalm 38:9). He comments: "There is another inward kind of prayer without ceasing, which is the desire of the heart." *New Advent*, "Exposition on Psalm 38," www.newadvent.org/fathers/1801038.htm.

18. Thomas Merton, *Day of a Stranger* (Salt Lake City, UT: Gibbs M. Smith, 1981), 41. For the earliest draft of this "typical day," written for a friend, Miguel Grinberg, see *Dancing in the Water of Life: The Journals of Thomas Merton*, vol. 5, 1963–1965, ed. Robert E. Daggy (San Francisco: Harper, 1997), 239–42.

19. See Jeremiah 29:13; Matthew 7:7; James 4:8; Matthew 11:28.

20. Thomas Merton, *The Sign of Jonas* (New York: Doubleday Image, 1956), 351–52.

A Qur'ānic Theology of Prayer

REZA SHAH-KAZEMI

"He is the Living One. There is no God save Him. So pray unto Him, making religion purely (sincerely) for Him" (40:65).[1] This verse may be said to sum up the basic theological attitude toward prayer in Islam. Prayer directed to the one true God is the logical concomitant of the fundamental tenet of the faith, that of *tawḥīd*: there is no divinity but the one God, *lā ilāha illā'Llah*. Praying to God and eschewing all other would-be partners is to make religion pure (*ikhlāṣ*), purifying it of *shirk*, belief in and orientation to many gods, the idolatry flowing from polytheism.

Prayer or worship (*ʿibāda*) takes many forms in Islam, each of which has a multitude of theological implications: the canonical prayer (*al-ṣalāt*); personal supplication (*duʿāʾ*); recitation of the Qur'ān (*qirāʾa*); invocation of blessings on the Prophet (*al-ṣalāt ʿalā'l-nabī*); repetition of certain formulae, usually on a rosary (*awrād*); and methodic invocation of the Name or Names of God (*dhikr Allāh*). To reduce the complexity of the different theological dimensions of these diverse modes of prayer, and to focus on the essence of theology as "knowledge of God," we could address to ourselves the simple question: how does prayer contribute to our knowledge of God? One answer is given by the traditional interpretation of the following verse of the Qur'ān that reveals to us the purpose of our creation: "I only created the jinn and mankind in order that they might worship Me" (51:56).

According to most Qur'ānic commentators, exoteric and esoteric alike, the meaning of "worship" in this verse is "knowledge." So the meaning of the verse becomes: "I only created the jinn and mankind in order that they might *know* Me." Praying to God and acquiring knowledge of God are thus complementary aspects of the divine intention underlying creation.

The great Ashʿarite theologian and exegete Fakhr al-Dīn al-Rāzī (d. 1209), in common with many other theological authorities, mentions this interpretation of the word *yaʿbudūni*, and concludes his comment on this verse by citing the following divine utterance (*ḥadīth qudsī*): "I was a hidden treasure and I willed [or loved] to be known."[2] This saying is one of the cornerstones of Sufi doctrine, and, although its chain of transmission (*isnād*) is not deemed authoritative by scholars of ḥadīth, its meaning is nonetheless accepted as theologically valid by these scholars, largely on account of their acceptance of the traditional interpretation of 51:56.[3] If God created us to worship Him, and if the deepest meaning of this worship is knowledge, then indeed it can be said that God was a hidden or unknown thing—a "treasure," if you will, known only to Himself; and He wished, or loved, to be known. In this light, worship becomes the primary means by which the divine purpose of creation is achieved, and by which knowledge of God—theology in the strict sense, *maʿrifatu'Llāh*—is attained.

Knowledge of God is innate within the human soul. This is explicitly expressed in the following verse, referring to the covenant between God and humankind at the very dawn of creation: "And when thy Lord brought forth from the Children of Adam, from their reins, their seed, and made them testify of themselves [saying], Am I not your Lord? They said: Yea, verily. We testify. [That was] lest ye say on the Day of Resurrection: Truly, of this we were unaware" (7:172).

The completeness of human knowledge of God is identified in another verse with all the "Names" or qualities of God, of which even the angels are ignorant (2:30–33); and it is also implied in the fact that God breathed His Spirit into the Adamic substance (15:29). Perfect knowledge of God resides in the heart as a spiritual seed that is brought to fruition by the conscious reaffirmation of our primordial covenant: bearing witness, in a myriad ways, to the divine reality. This heartfelt reaffirmation of God as our Lord is the very essence of prayer: "Truly those who say: our Lord is God, and are upright, the angels descend upon them, saying: fear not, and grieve not, and receive the good tidings of the Garden which ye are promised. We are your guiding friends [*awliyā'*] in the life of this world and in the Hereafter" (41:30–31). The angelic presence that is magnetically attracted to souls in prayer is not only a foreshadowing of the posthumous Paradisal reward for the pious; it can also be understood as the radiant presence of an already celestial reality experienced, here and now, through heartfelt prayer. We are your *awliyā'*, the angels say, in the life of this world as well as in the Hereafter.

The human *awliyā'*, the saints, are described by Imam ʿAlī as those whose hearts are in Paradise already; their bodies alone are at work in this world.[4] Prayer is the chief means by which this ascent of the heart to Paradise is accomplished while still alive. For the Prophet said: "The Prayer is the celestial ascent of the believer."[5] The reference here is to the miraculous ascent (*miʿrāj*) of the Prophet through the heavens from the Masjid al-Aqṣā in Jerusalem to the very presence of God, where he witnessed what the Qur'ān refers to as "the greatest of the signs of his Lord" (53:18). It was during the *miʿrāj* that God ordained that Muslims were to pray five times each day; this fact alerts us to the significance of the Prophetic equation of the daily prayer, *al-ṣalāt*, with the celestial ascent. The canonical prayer is thus as it were "winged" for spiritual flight, carrying us up through the heavens and into the very presence of God. Indeed, it is remarkable that the sūra titled "The Angels" (Sūrat al-Malā'ika) begins with a reference to the angels as having wings "two, three and four" (35:1), precisely the number of prayer cycles performed during each day: two for the morning prayer (*fajr*); three for the evening prayer (*maghrib*); and four for the noon (*ẓuhr*), afternoon (*ʿaṣr*), and night prayer (*ʿishā'*). Very important here is the Prophet's statement that of the three things beloved to him in this world—women, perfume, and prayer—it is the prayer that gave him his greatest delight (*qurrat al-ʿayn*).

The intimate relationship between prayer and the vision of God is affirmed in the Prophet's definition of *iḥsān*—which can be translated as "virtue," "spiritual excellence," or more literally as "making beautiful": "*Al-iḥsān*," he said, "is that you worship God as if you could see Him and if you see Him not, [know that] He sees you."[6] Imam ʿAlī, when asked whether he had seen his Lord, replied that he would not worship a Lord he had not seen. When asked how he saw his Lord he replied: "Eyes see Him not according to outward vision, but hearts see Him according to the verities of faith."[7] It is because the heart can be understood as containing the Spirit—breathed into man by God—that the vision of God becomes possible. Ibn al-ʿArabī affirms that the one who sees is identical to the one seen.[8] It is the divine consciousness within the heart that comes to "see" God because it is identical to that which is seen. If we ask how the heart can come to acquire this vision, the answer takes us straight back to prayer. The Prophet said that "for everything there is a polish, and the polish of the hearts is the remembrance of God, *dhikr Allāh*."[9] The word "dhikr" denotes not only the consciousness of God per se but also the means of attaining this consciousness, namely, the invocation of the Name of God, described by the Prophet in many sayings as being the quintessence of prayer. Likewise, the Qur'ān affirms the primacy of the dhikr in many verses. For example: "Establish the canonical prayer for the sake of My remembrance" (20:14). The very purpose of the prayer is to generate *dhikr Allāh*. "Truly the prayer keepeth one away from evil and iniquity; but the remembrance of God is greater" (29:45).[10] The Name of God, *Allāh*, unlike the names of false gods, has what the Qur'ān calls *sulṭān*, not just an "authoritative warrant" but a properly theurgic power: God is fully present in His Name. The divine Name is also likened, by Imam

ʿAlī, to the ultimate medicine for the ailments of the soul; and invoking the Name is the cure (*yā man ismuhu dawā' wa dhikruhu shifā'*).[11] In terms of spiritual praxis, "The Name is the Named," *al-Ism huwa'l-musammā*: this Sufi formulation, rendering explicit what is implicit in several verses of the Qur'ān, is the basis of the methodic discipline of invocation.[12] To devote oneself to the Name is to devote oneself to the Named.

Our sense of the mysterious power of the invocation of the divine Name is deepened when we ask ourselves who or what the agent of this supreme form of prayer is. In the Sufi tradition, it is asserted that God is Himself the invoker, *al-dhākir*, and is the one who is invoked, *al-madhkūr*. One of the Qur'ānic foundations for this idea is the following verse: "Hath there come upon man any moment in time when he was not a thing remembered?" (76:1). Here, it is the human being, *al-insān*, that is the object of remembrance, *al-madhkūr*: man's being created by God is identical with his being invoked by God. The agent of invocation, *al-dhākir*, is God. In Ibn al-ʿArabi's metaphysical imagery, creation is renewed with each breath (*tajdīd al-khalq bi'l-anfās*), with each "breath of the All-Merciful" *nafas al-Raḥmān*. Creation is thus not a single act at the beginning of time but the perpetual reverberation of the merciful invocation of God. To quote Ibn al-ʿArabī: 'His is the remembrance . . . a thing has being in the remembrance of the one who remembers it."[13] Imam ʿAlī, similarly, tells us that the invocation comes forth firstly from the Invoked, God, and only secondly from the invoker, man.[14] Rumi expresses a kindred truth in his *Masnavi*, when he tells the story of a man who spent night after night invoking God's Name. Satan appears to him and taunts him: Have you ever heard God's reply to your incessant calls? Despondent, the man falls asleep. He then dreams of al-Khiḍr, a mysterious saint alluded to in the Qur'ān, who remonstrates with him, telling him that God said: "That *Allāh* of thine is My 'Here am I' . . . beneath every 'O Lord' of thine is many 'Here am I' from Me."[15] Our invocation of God is therefore a response to His "call" to us: "O ye who believe, respond to God and the Messenger when He calleth you to that which giveth you life" (8:24). It is God Himself who performs the invocation, creatively and ontologically; human invocation is a response, a shadow or reflection, a particular consequence of this universal divine invocation.

Returning to the ḥadīth of the hidden treasure: It is by means of this divine dhikr, constituted by the entirety of existence, that the hidden treasure becomes known outwardly and objectively. From the human point of view, it is by means of this dhikr that the illusion of egocentric alterity is effaced, and by virtue of this effacement, God comes to know Himself through the now transparent veil of our own creaturehood. He knows Himself through us in the very measure of our self-effacement. This divine self-knowledge that is consummated through us is thus identical to our self-realization through Him: the famous dictum of the Prophet "he who knows himself knows his Lord" can be interpreted as follows: knowledge that the self is unreal foreshadows and leads to knowledge of the Real.[16] *Fanā'*, extinction or effacement, is not only a particular state, a *ḥāl*; it is also, and more accessibly, the prefiguration of this state: humility, a permanent awareness of our nothingness before God. The power of the *dhikr* to effect this extinction of the illusion of one's apparent autonomy is derived from the very power of the divine creative *dhikr*, human remembrance being as it were its inverted reflection within creation.[17]

The possibility of our attaining this extinction in invocation is well expressed by Ibn ʿAṭā'illāh al-Iskandarī (d. 1309), one of the principal exponents of spiritual wisdom, *maʿrifa*, in the Sufi tradition: "Do not abandon the invocation because you do not feel the Presence of God therein. For your forgetfulness *of* the invocation of Him is worse than your forgetfulness *in* the invocation of Him. Perhaps he will take you from an invocation with forgetfulness (*ghafla*) to one with vigilance (*yaqaẓa*), and from one with vigilance to one with the Presence of God (*ḥuḍūr*), and from one with the Presence of God to one wherein everything but the Invoked (*al-Madhkūr*) is absent. 'And that is not difficult for God.'"[18] The last words are a citation from the Qur'ān, words that conclude a passage of central significance to Sufism: "O mankind, ye are the poor in relation to God, and God, He is the Rich, the Praised. If He wishes, He would remove you and bring about a new creation; and that is not difficult for God" (35:15–17).

Read in the light of Ibn ʿAṭā'illāh's aphorism, one comes to sense the deeper meaning of the poverty (*faqr*) in question here, and to understand better what it means to be a *faqīr*, one who is "poor" in relation to God. Ibn ʿAṭā'illāh clearly intends us to understand by this allusion to the "new creation" the principle of "subsistence after extinction," which defines the perfected saint, the "friend of God," *walī Allāh*. The saint is he or she through whom divine life and love pulsates and radiates to the whole of creation. This function of the saint is alluded to in the following highly authenticated *ḥadīth qudsī*, a prophetic utterance through which God speaks in the first person: "My servant draws near to Me through nothing I love more than that which I have made legally incumbent upon him. My servant never ceases to draw near to Me through supererogatory acts until I love him. And when I love him, I am[19] his hearing by which he hears, his sight by which he sees, his hand by which he grasps, and his foot by which he walks."[20] Supererogatory acts (*al-nawāfil*) refer to the various forms of *dhikr* as well as extra cycles of formal prayer added to the canonical, obligatory cycles of prayer (*ṣalāt*).

By means of the loving grace attracted to the soul by these voluntary devotions, a mode of identity or union is attained. By "union" here should be understood metaphysical *tawḥīd*, "realization of oneness," and not existential *ittiḥād*, which implies that two entities, the soul and God, become one.[21] The deepest meaning of *tawḥīd* is revealed through the realization of a Oneness, or unicity, that has no "other" and thus infinitely transcends the realm of number. Here the succinct description of divine unity given by Imam ʿAlī is highly instructive: God is One, he said, not in the sense of number, "for that which has no second does not enter into the category of number."[22]

Returning to the *dhikr* as the unitive prayer par excellence, the Qurʾān contains several exhortations to perform the invocation in various modes and degrees, to invoke God "much," to do so "early and late," to invoke under one's breath, "in humility and in secret," and so on; but it is particularly galvanizing when it describes the Prophet's own devotional practice: "Verily thy Lord knoweth that thou keepest vigil in prayer almost two-thirds of the night, and half of it and a third of it, as doth a group among those with thee . . ." (73:20). Earlier in this sūra[23]—the Prophet is instructed to recite the Qurʾān in "measured recitation" (73:4)[24] and to invoke the Name of the Lord, doing so with "utter dedication" (73:8).

One is to invoke the Name of God not only with total concentration but also for long hours each night, if one wishes to abide by this most challenging—but infinitely rewarding—aspect of the Prophetic example. But it is not so much out of a desire for reward that one invokes; rather, one invokes in the grateful awareness that it is in reality the divine reality that is invoking itself through us; or, at least, with the grateful acknowledgment that one's very act of invocation is already the sign or consequence of divine attraction: "When My servants ask thee about Me, say: I am indeed near. I answer the call of the suppliant when he prayeth to Me. So let them answer Me and believe in Me, that they might be led aright" (2:186). And again: "God summoneth to the abode of peace" (10:25). Our prayers are grateful responses to this summons, and at a higher level, a unitive participation in the universal rhythm of divine invocation. In order to highlight this quality of gratitude that should infuse our prayer, Imam ʿAlī distinguishes between three kinds of worship: worship based on desire, which he calls that of the merchants (*al-tujjār*); worship based on fear, which is that of the enslaved (*al-ʿabīd*); and worship based on gratitude: the worship of the liberated (*al-aḥrār*).[25]

Those who have been liberated from the limitations of their own individuality are the ones who have been granted a taste of the beatitude at the heart of reality; they are granted this taste through the grace of God responding to their gift of self in pure prayer. All subsequent prayer is thus an expression of pure gratitude, devoid of desire for anything—even Paradise. Such prayer is wonderfully exemplified in the following incident in the life of the Prophet. In the early hours of the morning, the Prophet's feet had become swollen after having stood for so long in prayer. His wife ʿĀ᾿isha asked him why he was praying so much.[26] "Am I not a grateful servant?"[27] came the reply: simple, disarming, and utterly inspiring. The Qur᾿ān refers to a virtuous circle set in motion by gratitude: be grateful, God says, and I will give you more (*la-in shakartum la-azīdannakum*; 14:7). The Paradisal fountain of Kāfūr might be seen as a symbol of this perpetually increasing abundance of grace made available through the communion of the prophets and the saints with their Lord. This fountain is mentioned in the sūra titled "Man," the opening verse of which we heard earlier. It states that the perfect servants of God drink directly from the fountain of Kāfūr whereas the righteous (*al-abrār*) drink only from a draught flavored with it. The more the "servants" drink—in terms of our image, the more they commune with God in grateful, selfless prayer—the more abundantly the fountain of grace flows (*yufajjirūnahā tafjīrā*; 76:6) from Heaven to earth. This image helps us to see the principle that prayer to the One is prayer for all: in the measure that one prays selflessly to the One without a second, one prays for all without exception; the purer our prayer, the greater the blessings to all of creation.

One of the Prophet's names is *dhikru'Llāh*: he is the personification of the purest prayer, the remembrance of God. Being nothing but the remembrance of God, he is not just a blessing to all believers, he is also and above all else "a mercy to the whole of creation" (*wa mā arsalnāka illā raḥmatan li'l-ʿālamīn*; 21:107). One of the aspects of his merciful gift to us is that his noble example is accessible to each and every one of us by virtue of our human nature, our *fitra*; the prophetic Sunna does not set unattainably high standards, on the contrary, it makes us aware of what we can be if we were true to our own nature: we are invited by him to become what we already are. So when we fall short of the Prophet's standards, it behoves each of us to lament with Imam al-Būṣīrī: "No optional devotions have I accumulated, ready for my demise; nor have I fasted, nor prayed, more than the minimum required. I've wronged the example of him who revived the black nights, praying until his feet complained of painful swelling."[28]

However, much more important than our failure to do justice to the example of the Prophet is our very capacity to emulate him as a "beautiful example" (*uswa ḥasana*): "Truly in the Messenger of God ye have a beautiful example for whosoever placeth his hope in God and the Last Day, and remembereth God much" (33:21). Our capacity to emulate the Prophet, then, is intimately bound up with our remembrance of God, which is both condition and consequence of our emulation. This capacity stems not from our own power, however, but by the prophetic presence within us, that presence which is more closely identified with our own true nature than we are: "The Prophet is closer to the believers than their own selves," the Qur'ān tells us (33:6). When we bless the Prophet, as we are instructed to do in the Qur'ān, we are at the same time attracting to ourselves a realizatory grace—expressed in formal terms by the Prophet's statement that one who invokes blessings upon him once receives a ten-fold blessing from God in return. This grace can be understood as the power to bring our own *fiṭra* from potentiality to actuality. God and His angels are perpetually showering the Prophet (33:56); in other words, his spiritual reality, the Ḥaqīqa Muḥammadiyya, which pre-exists the creation of Adam, ceaselessly receives and transmits immeasurable graces.[29] The Prophet is therefore grasped in Islamic spirituality not simply as a person whom we love more than any other; rather, our unsurpassable love for him arises out of the fact that his transpersonal presence is the key to our remembrance, and hence love of God, and thereby the key to God's love for us: "If ye love God, follow me," the Prophet is told to say to us; "God will love you" (3:31).

Our loving remembrance of God, in harmony with the interiorizing presence of the Prophet, opens us up to the merciful grace that leads from the darkness of our own souls to the one and only light, that of God.[30] Such enlightenment is the consummation of "theology" in the true sense of the word. These relationships are alluded to in the following verses, with which we shall conclude:

> Muḥammad is not the father of any man among you, rather, he is the Messenger of God and the Seal of the Prophets; and God is ever Aware of all things.
> O ye who believe, remember God with much remembrance.
> And glorify Him early and late.
> He it is Who blesseth you, and His angels (bless you), that He may bring you forth from darkness unto light; and He is ever Merciful to the believers. (33:40–43)[31]

Notes

1. All translations of Qur'ānic verses are mine, based substantially on the translation of M. M. Pickthall (London: George Allen & Unwin, and Fine Books, 1976); the translations of M. A. S. Abdel-Haleem (Oxford: Oxford University Press, 2004) and Ali Quli-Qara'i (London: Islamic College of Advanced Studies, 2004) were also consulted.

2. Fakhr al-Dīn al-Rāzī, *al-Tafsīr al-kabīr* (Beirut: Dār Iḥyā' al-Turāth al-ʿArabī, 2001), 10:194.

3. The interpretation found here is given also by several other prominent Sufi authorities, for example, Abū Naṣr al-Sarrāj (d. 378/988), *Kitāb al-lumaʿ*, ed. R. A. Nicholson

(London: Luzac, 1963), 40 (of the Arabic text). See also al-Qushayrī's (d. 465/1074) *Risāla*, translated by B. R. von Schlegell as *Principles of Sufism* (Berkeley, CA: Mizan Press, 1990), 316.

4. *Nahj al-balāgha* (Tehran: Nahj al-balāgha Foundation, 1993), 302. See R. Shah-Kazemi, *Justice and Remembrance—Introducing the Spirituality of Imam ʿAlī* (London: I. B. Tauris, 2006), 36–72, for discussion of this and other similar sayings.

5. For discussion of this important saying, see William Chittick, *In Search of the Lost Heart: Explorations in Islamic Thought*, eds. Mohammed Rustom, Atif Khalil, and Kazuyo Murata (Albany, NY: State University of New York Press, 2012), 23–26.

6. Ḥadīth no. 2 of *An-Nawawī's Forty Hadith*, trans. E. Ibrahim, D. Johnson-Davies (Damascus: Holy Koran Publishing House, 1976), 28.

7. For the translation of the dialogue in which this statement appears, see William Chittick, *A Shiʿite Anthology* (London: Muhammadi Trust, 1980), 38–39.

8. In Michel Valsan "Le Livre du Nom de Majesté," in *Études Traditionelles*, no. 2 (1948): 214. In relation to the Prophet's vision of God at the summit of his *miʿrāj*, the Sufi Abū Bakr al-Wāsiṭī (d. 932) similarly states that "God took Muḥammad away from himself, and made him witness God. Therefore, in reality, it was God's essence witnessing His own essence." Cited in Gerhard Böwering, "From the Word of God to the Vision of God—Muḥammad's Heavenly Journey in Classical Ṣūfī Qur'ān Commentary," in *Le Voyage Initiatique en Terre d'Islam—Ascensions célestes et itinéraires spirituels*, ed. Mohammad Ali Amir-Moezzi (Paris: Peeters, 1996), 215.

9. This saying is found in the collection of Ibn Ḥanbal, among others. See al-Suyūṭī, *Jāmiʿ al-aḥādīth li al-Jāmiʿ al-ṣaghīr wa zawā᾿idihi wa al-Jāmiʿ al-kabīr*, vol. 2 (Damascus: Matbaʿat Muhammad Hashim al-Kutubi, 1979–81), 440.

10. Martin Lings refers to the following saying of the Shaykh al-ʿAlawī as a commentary on 29:45: "Our performance of the rites of worship is considered strong or weak according to the degree of our remembrance of God while performing them." Lings, *What Is Sufism?* (Cambridge: Islamic Texts Society, 1993), 37. This comment helps us to see that what is in question in verse 29:45 is not simply the affirmation that the invocation of the Name of God is greater than the canonical prayer but that the principle of the remembrance of God—consciousness of God—is "greater" than any particular form of worship.

11. This is verse 156 from his famous supplication, *Duʿā᾿ Kumayl*; see the translation by William C. Chittick, *Supplications* (Duʿā᾿) (London: Muhammadi Trust, 1990).

12. For example, "Glorify the Name of thy Lord Most High" (87:1); "Invoke the Name of thy Lord, and devote thyself to Him [or "it" the Name of thy Lord] with utter devotion" (73:8).

13. Ibn al-ʿArabī, *al-Futūḥāt al-makkiyya*, vol. 4 (Cairo, 1911), 315, lines 21–24. See the important points made in this regard by M. Chodkiewicz in his essay "Une Introduction à la Lecture des *Futūḥāt Makkiyya*," in *Les Illuminations de La Mecque* (Paris: Sindbad, 1988), especially 37, where he comments on Ibn al-ʿArabī's interpretation of 76:1 in the context of his metaphysics: the "moment" in time when man was not is an ontological "degree," that of *aḥadiyya*, absolutely unconditioned oneness.

14. *Ghurar al-ḥikam*, compiled by ʿAbd al-Wāḥid Āmidi, ed. Muḥammad ʿAlī Anṣārī (Qom: Imām-e ʿAsr, 2001), 135, no. 2098, as cited in Shah-Kazemi, *Justice and Remembrance*, 168.

15. Reynold A. Nicholson, *The Mathnawi of Jalaluddin Rūmī* (London: Luzac & Co., 1930), Book 3, 14, lines 189ff.

16. For discussion of this saying of the Prophet in the spiritual tradition of Islam, see R. Shah-Kazemi, "The Concept and Significance of *Maʿrifa* in Sufism," *Journal of Islamic Studies* 13, no. 2 (2002): 155–81.

17. For discussion of this principle and a profound exposition of the metaphysical dimensions of the invocation, see Frithjof Schuon, *Stations of Wisdom* (Bloomington, IN: World Wisdom, 1995), 125–35.

18. Ibn ʿAṭāʾillāh, *Sufi Aphorisms*, trans. Victor Danner (Leiden: E. J. Brill, 1973), 32; emphasis added. The final quotation is from the Qurʾān, 14:20. See also Ibn ʿAṭāʾillāh's volume devoted entirely to the invocation, *Miftāḥ al-falāḥ wa miṣbāḥ al-arwāḥ* (*The Key to Salvation: A Sufi Manual of Invocation*), trans. Mary A. K. Danner (Cambridge: Islamic Texts Society, 1996).

19. Most translators translate "*kuntu*" here as "I become," but we prefer the more literal translation, especially in light of what Ibn ʿArabī says about this saying: "God's words 'I am' show that this was already the situation, but the servant was not aware. Hence the generous gift which this nearness gives to him is the unveiling of the knowledge that God is his hearing and his sight." Cited in William C. Chittick, *The Sufi Path of Knowledge: Ibn al-ʿArabī and the Metaphysics of the Imagination* (Albany: State University of New York, 1989), 326, citing *al-Futūḥāt al-Makkiyya*, III.67.29. God is the sole ontological agent, acting through the appearance of the servant as the locus (*maẓhar*) of divine manifestation (*ẓuhūr*). The only change is in the knowledge of the servant, who now comes to understand concretely that "there is nothing in being but God" (*laysa fi'l-wujūd siwa'Llāh*), according to one of the most fundamental teachings of Sufism.

20. *Ṣaḥīḥ al-Bukhārī, Kitāb al-riqāq*, no. 2117, p. 992; cited in *Forty Hadith Qudsi*, selected and translated by Ezzeddin Ibrahim, Denys Johnson-Davies (Beirut: Dar al-Koran al-Kareem, 1980), 104 (translation modified).

21. As al-Ghazālī puts it, the highest state is called "unification" (*ittiḥād*) in metaphorical terms, but "*tawḥīd*, according to the language of reality." David Buchman, trans., *Al-Ghazālī—The Niche of Lights* (Provo, UT: Brigham Young University Press, 1998), 17–18.

22. For discussion of this saying see Shah-Kazemi, *Justice and Remembrance*, 24–25.

23. The first part of this sūra was revealed in the early period of the Prophet's mission in Mecca; the long concluding verse, no. 20—about one-third of the sūra—was revealed much later, during the Medina period, when the range of roles performed by the Prophet—head of state, lawgiver, general, husband to several wives, and so on—made his regular night vigils all the more remarkable. As Martin Lings notes, "it was the destiny of Muḥammad to penetrate with exceptional versatility into the domain of human experience" and to direct this domain in its totality toward God. At its deepest, this calls for a sacralisation of the whole of life: "Islam's deep penetration into the affairs of this world demands that its mysticism shall be correspondingly exalted." Lings, *What Is Sufism?*, 34 and 43.

24. The recitation of the Qurʾān plays a fundamental role in Islamic spirituality. According to Imam ʿAlī, "For one who recites the Qurʾān, it is as if prophethood is being woven into his very being (*fa-kaʾannamā udrijat al-nubuwwa bayn janbayhi*), except that he cannot be the recipient of the Revelation [i.e., cannot be regarded as a prophet in the

strict sense]." Cited in Ayatollah Javādī-Āmulī, in his ongoing voluminous commentary on the Qur'ān, *Tasnīm: Tafsīr-i Qur'ān-i karīm*, vol. 1 (Qom: Isrā, 2008), 247. Ibn al-'Arabī writes that when the Qur'ān truly descends upon the heart, rather than just being recited by the tongue, the result is "a sweetness (*ḥalāwa*) beyond all measure, surpassing all delight (*ladhdha*)." In the same passage he quotes the statement by Abū Madyan (d. 1198), the seminal Maghribi spiritual authority from whom many Sufi orders claim descent: "The aspirant (*al-murīd*) is not a true aspirant until he finds in the Qur'ān everything to which he aspires." Cited in Michel Chodkiewicz, *Un Océan sans rivage: Ibn Arabî, le livre et le loi* (Paris: Éditions du Seuil, 1992), 47.

25. See, for discussion, Shah-Kazemi, *Justice and Remembrance*, 111.

26. In fact, she quotes to him a Qur'ānic verse, reminding him that God had forgiven him whatever "sins" he had committed or might yet commit, referring to the opening verses of Sūrat al-Fatḥ (48:1–2): "We have established for you a clear victory, that God may forgive thee what is past of thy sin and what is to come."

27. Cited in Qāḍī 'Iyāḍ, *al-Shifā'*, trans. Aisha A. Bewley, *Muḥammad—Messenger of Allah* (Inverness: Madinah Press, 1991), 74.

28. Abdal Hakim Murad, trans., *The Mantle Adorned—Imam Būsīrī's Burda* (London: Quilliam Press, 2009), 44–45. This poem is arguably the single most influential work in Muslim devotional literature dedicated to the Prophet. As Shaykh Hamza Yusuf notes in the insightful introduction to his own translation, the *Burda* "is arguably the most memorized and recited poem in the Muslim world." Yusuf, *The Burda of al-Busiri* (Thaxted: Sandala, 2002), xvii.

29. "I was a Prophet while Adam was still between water and clay," the Prophet tells us in a famous ḥadīth. See Seyyed Hossein Nasr's fine discussion of the spiritual reality of the Prophet in his *Ideals and Realities of Islam* (London: George Allen & Unwin, 1988), ch. 3, "The Prophet and Prophetic Tradition", 67–93; see also Eric Geoffroy, *Introduction to Sufism—The Inner Path of Islam*, trans. Roger Gaetani (Bloomington, IN: World Wisdom, 2010), 43–55, for discussion of this ḥadīth in the context of a succinct presentation of the role played by the Prophet in Islamic spirituality.

30. What we mean by being in harmony with the prophetic presence is beautifully expressed by Martin Lings in terms of waves in the ocean ebbing back to the infinite whence they flowed: our individual "wave" must reach the "culminating point of the great wave," constituted by the prophetic presence, "in order that its own relatively feeble current may be overpowered by the great current and drawn along with it." Lings, *What Is Sufism*, 38. Rumi's image of the ordinary soul as "muddy water" remembering its own natural state of limpidity when it sees the "clear water" of the prophetic souls is also very instructive: "The prophets and the saints therefore remind him of his former state; they do not implant anything new in his substance. Now every dark water that recognises that great water, saying, 'I come from this and I belong to this,' mingles with that water. . . . It was on this account that God declared: *Truly there hath come unto you a Prophet from yourselves* (9:128)." A. J. Arberry, trans., *The Discourses of Rūmī* (Fīhi mā fīhi) (London: John Murray, 1961), 45.

31. The extent to which the enlightening function of the Qur'ān is interwoven with the spiritual reality of the Prophet is either overtly expressed or alluded to in several verses of the Qur'ān. To give just one example: "O ye who believe! Now God hath sent down unto you a reminder (*dhikrā*), a messenger reciting unto you the verses of God making clear [all things], that He may bring forth from darkness into light those who believe and do virtuous deeds" (65:10–11).

Muslim Prayer in Practice

M. M. DHEEN MOHAMED

PRAYER IN ISLAM is understood in at least three different ways, with each linked organically to the others: (1) *ṣalāt* (ritual prayer), (2) *duʿāʾ* (personal supplication), and (3) *dhikr* (prayer of the heart, recollection, or remembrance of God). All three forms and the manner in which Muslims have practiced them derive from the Qurʾān and the Sunna (the prophetic tradition).

Ṣalāt

Essentially meaning to pray, glorify, and bless, ṣalāt occurs in the Qurʾān in at least four forms:

1. All God's creation in the heavens and the earth perform ṣalāt. God says in the Qurʾān:
   "Do you not see that all that is in the heavens and the earth, even the birds that go about spreading their wings in flight, extol His glory? Each knows the way of its prayer [its ṣalāt] and of its extolling God's glory" (24:41).
2. All prophets of God performed the ṣalāt in a manner revealed to each: "And We saved him [Abraham] and Lot and brought him to the land. . . . And We bestowed upon him Isaac and Jacob as an additional gift, making each of them righteous . . . and We inspired them to good deeds and to establish ṣalāt" (21:71–73).[1]
3. God and the angels perform ṣalāt through which they bless God's servants:
   "It is He Who performs ṣalāt over you, as do His angels, that He may lead you out of darkness into light" (33:43).

Commentators on the Qur'ān quote several scholars who explain the ṣalāt performed by God over His creatures as the showering of His mercy upon them, while the ṣalāt of the angels is their invoking of blessings upon His creatures.

4. Finally, ṣalāt refers to the ritual prayer that Muslims are to perform five times a day at set times. References to this form of prayer are abundant in the Qur'ān (e.g., 2:3; 2:238; 4:43; 4:103) as well as in the Sunna.

There is evidence to indicate that during the period of Jāhiliyya (the Age of Ignorance before Islam), some Arabs (the *ḥunafā'*) performed prayers that they likened to Abrahamic prayer; even the Prophet (peace be upon him) is reported to have prayed before being granted the mantle of prophethood, in particular in the cave of Ḥirā'.[2] The Qur'ān hails the nascent Muslim community in the early revelations as those who establish prayers (e.g., 20:14; 73:20; 70:34), which indicates that Muslims used to pray from the very beginning of the prophetic mission. However, the ritual prayers five times a day were only authorized in the eleventh year of the prophetic mission in Mecca when the Prophet was taken on a miraculous nocturnal journey (*al-isrā' wa al-miʿrāj*) from Mecca to Jerusalem and from Jerusalem to the heavens, where he met his Lord and then came back.

It was on this journey that the Prophet was gifted with fifty prayers, which were finally reduced to five carrying the reward of fifty.[3] These prayers were to be established at specific times indicated by their names: *fajr* (dawn, before sunrise), *ẓuhr* (noon), *ʿaṣr* (afternoon), *maghrib* (sunset), and *ʿishā'* (night). The Qur'ān simply exhorts Muslims to pray and offers scant details about prayer times and the conditions to be fulfilled for prayers to be acceptable. Most of the instructions regarding the manner of prayer are only available in the ḥadīth literature, which makes emulation of the Prophet (peace be upon him) an absolute necessity not only with regard to prayers but also for any detail regarding a Muslim's life from birth to death.[4]

Performing Ṣalāt

Each performance of ṣalāt consists of a specific number of fixed cycles of movements and recitations (all in Arabic) that begin and end in established ways. Each such cycle is called a *rakʿa*. Fajr consists of two rakʿas; ẓuhr, four; ʿaṣr, four; maghrib, three; and ʿishā', four. It is compulsory for all Muslims to fulfill the established conditions, which include being Muslim, being ritually clean and pure through *wuḍū'* (ritual ablution) or *ghusl* (full ritual bath), being mentally sound, facing the *qibla* (the direction of the Kaʿba), declaring one's *niyya* (intention), and a few more that can easily be traced in manuals of Muslim prayer. Although Muslims usually pray in mosques, in other places used as prayer halls, or at home, the general rule is that the place of prayer ought to be clean and ritually pure. The Prophet (peace be upon him) said, "The whole earth has been made for me a place of prostration and has been purified for me."[5] It is little wonder, therefore, that Muslims can be seen praying in all kinds of places, even at sea or when flying in airplanes.

The ritual ablution (*wuḍū'*) consists mainly of washing one's hands up to the elbows, one's face (including rinsing the mouth and the inside of the nose), stroking one's head with a wet palm (and in the same rhythm and stroke also cleaning one's ears), and washing one's feet. Since *wuḍū'* is performed before praying, the general idea is that because I am about to meet my Lord, I should cleanse myself of the dirt and contamination of the world physically, spiritually, and psychologically and so purify myself to stand in the presence of my Lord.[6]

Ṣalāt is performed in the following way, with slight variations among different Muslim traditions. The worshipper begins by standing upright and facing the qibla and then raises his hands to his ears and folds them on his stomach or lower chest with the right palm over the back of the left hand. The recognized formula of recitations follows, among which the most fundamental is al-Fātiḥa (the opening sūra of the Qur'ān), followed by any other sūra or verses from the Qur'ān. After the recitation, the worshipper bows down so that both his palms rest firmly on both knees and his torso is perpendicular to his legs. Here also a short formula of glorification of God is recited after which the worshipper stands and then prostrates on the ground with toes, knees, palms, and forehead (including the nose) touching the ground. The worshipper then sits up, prostrates again and then stands up again, thus completing one rakʿa. A second rakʿa has now started. Unlike the first rakʿa, which ends with the worshipper standing, the second rakʿa ends by sitting after the second prostration (on the sole of his feet with the shin flat on the ground and his hands placed on his thighs) and reciting a standard formula that begins with praise to God and ends with blessings upon the Prophet (peace be upon him). Depending upon the prayer being offered, the worshipper can either continue the third and fourth rakʿas in exactly the same way or terminate his prayer with the second rakʿa (if praying the fajr prayer, for instance) by turning his face first to the right and then to the left. This whole process is punctuated by the recitation of various standard formulas glorifying and praising God explicitly taught by the Prophet (peace by upon him) for each position, such as: *subḥāna Rabbi al-ʿAẓīm* (Glory be to my Lord, the Great) while bowing, *Rabbanā wa laka al-ḥamd* (Our Lord, for You is all the Praise) after standing straight before prostration, and *subḥāna Rabbi al-Aʿlā* (Glory be to my Lord, the Most High) while prostrating.

In addition to the compulsory five daily prayers, Muslims perform a number of other ritual prayers, some of which are obligatory while others are supererogatory. Obligatory prayers include the *jumʿā* (offered in place of the noon prayer on Friday, including a sermon) and the *ʿīdayn* (the two festival prayers, one at the end of Ramaḍān and the other on the tenth of Dhu al-Ḥijj). Among many forms of supererogatory prayer, the most common and important include *tahajjud* (late night prayers highly recommended for attaining spiritual excellence)[7]; *janāza* (prayer for a deceased person); *kusūf* (prayer during an eclipse), *istisqāʾ* (prayer for rain); *safar* (prayer before a journey), *khawf* (prayer when afflicted with fear), and *ḥājah* (prayer to fulfill a certain purpose). Although this list is not exhaustive, most of the prayers mentioned are attested to by the actions of the Prophet himself (peace be upon him).

Duʿāʾ

Although originally ṣalāt and duʿāʾ had the same meanings, perhaps the clearest distinction between them occurs in the following prayer of Abraham: "Lord! Make me one who establishes ṣalāt and (let it be so) for my progeny. Lord! Accept my duʿāʾ" (Qurʾān 14:40). Although the general sense of duʿāʾ in the Qurʾān is to make an appeal to God for something, as in the passage above, some ḥadīths add some interesting details that are mentioned with relish in many Sufi works. The Prophet (peace be upon him) is reported to have said: "Prayer (duʿāʾ) is worship (*ʿibāda*)"[8]; and in another ḥadīth: "Prayer (duʿāʾ) is the *mukh* (literally, bone marrow—essence) of worship (ʿibāda)."[9] How this prayer is to be made and what ought to be its structure and content was also decided by God Himself in the very first sūra of the Qurʾān, *al-Fātiḥa.*[10] This sūra, which epitomizes prayer as duʿāʾ, constitutes the ideal structure, manner, and tone of a Muslim's prayer. Owing to its brevity we shall include it here: "(1) Praise be to Allah, the Lord of the worlds, (2) the Most Merciful, the Most Compassionate; (3) Master of the Day of Recompense. (4) You alone do we worship and You alone do we turn to for help. (5) Guide us to the Straight Path, (6) the path of those whom You have favoured, (7) not those on whom Your anger rests, nor those who are astray." Any appeal to God should start with the praise of God, which is what the first three verses do. Although these are the words of God, it is for the human being to recite them. If one seeks the bounties and mercy of God, it makes sense to let one's Lord know that it is He who possesses the requisite attributes to grant the request and, hence, receive the praise. The praise of God is immediately followed by a humble acknowledgment of the human need for divine help and guidance. That is the second part of an ideal prayer. It is only at the end (making this the last part of the prayer) that one actually makes the request for which one turned to God.

In line with the *adab* (etiquette) that God taught His Prophet (peace be upon him) in this sūra for imploring Him, the most sublime prayers that the Prophet (peace be upon him) made and taught his people even during trying times are nothing more than praise and glorification of God and His beautiful names without any pleas. For example:

> Ibn ʿAbbās reported that when faced with any tribulation, the Prophet (peace be upon him) used to recite, "There is no God but Allah, the Great, the Forbearing; there is no god but Allah, Lord of the Great Throne, there is no god but Allah, Lord of the heavens and Lord of the earth and Lord of the Generous Throne.[11]
>
> A man came to the Prophet (peace be upon him) and said, "I can't take (memorize) anything from the Qurʾān so teach me something that will recompense me." The Prophet (peace be upon him) replied, "Say! 'Glory be to God, all Praise be to God, there is no god but God, God is the Greatest, there is no power nor strength except through God, the High, the Great.'"[12]

Even when the Prophet (peace be upon him) would raise his hands in supplication, he would start it with a litany of praise and glory to God, would make his plea, and would persistently punctuate his pleas with God's praise.[13]

Dhikr

Dhikr literally means to remember or remind oneself of something—here, of course, God. The Qurʾān is replete with exhortations to remember God frequently, and it unequivocally claims that the very purpose of ṣalāt is dhikr: "Indeed I am Allah. There is no god beside Me, so worship Me and establish prayer to remember Me (*li-dhikrī*)." (20:14) Needless to say, it is only dhikr that makes it possible for Muslims to combat the forgetfulness that so plagues man.[14] The Qurʾān persistently warns its readers not to fall prey to this forgetfulness by exhorting them to remember God. It is little wonder that one of the names of the Qurʾān is *al-dhikr*.[15] In fact, dhikr seems to be its most oft-repeated theme.[16] Dhikr in one sense is the supreme form of prayer, far superior to any other form of worship, as is particularly stressed by the Sufis: "Recite what has been revealed to you from the Book and establish prayer (ṣalāt). Surely prayer forbids licentiousness and evil. And Allah's remembrance (dhikr) is the greatest!" (29:45). Perhaps dhikr is here described as "the greatest" (*akbar*) because it has been prescribed for every moment, whereas other rites and rituals such as ṣalāt, *ṣawm* (fasting), or *ḥajj* (pilgrimage) have set times; indeed, there are times when one should not perform these rituals.

In addition to drawing on the many references to it in the Qurʾān, Muslim understanding of dhikr is hugely dependent upon ḥadīths such as the following:"I am close to the idea that My servant forms of Me, and I am with him when he remembers Me; if he remembers Me within himself, I remember him in Myself and if he remembers me in an assembly, I remember him in an assembly better than his; if he moves close to Me by the span of a hand, I move close to him an arm's length; if he moves close to Me an arm's length, I move close to him the span of outstretched arms; if he approaches me walking, I run toward him."[17]

Tawba

A fundamental theme related to the issue of both duʿāʾ and dhikr is that of *tawba*, which merits separate mention here. Derived from the root *tawaba*, it literally means to repent or to return. When applied to creatures, it denotes repentance from sins; when applied to God, it denotes the idea of God as Oft-Returning. By their very nature, human beings are weak and forgetful. It is this weakness that prompts them so often to fall into sin and therefore distance themselves from their Lord. Tawba is the first step that a Muslim is required to take when starting his or her journey to God. The Qurʾān and the Sunna frequently employ various terms to emphasize the idea of repentance, such as *ināba* (return) and *istighfār* (seeking forgiveness). Before raising one's hands to make a plea to God or deciding to remember God, one must show profound sorrow for having sinned against God, whether the sin be great or small.

God exhorts people to repent in several verses of the Qurʾān. "Tell them, (O Prophet): "My servants who have committed excesses against themselves, do not despair of Allah's Mercy. Surely Allah forgives all sins. He is Most Forgiving, Most Merciful." (39:53). Similarly tawba is also a frequent theme in the ḥadīth. The Prophet (peace be upon him) would often say: "By God! Indeed I seek Allah's forgiveness and turn to him (*atūbu ilayhi*) more than seventy times in a day."[18] Moreover, "All of Adam's children are sinners and the best of sinners are those who are the oft-repenting."[19]

Tawba can be beneficial only when the one who repents fulfills three essential conditions: withdrawing immediately from committing sin, feeling remorse for the sin, and committing not to return to it. If one has perpetrated a sin against another person, then a fourth condition is to compensate immediately for the loss that one has caused his fellow being.[20]

As a result of repentance and prayer in all its aspects, one is immediately reconciled with God and one also learns humility. Humility in turn reminds one of one's actual worth as a servant of God (*ʿabd*) and thus puts a rein on one's ego, the root cause of all iniquity and evil. If further developed, humility eventually leads people to love God's creatures and goes a long way in achieving peace and harmony in the society.

The Significance of Ṣalāt

Traditionally Muslims have viewed ṣalāt as the most fundamental aspect of their religion. It is little wonder that the sight of Muslims bowing or prostrating in unison has come to signify an important image of Islam and Muslim religious life in the media. The fact of the matter is that ṣalāt is the core of what it means to be Muslim. It is a continuous reminder (at least five times a day) to Muslims of the ultimate purpose of their creation as human beings—to worship God. God says in the Qur'ān, "I did not create the jinn and human beings except that they should worship me (*yaʿbudūni*)." (51:56) The word that the Qur'ān uses for worship is ʿibāda, derived from the root *ʿabada*, meaning to serve or to be a slave or servant. Thus, both jinn and human beings are to live as obedient servants of God, glorifying Him, bowing and prostrating to Him, and displaying complete submission to Him. It must be clarified, however, that the sort of servitude implied here is not of the involuntary kind mentioned in the Qur'ānic verse: "There is none in the heavens and the earth but shall come to the Most Compassionate Lord as a servant (*ʿabdan*)" (19:93). Rather, a true servant of God has decided voluntarily and with full love and devotion to submit to the will of God. This requires total effacement of one's own will and desires—indeed, of one's very self.

ʿAbd is also the title given in the Qur'ān to the prophets Muḥammad and Jesus (peace be upon them) (17:1; 19:30). Interestingly, when Muslims recite the Shaḥada in their ritual prayer they say, "and I testify that Muḥammad (peace be upon him) is His [God's] servant and messenger." The Prophet (peace be upon him) is first mentioned as a servant and then as a prophet, suggesting that his capacity as a servant of God takes precedence over his capacity as a messenger of God. It is no accident that Jesus also refers to himself as a servant of God before announcing that he is a prophet (19:30).

So, true and complete submission to the Lord is only possible when the Lord's will and desire is voluntarily acquired as one's own will and desire; in other words, one does not possess a will or desire of one's own and hence stands unified with God. This is called the level of *ʿubūdiyya* (servitude) in Islam. Sufis have generally called this phenomenon *waṣl*, or spiritual reunion with God. It is also known as the "station of annihilation" (*maqām al-fanāʾ*), in which the servant no longer sees himself or herself, no longer sees anything, but only sees, feels, and is totally immersed in the Presence of his Lord.

The fact that ṣalāt was prescribed for the Prophet (peace be upon him) and his people during the *isrāʾ* and *miʿrāj* is of great significance for Muslims. While the overwhelming majority of Muslims have traditionally understood this nocturnal journey to be both spiritual and physical, all have unanimously acknowledged its symbolic nature. The Prophet (peace be upon him) rose through the seven heavens (symbolizing varying levels of closeness to God) with the archangel Gabriel. At a certain point, the ritual prayers were prescribed by God. The Prophet (peace be upon him) proceeded further to a point beyond which Gabriel could not accompany him and became so intimately close to God that he was unified with Him or was even closer. The Qurʾān has captured this moment in a sequence of very powerful verses at 53:1–18.

Having witnessed union with Allah, the Prophet (peace be upon him) returned to earth with the good news that "prayer is the ascension (*miʿrāj*) of the believer." The witnessing of this union with God was not the prerogative of the Prophet alone. All believers could witness this intimacy with God through the ritual prayer. This has been testified to by the Prophet (peace be upon him) in "the ḥadīth of the *walī*" (saint or friend):

> The Prophet (peace be upon him) said: "Verily, God says, 'whoever is hostile to my friend (*walī*), I declare war upon him. No servant of mine comes close to me in a way more beloved to me than through that which I have made obligatory for him. And my servant keeps drawing nearer to Me through the supererogatory practices until I love him. When I love him, I become his hearing with which he hears, and his sight with which he sees, and his hand with which he grips and his leg with which he walks. Indeed if he entreats Me, I will certainly grant him [his plea] and if he seeks My refuge, I will certainly take him in My refuge."[21]

Although such verses and prophetic traditions are much quoted by a wide range of Muslims, it is the Sufis in particular who have delved into their deeper meanings and brought out the gems of wisdom hidden in them. The Sufis have done this through contemplation (*fikr*) and remembrance of the names of Allah (dhikr). It is for this reason that Seyyed Hossein Nasr rightly points out that dhikr is considered to be the prayer of the heart by the Sufis.[22] It needs to be mentioned, however, that no Sufi worth the name has ever understood the performance of dhikr to mean a level or state of prayer where ṣalāt may be discarded under the ruse that dhikr is the spirit while ritual prayers are the form and spirit inevitably takes precedence over form.[23]

Ṣalāt is compulsory for Sufis, as for all Muslims; the marked difference is that Sufis busy themselves with the idea of being in a perpetual state of prayer in accordance with the ultimate purpose of their creation—that is, worship. This ultimate purpose is to have arrived at a level that the Qur'ān and ḥadīth call *iḥsān*, literally, doing what is beautiful. In a famous ḥadīth the Prophet (peace be upon him) described iḥsān as when "you worship God as if you see Him; if you can't see Him then He certainly sees you."[24]

Since a Muslim is to spend all his life in a state of worship, it makes sense that he should perpetually be in a state of beholding God. That requires God-wariness (*taqwā*) and sincerity, both states of the heart.[25] Purity of heart is the only way one can attain these two states, and, as far as Sufis are concerned, that is only possible through dhikr.

Traditionally, Muslim societies were keen to uphold all three forms of prayer simultaneously. In addition to ṣalāt, the companions of the Prophet (peace be upon him) would often get together to make dhikr. Similarly, a whole tradition of *munājāt* developed in early Muslim society whereby the supplications (duʿā') of the Prophet (peace be upon him), his family members and companions, and later saints were collected. The memorization and recitation of these supplications was considered extremely auspicious.

Even in huge urban centers contaminated by the profanity of modern lifestyles one can observe the impact that ṣalāt has on Muslims. The fact that Muslims break the rhythm of their work five times a day and go to the mosque to pray deeply colors their lifestyle in all its complexities. Moreover, the Prophetic tradition mentions prayer in congregation as twenty-seven times better than praying individually. The social, psychological, and emotional benefits of congregational prayer are a favorite theme in manuals of Muslim prayer; praying together continues to provide strong social bonds of love, collegiality, equality, and brotherhood among Muslims and dissipates hatred and unhealthy competition among individuals.

Muslim Prayer Today

One often hears people posing questions about why one should pray and what the benefits are. These are by no means traditional questions. It is only modern man who has had the audacity to raise such questions, casting aside the spiritual perspective for the profanity of a secularist and materialist perspective, which boasts of apprehending reality through the power of modern science. In this perspective humankind is not the microcosm into whom the whole macrocosm folds.[26] Rather, humankind is the product of an evolutionary process that continues to unfold into the unknown future. Things in such a worldview can be classified as either mechanical or accidental—both states where prayer has little role to play, if any at all. In either case, it is only natural that people concern themselves with the here and now, focusing all their attention on fulfilling their immediate desires. We have seen earlier that prayer necessitates a diametrically opposed view since it leads one to submit oneself totally to the will and command of God. It therefore comes as no surprise that today, particularly in urban settings, most people feel no need to pray regularly simply because this new way of thinking, exclusively the product of the modern Western world, has inundated the whole world thanks to an unprecedented rise in ever quicker and more effective ways of communication.[27] Modernity has created too many other gods on whose altars human beings sacrifice their most priceless gift, the ability to know and communicate with God.

The point made in the last paragraph is just one side of the whole story, and it applies to almost all religions and cultures of the modern world. There is, however, another aspect of the modern Muslim practice of prayer that has risen from within the Muslim community itself: the growth of puritanical reform movements that apparently rose to correct the situation of the Muslim world by doing away with all innovations that in their perspective were the main cause of the backwardness of Muslims and their having fallen out of favor with God. Whatever their declared intentions, these puritanical movements did great disservice to Muslim communities through their hostility to tradition.

All traditional Muslim societies had developed a living tradition of prayer over many centuries on the basis of their understanding of the Qur'ān and prophetic tradition and the cumulative understanding and practice of the early Muslim community. Various scholars derived and developed their own principles for a judicious understanding of the texts—hence the slight variations in the way Muslims pray. Similarly, various spiritual orders also developed that paid close attention to other forms of prayer, in particular, dhikr and duʿā'. Ṣalāt had always been practiced in Muslim communities but at the times specified. The idea of being in a perpetual state of prayer and thus in the remembrance of God was only possible through dhikr. For this, each spiritual order developed formulas, litanies (*awrād* and *aḥzāb*), and other practices that would ensure that the whole Muslim community might not lose sight of its ultimate purpose—to worship God. There were several additional social, economic, psychological, and even political benefits attached to the tradition of dhikr.[28] It was these dhikr practices that the puritanical movements attacked as innovations, leading to disastrous results wherever these movements have held sway.[29] This is because group dhikr produces an effect that is more likely to "melt hearts" and to "lift the veils" that separate man from God. Usually performed under the tutelage of a *shaykh*, these dhikr *majālis* (gatherings) are perhaps the most effective way of setting a person individually, and the whole gathering collectively, on the path to God. Once such gatherings were declared heretical innovations, it was only a matter of time before the religious fabric of traditional Muslim society was torn apart. Here is how that happened in my native land, Sri Lanka.

A Personal Perspective from Sri Lanka

I belong to Sri Lanka, a land whose very environs are enmeshed in spirituality, and a land that Hindus, Buddhists, and Muslims consider the place where Adam came to earth from Paradise. My forefathers trace their religious heritage back to the Muslims of Yemen and Morocco, both enjoying a significant place in the intellectual and spiritual tradition of Islam; other Muslims trace their roots to the early Muslim communities of South India. Ours was a Muslim majority area in the east of the country punctuated by pockets of Hindu and Buddhist settlements all around us. We were all Shāfiʿī as far as our juristic school of thought was concerned, and the majority of us subscribed to one of the major Sufi orders prevalent in the Islamic world. Until the 1970s our rural community had been virtually untouched by the ravages of modern culture, and we were very proud of this.

I vividly remember that my childhood was spent trying to keep abreast of our lunar calendar, which was full of dates commemorating the three major Islamic festivals but also other important events in the life of the Prophet and the saints and sages of the Islamic tradition. The main feature of all these occasions was dhikr, in keeping with the Qur'ānic injunction "and remind them of the Days of Allah" (14:5).[30]

God was to be remembered in Himself and through His creation.[31] In particular, it was by following the path of His prophets and saints, who had traversed the difficult terrains of the soul and had put the reins of abstinence right through its nostrils leading it to its creator, that one could stand face to face with the Lord of the universe. Generally known as *mawlid* or *ʿurs*, these occasions were marked by solemn recitation of the Qur'ān, *istighfār*, remembering God through one or more of His names, reciting prayers of blessing on the Prophet (peace be upon him), and finally reciting a few stories from the life of the Prophet (peace be upon him) or the relevant saint. Although the sequence might be different in various spiritual orders, with a few additions or deletions here and there, this was the general pattern of recitation on most of these occasions. These were not merely solemn religious occasions; rather, they were also occasions of festivity and celebration and, hence, the source of abundant social, psychological, emotional, and religious benefits. It was in an advanced state of spirituality and remembrance of God that I left my community in 1976.

When I returned in the late 1980s things had changed considerably. Modernity had sunk its fangs into my community, and its impact on our religious culture was most evident in the mosques. Except for an odd youngster here and there, only the elderly came to the mosque. I soon discovered that the young folk were in the cafés, glued to the TV screens. And whereas in my time we youngsters spent our afternoons on the beach, on the playground, or in the fields discussing every topic under the blue sky, now our youngsters spent the afternoon taking extra classes. Education had become their new god.

Similarly, when I attended dhikr gatherings, which usually took place after the night prayer, I was once again stupefied to see very few youngsters. Obviously, our young folks had more important things to do than remembering God. While I was still recovering from this shock, I noticed that some of our youth were expressing their discomfort with the dhikr gatherings, calling them innovations of later generations. It turned out that the "puritans" had penetrated my community as well. Fresh from Al-Azhar University, the citadel of traditional learning in the Islamic world, I was well aware of the whole range of evidence that these young puritans built their foundations on, so I decided to talk to them. As it turned out, these were very young boys, many of them just teenagers, who seemed sincerely concerned about the waywardness of the whole Muslim *umma*. They were keen to outdo each other in the performance of the basic practices of Islam, particularly ṣalāt, but had not even the basic knowledge of Arabic necessary to be able to understand the Qur'ān and ḥadīth firsthand. They were far too concerned with the exoteric form of prayer to even ponder what prayer is all about. They were pathetically ignorant about the *sīra* of the Prophet (peace be upon him) and the history of Islam in general. To top it all, each of them considered himself a jurist of the highest caliber. They regarded Shāfiʿī, Mālik, and Abū Ḥanīfah as mere toddlers, unable to understand the prophetic traditions, which is why they dared to bring in their own opinions.[32]

My claim is that this sad state of affairs has arisen out of a multitude of factors, the most important being that the significance of prayer has been totally misunderstood. Prayer, in all its three aspects explored in this essay, has an individual as well as a collective dimension. The collective dimension of prayer stands thoroughly compromised in modern times as far as duʿāʾ and dhikr are concerned. It was these two aspects of prayer that kept the Muslim community continuously attached to God, or at least wary of being neglectful of God.

Perhaps, as many would have us believe, the tides of time cannot be reversed; perhaps modernity and the puritans have made their mark and are predestined to stay to wreak havoc in other traditional religious societies. Fortunately, Prophet Muḥammad (peace be upon him) taught otherwise, "Nothing can change destiny except prayer (duʿāʾ)."[33]

Notes

1. See also 19:31 (for the prayer of Jesus) and 19:58–59.

2. Muhammad Said Ramadan al-Buti, *Fiqh al-Sīra* (Beirut: Dār al-Fikr, 1994), 48.

3. For more details, see Bukhārī, *Ṣaḥīḥ al-Bukhārī*, "Bāb ḥadīth al-miʿrāj," ḥadīth 3598; and Muslim, *Ṣaḥīḥ Muslim*, "Bāb al-isrāʾ bi rasūl Allāh ṣalla Allāhu ʿalayhi wa sallam ila al-samāwāt wa al-arḍ," ḥadīth 234. Wherever I have quoted a ḥadīth, I have used the CD version of al-Maktabah al-Shāmilah, version 2. All volume numbers, page numbers, and ḥadīth numbers are strictly according to this version.

4. This idea can hardly be overemphasized. Perhaps the closest corresponding idea in Christianity is the Christian ideal of "living in Jesus Christ."

5. Al-Tirmidhī, *Sunan al-Tirmidhī*, "Bāb mā jāʾa fī al-ghanīma," ḥadīth 1474.

6. Owing to several traditions that emphasize the excellence of performing *wuḍūʾ* and the merits that one thereby accrues, many pious Muslims strive to constantly remain in this state of ritual purity. Moreover, in the Islamic spiritual tradition, one finds compelling details regarding the symbolic significance of washing the concerned body parts.

7. The late night prayers in Ramaḍān called *tarāwīḥ* that have become so popularized in the media lately can be categorized under *tahajjud*.

8. Abū Dāʾūd, *Sunan Abī Dāʾūd*, "Bāb al-duʿāʾ," ḥadīth 1264.

9. Al-Tirmidhī, *Sunan al-Tirmidhī*, "Bāb minhu (Mā jāʾa fī faḍl al-duʿāʾ)," ḥadīth 3293.

10. The Prophet called the Fātiḥa "*Umm al-Kitāb*" and "*Umm al-Qurʾān*," literally, the mother of all books and the mother of the Qurʾān. The recitation of this sūra in every cycle of the ritual prayer is enough evidence of its significance in Islamic worship. In fact, its recitation is considered obligatory for the correct performance of the ritual prayer by many Muslim jurists. Known for its immense power and impact, this brief chapter of the Qurʾān is recited by people on all sorts of occasions from childbirth to death, at the beginning of speeches, before exams, in times of tribulation and misery, on festive occasions like marriage and circumcision, and during *mawālīd* and *aʿrās* of notable saintly figures.

11. Bukhārī, *Ṣaḥīḥ al-Bukhārī*, "Bāb al-duʿāʾ ʿind al-karb," ḥadīth 5870.

12. Abū Dāʾūd, *Sunan Abī Dāʾūd*, "Bāb mā yujziʾu al-ummiyy wa al-ʿajamiyy min al-qirāʾah," ḥadīth 708.

13. For more on the prayer of the Prophet (peace be upon him), see Shāh Walī Allāh al-Dhelvī, *Ḥujjat Allāh al-Bālighah* (Karachi: Nūr Muḥammad, Kārkhāna-i Tijārat-i Kutub, n.d.), 70–81.

14. Humankind is forgetful of the covenant made with God in the spiritual realm prior to creation: "And [recall], when your Lord brought forth descendants from the loins of the sons of Adam, and made them witnesses against their own selves, asking them: 'Am I not your Lord?' They said: 'Yes, we do testify.' We did so lest you claim on the Day of Resurrection: 'We were unaware of this.' (7:172).

15. "Indeed it is We Who revealed the Reminder (*al-dhikr*) and it is indeed We Who are its guardians." (15:9).

16. Among many other examples, see 2:152; 18:24; 33:41–42; 3:191.

17. Bukhārī, *Ṣaḥīḥ al-Bukhārī*, "Bāb qawl Allāhu taʿāla wa yuḥadhdhirukum Allāhu nafsahu," ḥadīth 6856. See also Aḥmad bin Ḥanbal, *Musnad Aḥmad*, "Bāb ḥadīth Muʿādh bin Jabal," ḥadīth 21065; and Tirmidhī, *Sunan Tirmidhī*, "Bāb minhu," ḥadīth 2244.

18. Bukhārī, *Ṣaḥīḥ al-Bukhārī*, "Bāb Istighfār al-Nabī ṣalla Allāhu ʿalayhi wa sallam fī al-yawm wa al-layla," ḥadīth 5832.

19. Ibn Majah, *Sunan Ibn Majah*, "Bab dhikr al-tawba," ḥadīth 4241. See also Muslim, *Ṣaḥīḥ Muslim*, "Bāb al-targhīb fī al-duʿā' wa al-dhikr fī ākhir al-layl," ḥadīth 1263.

20. See Nawawī, *Riyāḍ al-Ṣāliḥīn* (Beirut: al-Maktab al-Islāmī, 1979), 37–38.

21. Bukhārī, *Ṣaḥīḥ al-Bukhārī*, "Bāb al-tawāḍuʿ," ḥadīth 6021.

22. Seyyed Hossein Nasr, *The Garden of Truth: The Vision and Promise of Sufism, Islam's Mystical Tradition* (New York: Harper Collins, 2007), 101.

23. Unfortunately, many modern "spiritualists" (and a few ancients as well) who generally go around under the deceptive garb of mysticism or Sufism would have us believe that it is only the spirit that matters; once one has attained a level of perfection, one can do away with the form. The threat that these "pseudos" pose for the whole religion where its internal and external forms coalesce into a harmonious whole can hardly be overemphasized. For a wonderful analysis and response to this thought pattern, see Christopher James Northbourne, *Religion in the Modern World* (Lahore, Pakistan: Suhail Academy, 2005).

24. See Muslim, *Ṣaḥīḥ Muslim*, "Bāb Bayān al-Īmān wa al-Islām wa al-Iḥsān," ḥadīth 9.

25. "The Prophet (peace be upon him) used to say, 'Islam is manifest and Īmān (faith) is in the hearts. Then he pointed to his heart with his hands thrice and said God-wariness is here, God-wariness is here.'" See Aḥmad bin Ḥanbal, *Musnad Aḥmad*, "Bāb Musnad Anas bin Mālik," vol. 24, 479.

26. This saying is attributed to ʿAlī (may God be pleased with him), the fourth rightly guided caliph.

27. It needs to be emphasized here that the premodern Western world was as religious as any other civilization of its time, with predominantly Judaism and Christianity catering for its religious needs.

28. The relation of the tombs of saints (where many dhikr circles were created) to the spread of Islam and to politics has captured the interest of several scholars. See, for instance, Vincent Cornell, *Realm of the Saint: Power and Authority in Moroccan Sufism* (Austin: University of Texas Press, 1998).

29. It is not that such communities have been spared the wrath of modernity. For example, Saudi Arabia, the most vocal champion of one such puritanical movement, also epitomizes a rapidly modernizing state where the fabric of traditional Muslim society has been torn apart.

30. The "Days of Allah" have been understood by scholars as all those occasions when God revealed His mercy by being bounteous to a people or His wrath by putting them through a trial or chastisement of some sort.

31. God says in the Qur'ān: "We shall show them Our signs on the horizons and in themselves until it becomes clear to them that this is the Truth." (32:53).

32. A quarter of a decade later my community stands further divided, with its tolerance level at its lowest. Muslims are busy hurling verdicts of infidelity at each other, and the last ten years have actually witnessed Muslims killing each other on religious grounds. Unfortunately, Hindu and Buddhist communities have not fared better.

33. Al-Tirmidhī, *Sunan al-Tirmidhī*, "Bāb mā jā'a lā yaruddu al-qadar illa al-du'ā'," ḥadīth 2065.

Christian Prayer in Practice

PHILIP SHELDRAKE

ALL FORMS OF PRAYER necessarily involve particular practices, whether brief or extended, complex or simple, alone or in common. However, from a Christian perspective, practices only make sense, spiritually and theologically, as explicit realizations of something more fundamental—our relationship with God. For this reason I want to begin with a few theoretical remarks. There are different Christian traditions with distinctive emphases, but what I will say reflects my own Western Catholic tradition.

Prayer as Relationship

How is the human relationship with God understood in Christianity? In brief, Christians believe that God, while the ultimate mystery, is nevertheless revealed to us as a personal rather than an impersonal force. This implies a relationship that, while challenging and transforming, is essentially characterized as "love." The Western Catholic tradition has a sacramental view of the created world and of everyday existence. In other words, the material world, human history, and everyday affairs are the media through which we are opened up to God's love and to God's transformative power. By implication, the divine can potentially be discerned not merely within explicitly religious contexts but within all aspects of life. The German Catholic theologian Karl Rahner, writing in the 1970s, defined prayer as "the explicit and positive realization of our natural and supernatural relationship with the personal God of salvation. It realizes the essence of the religious act." Rahner further notes, "All positive religious acts which are directly and explicitly related, both knowingly and willingly, to God may be called prayer."[1]

Two American theologians, Lawrence Cunningham and Keith Egan, who have written extensively on Christian mysticism and spirituality jointly offer other useful pointers.[2] They begin by discussing prayer as an activity but see this as "a fundamental gesture of belief, faith, dependence and connectedness."[3] In their comments on practices of prayer they write of "Making Ordinary Life a Prayer."[4] However, as with Karl Rahner, they state that this is not automatic but demands a conscious act of placing oneself in the presence of God in the midst of action. Finally, in their section "Prayer as Activity" they move beyond "prayer as practices" to a sense that, because prayer is a gesture that relates us to God, all that we purposefully do as Christians is a form of prayer: "In other words, it is possible to think of our lives as Christians as a form of prayer and the moments when we formally stop to pray either individually or in common as 'summing up' or 'articulating' our larger, less-consciously-prayerful acts which make up the business of living."[5]

Prayer as Theology

In summary, how and why we pray expresses important beliefs about God, human nature, and the world. Conversely, it is our relationship with God in prayer that creates our theology. We talk about God in certain ways because before this we have talked to and listened to God.

Worshipping and honoring God as well as notions of duty and obedience certainly appear in Christian understandings of the practice of prayer. Yet our relationship with God is not one-sidedly deferential or passively accepting. In the Book of Psalms, widely used in Christian worship, God is praised and thanked but also sometimes challenged. "How long, O LORD? Will you forget me for ever?" (13:1). "O God, why do you cast us off for ever?" (74:1). In the Book of Job, as theologian Gustavo Gutiérrez reminds us, the difference between Job and his friends is that the former does not live by abstract principles but risks a face-to-face encounter with God—even confronting God fearlessly.[6] A similar point is made by another theologian, Johannes Baptist Metz, that prayer is a kind of limitless language. Everything may safely be said to God in prayer including rage, frustration, and even accusation.[7]

The Practice of Prayer

When we turn to the practice of prayer in Christianity, the concept of relationship is central but we confront a significant range of prayer styles. Some of these are perennial, but other styles predominate in specific contexts and express the preoccupations of their time or place. Any attempt to summarize Christian prayer practices is selective, but I want to suggest six broad headings for consideration.[8] At the end of this essay I will also briefly take the tradition of prayer associated with Ignatius Loyola in the sixteenth century as one specific illustration.

Worship and Common Prayer

All Christian traditions have forms of regular public worship or common prayer. Sometimes this is ritualistic and structured while in other traditions it is more spontaneous. Common prayer expresses a fundamental sense that the practice of Christianity is inherently social rather than individualistic. From birth onward we develop within a network of human relationships. In terms of prayer, we may recall the words of the great seventeenth-century English poet and priest, George Herbert: "Though private prayer be a brave design, / Yet public hath more promises, more love" (*Perirrhanterium* lines 397–98).

Formal liturgy has two main characteristics. First, it divides the flow of time and marks particular times. Thus each day may be punctuated with sessions of prayer. Liturgy also marks out the week with different formats of scripture and prayers on a Sunday and on each weekday. Common worship also marks the seasons of the year, both the natural seasons and religious seasons related to the life and death of Jesus Christ. In some Christian traditions the year is also filled with memorial days of the Virgin Mary and other saints. Second, liturgy is repetitious in the sense that the same rituals, cycles of prayer, and readings appear again and again each year. Yet, importantly, those who gather for worship are never the same either as individuals or as a community. Thus, the way that liturgy and the existential reality of people interact means that the event of worship is never the same.

Lectio Divina

Lectio divina (literally, spiritual reading) is a form of scriptural study and prayer that derives originally from early monasticism in the fourth and fifth centuries CE, later influenced by patristic and medieval scriptural commentaries. It involved reflective study of scripture passages, the repetition of certain words or phrases, and then rumination on them. Originally this prayerful reading, which was both devotional and intellectual, was a fluid process. However, in the West it gradually developed four clear dimensions. These are known as *lectio* (the reading of a scripture passage), *meditatio* (repetition of words or phrases), *oratio* (or personal prayerful response), and *contemplatio* (the point at which words and thoughts dissolve before the mystery of God). These dimensions were eventually turned into a more systematic method during the twelfth century in the writings of a Carthusian monk, Guigo II. This move also paved the way to some extent for the later development of systematic forms of Christian meditation.[9]

Unceasing or Constant Prayer

From the early monastic practices of the Egyptian desert also arose a tradition of unceasing prayer encapsulated in what became known in Eastern Christianity as the Jesus Prayer or the Prayer of the Name. This was promoted in the seventh century CE by John Climacus, who specifically taught the link between breathing and the name of Jesus. The practice blended into an important strand of Eastern Christian spirituality known as hesychasm (from Greek *hēsychia*, stillness). The classic form of the Jesus Prayer was a phrase from Matthew 9:27, "Lord Jesus Christ, Son of God, have mercy on me a sinner," sometimes reduced simply to the name "Jesus." The practice became known in the West especially through nineteenth-century Russian writings. Importantly, this form of prayer is not purely mechanistic but involves a complex process of inner transformation and demands careful spiritual guidance.[10] There is also at least one example of this form of repetitive breathing prayer in the West in the writings of Ignatius Loyola, as we shall see later.

Popular Devotions

Popular devotions have often been underestimated in studies of Christian prayer. This devotional strand goes back to the early church—to the world of martyrs and their tombs, to the consequent growth of shrines, the cult of saints and their relics, the production of religious art and iconography, outdoor religious dramas such as the medieval English Mystery Plays, feast-day processions through city streets, and, of course, pilgrimage journeys to holy places. Popular devotion existed in both Eastern and Western Christianity and, while seriously questioned during the Reformation, is still current today. The great age of Western devotional development was from 1150 to 1450 and reflects three important factors. First, culturally there was a growing emphasis on human subjectivity and a resulting spiritual focus on the humanity of Jesus. This is notable in the development of Eucharistic devotions. Second, devotions channeled the popular fervor provoked by medieval church reform movements. Third, there was a growing democratization of spirituality outside monastic circles, linked to the renewed expansion of cities and an increasingly educated laity. The rosary, involving the use of beads, the repetition of the prayers "Our Father," "Hail Mary," and "Glory be," accompanied by reflection on aspects of Jesus's life, was in effect a lay adaptation of the monastic offices combined with elements of *lectio divina*. The Stations of the Cross, involving a mini pilgrimage around a church building while meditating on Jesus's passion and death, also combined elements of *lectio* with a microcosm of the great pilgrimage to the holy places of Jerusalem.[11]

Meditation: Historic and Contemporary

The development of structured meditation is mainly associated with the Western church although there is evidence for its presence in eighteenth-century Eastern Orthodoxy in translations of Western spiritual texts by Nicodemos of Mount Athos (1749–1809).

Methodical meditation first became popular in the late fourteenth century CE through a spiritual movement in present-day Belgium, The Netherlands, and North Germany known as the *Devotio Moderna*.[12] The *Devotio* taught a form of interior rather than vocal prayer broadly based on monastic *lectio*. However the movement recommended a systematic order to meditation to give cohesion to the process. This consisted of specific material to be meditated upon (either scriptural, devotional, or from the Christian creeds), suggestions as to how to use this material (what were called "points"), the provision of "colloquies" or personal prayer at the end of meditation, and a schedule of meditative themes over a week or longer. One of the founders of the movement, Geert Groote, wrote in his Letter 62 of reading scripture, then meditating on it and using the mind (including the imagination) to consider certain points. In his *Treatise on Four Classes of Subjects Suitable for Meditation* he again writes about the use of imagination and of the movement from outer imagination to the "inner senses," which he sees as contemplative or even mystical. Thus, just as the Christian sacraments (for example, the Eucharist) were intended to lead the worshipper from outer signs to what is signified, so, according to Groote, "the images of sensible things" in meditation also lead us to what is beyond the senses. Other writers in the movement, such as Salome Sticken in her *Way of Life for Sisters* and Gerard Zerbolt in *The Spiritual Ascents*, describe a short meditative review of each day, or what they called the examen.[13] All of these features had an explicit impact on the spirituality of Ignatius Loyola, as we shall see.

The practice of meditation is once again increasingly popular in Western countries both inside and outside conventional religion. A variety of techniques are used, sometimes borrowed from Buddhism (for example, Zen "sitting") or Hinduism (for example, yoga). Within Christianity similar borrowings may also be present. However, one of the best-known Christian meditation movements is the World Community for Christian Meditation founded by an English Benedictine monk, John Main, OSB.[14] He recommended sitting still and upright with eyes closed, emptying the mind while repeating a single word such as "Maranatha" ("Our Lord, come!"), which appears at the end of St Paul's first letter to the Corinthians (16:22). Main had originally been influenced in the 1950s by the Hindu teacher Swami Satyananda. However, after becoming a Christian monk he studied further and believed that he had found parallel teachings in the writings of John Cassian, the great early monastic teacher. In fact Cassian's Tenth Conference does not really describe systematic meditation in a modern sense. He recommends repeating "in the heart" the opening verse of Psalm 70, "O God come to my aid; O Lord make haste to help me," when in trouble, while working, or while on a journey.[15]

Informal, Brief, or Conversational Prayer

The final form of prayer practice cannot really be described as a method. This is the long tradition of informal, brief, and spontaneous "conversational" prayer. Many Christians, whether aware of more structured practices or not, express their sense of intimate relationship with God in spontaneous moments of conversation, petition, or praise. The immediacy and "honesty" of such prayer reflects Metz's idea of prayer as a limitless language. It has a long pedigree, for example in chapter 20 of the monastic Rule of St Benedict, which suggests that ideally prayer should be short and "pure" with resonances here of both "distilled" and "honest." Equally, St. Augustine in his spiritual treatise for the widow Proba suggests that longer prayer is good but not necessary. He therefore commends "very brief, quickly dispatched prayers" (*orationes brevissimas et raptim quodammodo jaculatas*).[16] It is also important to acknowledge the tradition of "charismatic" prayer that began in Protestant churches but later provoked a movement of fervor from the 1960s onward in more formal liturgical traditions such as those of Roman Catholicism or Anglicanism. The charismatic movement involves more than prayer forms. However, prayer is essentially a communal practice best known for its spontaneous praise related to being "filled with the Holy Spirit." This sometimes involves "speaking in tongues" or glossolalia—that is, praying in an ecstatic language that is not immediately intelligible unless interpreted.

Contemplative-Mystical Prayer

What of contemplative-mystical prayer? I suggest that while it is in some sense possible to talk of "contemplative practice," it is misleading to see contemplation as merely another method of prayer alongside others. Whatever our prayer practices, "contemplation" (for example, the fourth dimension of monastic *lectio*) is not something we simply choose to perform. Rather, the word "contemplation" expresses a movement beyond structures and the complexities of method. Externally it tends to be a movement into silence or stillness but is essentially a process of being drawn into an immediacy of presence to God. Christians understand this to be wholly a gift. Admittedly, contemplation arises from a consistent practice of prayer, but it is not the guaranteed result of any practice. It implies a transformative process that leads to a deepening of the fundamental relationship with God. In its mystical forms, it may involve transformations of consciousness or certain experiential phenomena, but these are incidental to a mysterious process of ever-closer union with the divine.

Ignatian Prayer

In the final part of this essay I shall refer briefly to one living Western spiritual tradition to illustrate some of what has gone before. This tradition is known as Ignatian spirituality and takes its name from St. Ignatius Loyola, the sixteenth century Basque founder of the Jesuit Order and author of the famous *Spiritual Exercises*.[17] This work is not intended for spiritual inspiration but offers detailed guidelines for those who guide others during a solitary retreat, usually lasting a month, but sometimes available over a more extended period in the midst of everyday life. These "Exercises" promote a structured process across four phases or "Weeks," focused on the quest for inner freedom (what Ignatius calls "detachment") from all that imprisons us spiritually. This freedom leads to an ever-greater capacity to respond with generosity to the call of God in Jesus Christ. This process is supported by a range of prayer practices. Apart from the fact that I am personally familiar with it, I have selected this tradition because it has such contemporary influence across a wide spectrum of Christian traditions.

Contrary to popular myth, Ignatius did not promote any one method of prayer. Even in the text of the Exercises there are at least ten. Outside the text, in his thousands of extant letters, Ignatius taught a very broad understanding of prayer. I want to focus on four practices drawn from the text of the Exercises.

The first practice is known as "gospel contemplation" and involves meditating on gospel texts that focus chronologically on the life and ministry of Jesus.[18] This is the predominant practice of prayer during much of the retreat. The formula for this practice is laid down in two successive meditations at the beginning of Week Two, the "Contemplation on the Incarnation" (Exx 101–9) and the "Contemplation on the Nativity" (Exx 110–17). The format of gospel prayer clearly echoes elements of monastic *lectio divina*, mediated through the *Devotio Moderna*, to which Ignatius was exposed while receiving spiritual guidance at the monastery of Montserrat and then during his theological studies in Paris. The person praying first asks God that prayer may be directed only at God's purposes. After that the next step is to recall the relevant scriptural narrative (*lectio*). Then follow two steps that correspond to *meditatio*. The first is a brief "composition of place," that is, by imagination to enter into the scriptural scene, followed by an invitation to focus on what one desires. The main body of the meditation consists of three to five points to guide the person praying to reflect on the scripture narrative and to "draw fruit" in a personal way. Finally, the contemplation ends with a "colloquy" as in the *Devotio Moderna*—a personal conversation with God "according to my inner feelings" in response to what has been meditated upon. This corresponds to *oratio* in the *lectio* tradition.

The second prayer practice is called the "Application of the Senses" and is the final period of prayer of the day from Week Two onward. Its formula is described at the start of Week Two (Exx 121–26). This is "to pass the five senses of the imagination over" key points, or insights, from earlier meditations. Thus, Ignatius invites the person praying "to see the persons [in the gospel narrative] with the imaginative sense of sight" and so on through all five senses. This practice has often been treated with a lack of clarity. Some people simply assume that it is a restful practice aimed at those who are weary at the end of a long retreat day. However, a correct understanding is reached if we recall what I described earlier about the movement from outer imagination to the "inner senses" in writings of the *Devotio Moderna* from which this practice is derived. Thus, "applying the senses" should be understood as an embodied approach to imagination, using the senses, that simplifies and synthesizes earlier prayer. This hopefully leads the person praying beyond images to a form of infused contemplation.

The third practice is known as the Examen. This appears in the Exercises in two forms, the Particular Examen and the General Examen (Exx 24–43). There was a time when the Examen was interpreted as a moral exercise aimed at the correction of faults. However, its richer meaning has been recovered in recent decades, not least by rediscovering its sources in the *Devotio Moderna*. Here, the Examen, as in Ignatius, is to be prayed daily. It is intended as an overall reflective review of each day. Contemporary versions recommend the following. Begin by asking for God's guidance to truly understand the past day, especially where God was particularly revealed in people and events. Then focus on the ways one recognized God and was led to respond, and thank God for that. Next focus on the moments when one failed to respond, and why, and ask pardon. Finally, seek the guidance of God for the following day. The Examen ends by asking for strength and insight to respond appropriately to God's call in the events of daily life. This practice of prayer grounds two values in Ignatian spirituality. First, it expands the process of "finding God in all things." Second, it sharpens a person's ability to exercise what Ignatius (and the longer Christian tradition) calls discernment or practical wisdom, in relation to everyday choices. Discernment is the ability, aided by God, to recognize the different influences from within ourselves and from outside and to be able to distinguish those that are life-giving from those that are destructive.[19]

The final Ignatian prayer practice is called "the third way of Praying" (Exx 258–60) in the section of additional material at the end of the Exercises. This practice of prayer is called variously "by rhythm" or "of the breath." It is regularly overlooked. Apart from the fact that it is an appendix to the text, I suspect it is overlooked because until the recent growth of a greater awareness of practices outside Western Christianity, this prayer form was not seen as mainstream. The practice itself is simple. Take a well-known prayer—for example, the Our Father—and link each word rhythmically to our breathing. Each word in succession is interiorly pronounced between each breath while the mind focuses quietly on the presence of God. Ignatius's sources for this practice are a mystery. Irenée Hausherr has suggested connections with Eastern Christian hesychasm.[20] Another possible source is the Andalusian Sufi influence on Spanish Christian mysticism during the fifteenth and sixteenth centuries.[21]

Conclusion

By way of conclusion, it is worth noting that different traditions of prayer practice emphasize certain physical locations. In some cases it is assumed that these will be religious buildings or in the presence of sacred objects such as a statue or icon. However, while Ignatius Loyola points out the importance of place for prayer, he does not specify where it should be and seems to imply that it need not be a chapel (Exx 75–79). Indeed, in one letter he commends responding to God's presence in all things as one walks around. In formal prayer, Ignatius suggests that people should adopt whatever posture helps them—kneeling, standing, sitting, or lying prostrate (Exx 76). He also recommends the varied use of light or dark, as seems helpful (Exx 79).

In recent decades there has been greater awareness that, if we believe that prayer is fundamentally a relationship, it seems likely that women's and men's spiritual experiences may vary to some degree. This awareness leads to a growing sensitivity about the language and imagery used or recommended for public worship or for individual meditation. Sometimes this awareness leads to greater reflection on actual practices of prayer. Thus, a recent commentary by women on the Ignatian prayer tradition suggests that the dominant emphasis during much of the nineteenth and twentieth centuries on analytical forms of mental prayer based on reason, will, and detachment from feelings was problematical while the rediscovery of the more fluid use of imagination has been positive for women.[22]

The variety of Ignatian prayer forms and, more importantly, Ignatius's teaching on the imperative of adapting prayer practices to persons and circumstances reminds us yet again of what I emphasized at the beginning. Prayer is ultimately a living relationship between humans and God and the practices of prayer are simply to express this relationship and to enable it to develop fruitfully. Methods, maxims, and disciplines undoubtedly have their role, but they are merely means to an end and as such must always be subordinate to the mysterious dynamics of the human encounter with God.

Notes

1. Karl Rahner, "Prayer," in *Encyclopedia of Theology* (London: Burns & Oates, 1975), 1275.
2. Lawrence S. Cunningham and Keith J. Egan, *Christian Spirituality: Themes from the Tradition* (New York: Paulist Press, 1996). See their section on prayer, 66–83.
3. Ibid., 67.
4. Ibid., 73.
5. Ibid., 78.
6. Gustavo Gutiérrez, *On Job: God-Talk and the Suffering of the Innocent* (Maryknoll, NY: Orbis Books, 1998), especially part 3, "The Language of Contemplation."
7. See the insightful study of Metz's theology in Spanish theologian Gaspar Martinez, *Confronting the Mystery of God* (New York: Continuum, 2001), ch. 2, especially Metz's approach to spirituality and prayer in the section "Theology and Theodicy," 82–88.
8. There are not many overall historical surveys of Christian prayer. One that, although originally written in 1969, is still useful is Joseph Jungmann, *Christian Prayer through the Centuries*, rev. ed. (London: SPCK/New York: Paulist Press 2007). For the foundations of the practice of prayer in Eastern and Western Christianity, see the important essays "Ways of Prayer and Contemplation," (i) Kallistos Ware, "Eastern" and (ii) Jean Leclercq, "Western" in *Christian Spirituality: Origins to the Twelfth Century*, eds. B. McGinn, J. Meyendorff, and J. Leclercq (New York: Crossroad, 1985), 395–426.
9. See E. Colledge and J. Walsh, eds., *Guigo II: The Ladder of Monks & Twelve Meditations* (New York: Doubleday, 1978). See also the more recent exposition of *lectio* by the Cistercian monk Michael Casey, *Sacred Reading* (Ligouri, MO: Triumph Books, 1996).

10. See Kallistos Ware, *The Power of the Name: The Jesus Prayer in Orthodox Spirituality* (Oxford: SLG Press, 1986); and for the nineteenth-century Russian tradition, see A. Pentkovsky, ed., *The Pilgrim's Tale*, Classics of Western Spirituality series (New York: Paulist Press, 1999).

11. See Richard Kieckhefer, "Major Currents in Late Medieval Devotions," in *Christian Spirituality II: High Middle Ages & Reformation*, ed. Jill Raitt, 75–108 (New York: Crossroad, 1987). See also Philip Sheldrake, *A Brief History of Spirituality* (Oxford/Malden MA: Wiley-Blackwell, 2007), 24–25, and ch. 3.

12. On the *Devotio Moderna* and the meditation movement, see Otto Gründler, "Devotio Moderna," in *Christian Spirituality II: High Middle Ages & Reformation*, ed. Jill Raitt, 176–93 (New York: Crossroad, 1987).

13. Translations of all these texts are available in John Van Engen, ed., *Devotio Moderna: Basic Writings*, Classics of Western Spirituality series (New York: Paulist Press, 1988).

14. Full details are available on the WCCM website: www.wccm.org.

15. See Boniface Ramsey, ed., *John Cassian: The Conferences*. Ancient Christian Writers (New York: Newman Press, 1997), Tenth Conference, 10.14, p. 382.

16. Augustine, *Ad Probam*, in Migne, *Patrologia Latina*, 33, col. 1075.

17. For an up-to-date translation and edition of the *Spiritual Exercises*, see J. Munitiz and P. Endean, eds., *Saint Ignatius Loyola: Personal Writings* (London: Penguin Classics, 1996). References are to the standard paragraph designation, e.g., Exx 200.

18. For a useful essay on the contemporary renewal of Ignatian contemplation, see John F. Wickham, "Ignatian Contemplation Today," in *The Way of Ignatius Loyola: Contemporary Approaches to the Spiritual Exercises*, ed. Philip Sheldrake (London: SPCK; St Louis MI: Institute of Jesuit Sources, 1991), 145–53.

19. For a contemporary study of the examen, see Donald St. Louis, "The Ignatian Examen," in *The Way of Ignatius Loyola: Contemporary Approaches to the Spiritual Exercises*, ed. Philip Sheldrake, 154–64 (London: SPCK; St Louis MI: Institute of Jesuit Sources, 1991).

20. See Irenée Hausherr, "Les exercises spirituels de Saint Ignace at la méthode d'oraison hésychaste," *Orientalia Christiana Periodica* 20 (1954): 7–26.

21. For a general study of such influences, see L. López-Baralt, *The Sufi 'trobar clus' and Spanish Mysticism: A Shared Symbolism* (Lahore, Pakistan: Iqbal Academy, 2000).

22. See K. Dyckman, M. Garvin, and E. Liebert, "Knowing Whose I Am: Prayer in the Spiritual Exercises," ch. 5 in *The Spiritual Exercises Reclaimed: Uncovering Liberating Possibilities for Women*, 113–49 (New York: Paulist Press, 2001).

A Muslim Response to Christian Prayer

CANER DAGLI

I RECALL THAT on one occasion my mother, a pious Muslim who grew up in a town in central Anatolia in Turkey, asked her professor son the basic question, "Do Christians pray to Jesus?" with a tone of puzzlement and, it must be said, impending disapproval. Her difficulty stemmed from thinking about her own daily prayers and supplications to God—forehead on the ground or hands raised toward the heavens—and what it would be like to direct those prayers to Jesus. For any Muslim, the substance of prayer consists in gratitude for blessings bestowed, repentance for wrongs committed, petitions for good in this world and the Hereafter, and glorification and remembrance. These pillars of prayer and devotion, for the typical Muslim, approach something like self-evidently good ideas that are uncomplicated and direct. My mother knew enough about Christianity to know there is this idea of the Trinity, and that it involves something about Jesus being the Son of God or Jesus being God, and in her own mind she put these ideas together with her own understanding of what makes prayer prayer and came up with that sincere question, "Do Christians pray to Jesus?"

What she said was hardly ever absent from my mind as I thought about how to approach writing a Muslim response to Christian prayer. The answer I gave her then, and that I would still give now, is no, Christians do not pray to Jesus in the way that Muslims pray to God when they stand and bow for the *ṣalāt* or raise their hands in supplication, nor do they say or believe, for example, that Jesus as such created the heavens and the earth. I told her that when Christians pray to God, they really are praying to God, to one God. But when Christians talk about God, they do say that He is triune, and that Jesus is the son of God, and God incarnate, and to a Muslim this is already and necessarily a tension.

For me the answer to the general question "To whom do Christians pray?" and, by extension, "How do Christians pray?" is from the Muslim point of view a complex one. The most important reason for this is that the Qurʾān, the basis for any Muslim's theological position, provides a picture of Christianity that is often misunderstood, and that is more nuanced and complex than many commentators and theologians—both Christian and Muslim—seem to allow. It is clear that the Qurʾān does not render just one judgment about Christians, neither always condemning them nor always praising them.

For example, if we were to ask what the Qurʾān says about monks, we would come across 5:82, which reads: "And you will find the nearest of them in affection toward those who believe to be those who say, 'We are Christians.' That is because among them are priests and monks, and because they are not arrogant."[1] But in 9:34 we read: "O you who believe! Verily many of the rabbis and monks consume the wealth of people falsely, and turn from the way of God. [As for] those who hoard gold and silver and spend it not in the way of God, give them glad tidings of a painful punishment." The complexity is perhaps evidenced most clearly in a single verse regarding Christian monasticism, 57:27: "Then We sent Our messengers to follow in their footsteps, and We sent Jesus Son of Mary and We gave him the Gospel and placed mercy and kindness in the hearts of those who follow him. And monasticism they invented—We did not ordain it for them—only to seek God's contentment. Yet they did not observe it with proper observance. So We gave those of them who believed their reward, yet many of them are iniquitous." This complexity comes out in the facts that (a) God characterizes followers of Christ as being kind and merciful; (b) Christians themselves, not God, ordained monasticism; (c) monastic practice was originally well intentioned, but Christians were not faithful to it (by which some commentators understand the introduction of the Trinity); (d) there was in fact a right way (*ḥaqq riʿāyatihi*) to be a monk; and (e) some of these who practice monasticism have a reward while others are iniquitous.

Finally, in light of all this, we read in 2:62 (and a similar verse at 5:69): "Truly those who believe, and those who are Jews, and the Christians, and the Sabeans—whosoever believes in God and the Last Day and works righteousness shall have their reward with their Lord. No fear shall come upon them, nor shall they grieve." There are many more relevant passages of the Qurʾān that I could cite, but for my purposes here it is enough to say that I view all of the Qurʾān's statements about Christians—in the framework of the Qurʾān's description of sacred history, sectarian disagreement, and uncompromising monotheism—as variations of two underlying principles: first, that for Christians who believe in God and perform righteous deeds, "no fear shall come upon them, nor shall they grieve"; and second, that

Christians utter *kufr* or unbelief when they say that Jesus was the Son of God or that he is God, and when they worship Jesus and Mary as gods. That is, I understand the Qur'ān to be saying that the Christians worship well but have terrible ideas. The challenge of approaching Christian worship and devotion is that these two principles or axioms exist in a kind of tension.

This basic distinction that the Qur'ān makes in its treatment of Christians and Christianity, and that can serve as a reliable basis for which to compose a Muslim response to Christian prayer, is the difference between devotional attitudes on the one hand and metaphysical propositions on the other. It is the difference between how one encounters God and how one describes God, and the Qur'ān generally praises Christians in their devotion to God while generally condemning them for their theology. It is within this framework, this tension, that I would like to explore some aspects of Christian worship and prayer from the point of view of a Muslim believer.

The Sacraments

Distinguishing between what one might call the theological background and the devotional foreground can be helpful when thinking carefully about Islam and Christianity. It is usually said that Islam has no sacraments. But it certainly has rituals that seem to have some overlap with what would be called sacraments in the Christian context—if not in their precise form, then in the attitude or posture one takes in performing them. Muslims tend to conceptualize the Christian sacraments against the backdrop of a drastic distinction between the sacred and the profane, between what is spiritual and what is merely natural. This impression is often reinforced by the limited number of "sacraments" that act as conduits of divine grace, and by statements such as, "Give unto Caesar what is Caesar's" and the Christian doctrine of original sin and the Fall; it is also exacerbated by the general lack of understanding by Muslims of the theological explanations of the sacraments. Moreover, there is a problem here of terminology. What are called "sacraments" in the West are in the East called "mysteries" (from the Greek *mystērion*), a more fluid term not restricted to the seven sacraments but also including, for example, the Incarnation itself. Indeed, posing a question using the word "sacrament" already has the potential to leave out too much and to lead to misunderstanding.

The Christian sacraments or "sacred mysteries" operate within a universe that is determined by the Christian view of the fallen state of human beings and the special manner in which they stand in need of God's grace. Because Muslims conceive of this fallen state and its remedies differently, there is often an assumption made by both Muslims and Christians that Islam has no sacraments. And because in Islam there is no priesthood and no church hierarchy, and because sacraments are typically (though not in all Christian traditions) administered through them, Muslims again will usually say there are no sacraments in Islam, and that Islam is not a sacramental religion.

My contention is that a Muslim can have a more positive appreciation of the sacraments than is typically afforded by conceiving of "sacraments" as a distinctively Christian feature of religion. To be sure, there are decisive differences between the theological and metaphysical apparatus surrounding these acts of worship in Christianity and their counterparts within Islam, but I believe we can understand the similarities and differences in liturgy and ritual between the two religions if we do not insist on categories such as "sacramental" and "nonsacramental."

After all, Christians describe a sacrament or sacred mystery as consisting of an outward sign (the form) and inward grace that is instituted by God. This latter is crucial because it distinguishes mysteries of the special kind from the general mysteries of the world as God's creation expressing His wisdom and power.

If we take the Christian definition of sacrament or "sacred mystery" and keep to these essentials, it turns out to be a decent rough-and-ready description of the Five Pillars—the testimony of faith, the canonical prayer, the fast, the pilgrimage, the alms. If one message comes out from reading the Qur'ān, it is that everything God created is a sign conveying a grace (we would say *baraka* or blessing), some being natural and others most certainly being instituted specifically by God. When I reflect upon the central practices of Islam as "sacraments," to my mind the description seems to fit—so long as we hold firm to the conception of an outward sign having an inward blessing or grace instituted by God.

In my own spiritual universe, I know what it is like to a believer to gravitate toward *baraka*, and I know that believers automatically conceive of some kind of inward element, often thought of as angelic support, that flows through the rites. In a ḥadīth, the Prophet said that God says, "My servant continues to approach Me with voluntary devotions until I love him, and when I love him I am the ear by which he hears, the eye by which he sees, the hand by which he grasps, and the foot by which he walks."

My remarks about the sacraments are more of an appreciation than anything else, since space and time do not allow me to address each of them individually. I would like to point out that the specifically Christian notion of what it means to be fallen and the transformation these sacraments or mysteries are meant to effect seem to be a major part of what makes Christian sacraments opaque and well-nigh impenetrable to Muslims, and it may be part of what masks the spiritual ambience of Islamic rites to some Christians. That is to say, if we get too lost in the respective theologies and hierarchies, we can lose sight of the obvious similarities in that actual moment and experience of prayer and ritual—when an infant is baptized and a father recites the *adhān* into his newborn's ear, when a Christian receives the Eucharist and a Muslim recites the Qur'ān, holy orders, and the bestowal of the Sufi cloak, not to mention matrimony.

The Lord's Prayer

Although I could have structured my entire essay as a Muslim response to the Lord's Prayer, the *Pater noster*, I would like to focus on two of its themes: fatherhood and forgiveness. The words "Our Father" already seem to complicate the plain sense of Trinitarian doctrine since Christ is not the Son of God the way that Christ describes believers as being sons and daughters of God in Matthew 5:9: "Blessed are the peacemakers: for they shall be called the children of God." Commentators on the Lord's Prayer (from Tertullian and Origen through Calvin and Luther to the Catholic Catechism) are placed in the position of elucidating how the "Our" spoken by believers in the "Our Father" does not change the "My" of "My Father" when spoken by Christ. In reading these meditations and explanations of the Lord's Prayer a Muslim reader such as myself is somewhat frustrated in not finding clearer solutions to the problem of equivocality when one encounters "Father" in the prayerful statement "Our Father," and when one reads it in what might be called the metaphysical statement, "I and the Father are one" (John 10:30). By equivocality I mean that the word "father" is not said univocally in these two instances, as when one says "man" of both Socrates and Plato, and neither is it a homonym, as when one speaks of the "bank" of money and the "bank" of a river. As they might say in Islamic philosophy, it lies between synonymy and homonymy.

In his commentary on Qur'ān 2:116 the theologian Fakhr al-Dīn al-Rāzī (d. 1210) notes that the appellation "father" must have originally denoted priority, authority, and love, not unlike the description of God as "Lord" or "King," and on this score he sees no irreconcilable problem with it, but in his view it then became exaggerated to the point of being a theologically untenable limitation of God, being bound up with the Incarnation and the Trinity.[2] It does seem significant to me that in this central prayer—taught to believers by Christ—the Father is the kind of father even an Ashʿarite theologian such as al-Rāzī would be able to pray to. One feels a tension between the doctrine bound up in the phrase "God the Father" and the natural attitude expressed in the prayer, "Our Father who art in Heaven." So to register a Muslim puzzlement on the matter: when a believer says, "Our Father" in the *Pater noster*, is it closer to the Father as al-Rāzī conceives of it, or is it closer to being the Father of the Nicene Creed? When one is actually praying, what does it actually mean to call God Father?

Later in the Lord's Prayer we find the petition, "And forgive us our debts, as we also have forgiven our debtors." In a Muslim's mind, a prayer for forgiveness is a hope that God will consider one to be forgiven, that He will show compassion and mercy and not take us to task for everything we have done. A Muslim knows that for a Christian forgiveness is bound up totally with Jesus' experience on the cross, but also beyond that with baptism, and moreover is intimately related to concepts such as justification and sanctification. Taking all this into account, and trying to capture the spirit of my mother's question, I would ask: when a Christian prays for forgiveness, what is he or she praying will happen? I formulate it in this way to highlight that, from the outside looking in, the economy of forgiveness, of getting right with God, of being reconciled—however one formulates it—seems complex and difficult to capture in a single insight.

For example, one has difficulty in juxtaposing the direct, intuitive forgiveness that seems to be described and hoped for in the Lord's Prayer with the various versions of atonement, whether it is the ransom theory, penal substitution, or variations thereof. I am not here trying to decode or decide between these theories; rather, I am trying to understand how, in the actual articulation of the Lord's Prayer and the petition for forgiveness, these theories (so intimately bound up with the central doctrines of the Trinity and Incarnation) actually guide and provide substance to the supplication for forgiveness in the moment of worship. The analogy that is bound up in this petition—"as we also have forgiven our debtors"—announces to my mind a certain simplicity of act: I know what it is like to forgive another human being, and it does not seem easily modeled on any of the mainstream theories of atonement (except perhaps that of Abelard, the moral influence theory). The plain sense of the Lord's Prayer strikes one as limpid and straightforward, providing a kind of commentary upon itself when it reads "as we also have forgiven our debtors." Often in the commentaries on this particular verse of the Lord's Prayer one is directed to Luke 6:37, "Forgive, and you will be forgiven," and Matthew 18:21–22, "Then Peter came and said to him, 'Lord, if another member of the church sins against me, how often should I forgive? As many as seven times?' Jesus said to him, 'Not seven times, but, I tell you, seventy-seven times.'"

Christian Theology and Devotion in Qur'ānic Perspective

It is now worth reconsidering, in light of this discussion of Christian worship and devotion, some significant Qur'ānic passages related to Christian theology and devotion: "And when God said, "O Jesus, son of Mary! Didst thou say unto mankind, 'Take me and my mother as gods besides God?'" (5:116); and "They certainly disbelieve, those who say, 'Truly God is the third of three,' while there is no god save One God" (5:73).

I would not be the first to see the possibility that the statement "Take me and my mother as gods" does not have to be interpreted as some version of a doctrinal Trinity but as a subjective association of objects of worship with God. Still, it is commonly thought that somehow the Qur'ān got the Trinity wrong here, or that this is referring to a long-dead sect that did in fact worship this Trinity of God, Jesus, and Mary. The same is often said of the statement "God is the third of three," again interpreted to be a misunderstanding or perhaps a way of describing Jesus that was common in Syriac at the time the Qur'ān was revealed. To me it is important to note that this verse critiques the assertion that "God," not "the Father," is the third of three. "God" is not the third of three for Christians; rather, God is the three. I interpret "God is the third of three" as I do the taking of Jesus and Mary as gods beside God: as describing an attitude of worship that the Islamic perspective cannot accept.

One key to interpreting these verses is 9:31: "They have taken their rabbis and monks as lords apart from God, as well as the Messiah, son of Mary, though they were only commanded to worship one God." No Christian theology places monks as objects of worship, and the grouping together of monks and Christ in this verse shows that what is at stake is an attitude, the orientation of the soul in the act of worship, not a matter of official theology. Is there any doubt that in the economy of Christian devotion there is a kind of devotional Trinity of God, Jesus, and Mary that is not coterminous with the doctrinal Trinity of Father, Son, and Spirit? Who receives prayers and devotions in the Christian tradition if not these three and in this order? From the Islamic perspective, when the veneration of Jesus and Mary go too far, God—and not the Father of the Trinity—becomes the third of three objects of worship.

I favor reading these verses as being critiques of the actual devotional posture of some Christians because elsewhere (4:171) the Qur'ān does provide a head-on critique of Christian theology: "O People of the Book! Do not exaggerate in your religion, nor utter anything concerning God save the truth. Verily the Messiah, Jesus son of Mary, was only a messenger of God, and His Word, that He committed to Mary, and a Spirit from Him. So believe in God and His messengers, and say not 'Three.' Refrain! It is better for you." This is a direct indication that the theology is at question, not the practice. The bare and unqualified command "say not 'Three'" does not implicate the devotional life of Christians or their acts of worship, drawing attention to what they say, not what they do, and does so in a remarkably gentle fashion.

The issue at hand is that a mainstream Christian does not view Trinitarian theology and Christology as theological afterthoughts to their encounter with God in prayer, to be toyed with in an armchair after the serious business is done. Rather, the Trinity is what God is, and one really cannot come to the Father but through the Son, who is God incarnate. A Muslim will wait in vain for the Christian to say that "Father" and "Holy Spirit" are just different names for God. They are not. And this is what leaves Muslims often baffled when looking closely at both Christian ritual life and Christian doctrine together. It leads people like my mother to ask, "Do Christians pray to Jesus?"

To the Muslim soul, the actual encounter between a human being and God, the attitude of devotion, and the resolve to a life of virtue are realities that converge upon a unity that is not analyzable or divisible into a conceptual trinity, and the Christian Trinity is, no matter how formulated, a conceptual three-ness since the minimum definition has at least three ideas in it—actually more because their relation must also be taken into account.

While Muslims famously attribute to God many Names, these are Attributes of one Object. When I bring my attention upon another human being—my wife for example, with all her attributes and actions—I am conceiving of her as a single person with those attributes. But the hypostases of Christian theological discourse are not attributes or names of a single essence. The "three" of the Trinity does not collapse or get transcended in mainstream Christian theology. And so the Muslim wonders how or whether Christians address themselves to three persons in prayer, or to one of three, and if so, how?

When an activity becomes most human and spiritual and most alive, it converges on simplicity—a simplicity of the whole, not of the part. When we first play a musical instrument, we necessarily visualize our actions as a sequence of motions and as an aggregate of parts. When we achieve true mastery, this complexity becomes simplicity. We no longer see ten different fingers on white and black keys, each key with a separate name and sound. We see an inseparable whole. In prayer, from the Muslim point of view, the conceptual oneness we ascribe to the object of our worship can accompany us, as it were, along every level of prayer and contemplation until we leave off the level of ideas and enter into pure contemplation or silence. But a Muslim has difficulty understanding how the conceptual nonunity of the Trinitarian idea ever becomes simple. That is, as we focus our attention and our heart upon God, does not the relationality of the three Persons have to give way to the immediacy and simplicity of the I–Thou encounter in prayer? And if so, does it not behoove the supplicant or worshipper to begin and end simply with that "Thou" and to conceive of it as simply as possible? Is there not a hiatus from the three elements in the mind to the unity of the lived encounter, to the oneness of the actually existing experience that happens in prayer?

The Islamic attitude in prayer originates from the content and indeed the very form of *lā ilāha illā Allāh*. As a matter of prayerful meditation or meditational prayer, the formula "No god but God" continuously wipes away all other objects of thought until one is left with only Allāh, and as the Sufis would say then the final "h" of Allāh, and finally just the breath and the death of the soul. The idea of "one" comes with us at each step of that spiritual journey, right up to the point where we cannot or should not any longer think our thoughts. But it seems, from the outside, that the Trinity as an idea in the mind (again, not as a reality that is encountered) cannot come so far with us. It must stay behind as the human being's consciousness of God becomes increasingly simple and integrated.

Conclusion

I am not here trying to solve any metaphysical puzzles, or even to mount a critique of Christian theology from the Muslim perspective, but to convey what I think is a faithful Islamic response to and appreciation of Christian worship. I base my reflections on what I think the Qur'ān literally says about Christians because I think that is the only legitimate starting point for a Muslim. My whole premise is that the Islamic attitude to this question is necessarily complex because what the Qur'ān says about Christians is not simple or lacking in nuance. And in reading what the Qur'ān has to say, I have found it most helpful to make a basic distinction between what human beings actually do in their souls when they worship or pray and the intellectual and symbolic framework within which they situate those actions. I am not trying to disentangle them because they are inseparable, like the dimensions of breadth and depth. But they are not the same thing, and they often exist in a state of tension. They usually do, in fact.

Postscript: Evangelism as Ritual

Although it does not fit neatly together with my foregoing remarks, I would also like to reflect briefly upon worship in the evangelical community, and here a Muslim is struck (indeed, I believe most Muslims have not the slightest inkling of this) by the fact that worship and ritual share the same plane of priority with evangelism and sharing the good news. Muslims naturally relate to the devotional structure of Catholicism, Orthodoxy, or Anglicanism, which assume that preaching and conversion of others is a special vocation that belongs to a select few. That is, Muslims easily conceive of a core of beliefs and practices, and although just and charitable behavior is part of that essential set of obligations, the specific imperative to find new converts and change the hearts of others is not thought of as an obligation upon every last believer. Rather, at a maximum it is a special vocation, and at a minimum one is called to be witness or human testimony to one's own faith by simply living it, leaving God to guide whomsoever He will.

The elevation of evangelism to what seems to be a core act of worship—one which a person cannot as a good Christian omit—does not, despite the facile assumptions made by some evangelicals, have any counterpart within the Islamic universe. You can find a certain current in the Muslim community who believe they have to justify their residence in so-called non-Muslim lands by preaching Islam, but this stems more from a distorted understanding of Islamic political structure than from a theological conviction about the saving of souls. And naturally there exist many Muslims who, because of a spiritual imperative and inner drive, make part of their life the preaching of Islam to others in hope that they will become Muslim, or become better Muslims.

To be frank, I think the vast majority of Muslims are unaware of this elevation of evangelism to the rank of a central ritual, and they assume that evangelicals situate the preaching of religion at a level of obligation akin to what one finds in Islam. From the outside looking in, this focus on what some have called "conversionism" has all the hallmarks of a sacrament or mystery: one does it as a kind of divine institution, one is guided or moved by the Spirit in doing so, where one's own person or the Gospel itself is the outward sign which conveys the inward grace that effects the conversion. It is hard to deny a certain ritual quality to the preaching that results from this conviction that the saving of souls is at the heart of religious obligation, which one may judge to be good or bad. I dwell upon it as part of a Muslim response to Christian worship and prayer because it is a dimension of Christian worship with which Muslims have to directly grapple as an ongoing matter, and it is not trivial. That Muslims are unaware that many of the

Christians with whom they interact view their evangelism this way is of utmost significance.

Notes

1. Translations from the Qur'ān and the ḥadīth are my own, drawing on various versions.
2. Fakhr al-Dīn al-Rāzī, *al-Tafsīr al-kabīr* (Beirut: Dār Iḥyā' al-Turāth al-'Arabī, 1999).

A Christian Perspective on Muslim Prayer

DANIEL A. MADIGAN

Whenever one talks about prayer, one is treading on holy ground, and that is particularly the case when one is speaking about others' prayer. One has no access to that secret space in which God and the believer encounter one another most intimately, and there is certainly no question of making judgments. In this chapter I hope to share some observations about my experience as a friend and admirer of Muslims who pray, particularly the insights that have been prompted by them—observations about things that seem to me to be common to us as well as those that offer some contrast by which we can know who we are in our particularity and difference. I must tread respectfully on the holy ground where Muslims pray; so, too, I must try to do justice to at least some of the variety of Christian understandings of prayer. I acknowledge that I am speaking from the Roman Catholic tradition within which my understanding and experience of prayer has been shaped. Still, I hope other Christians will recognize in what I say at least some of their experience of praying.

It is a great pity—indeed, a gross injustice—that almost the only images of the Muslim ritual prayer seen by people in the West are the accompaniment to television news reports of violence and radicalism. Those who lived through the violent decades of the Irish "Troubles" can imagine what the corrosive effect would have been if every report of an IRA attack had been illustrated by images of Catholics at Mass.

One of the most striking aspects of Muslims at prayer is the prescribed communal prayer—the *ṣalāt*—with its row upon row of believers standing shoulder to shoulder before God. Yet these prayer lines are straight only on a micro level. The *ahl al-qibla*, or, as Kenneth Cragg liked to translate the term, the People of the Point, are actually praying, Cragg observed, not in serried ranks but rather in concentric circles when looked at on a global scale.[1] The turning of one's face as a whole community toward a single point on the face of the earth five times daily is the physical analogue of the constant spiritual reorientation that any believer needs. One repeatedly pauses to get one's bearings on the journey on which we are led by God. Those who pray are, in Qur'ānic terms, the *muhtadūn*, the ones who accept to be guided, rather than choose proudly their own path and end up wandering, lost. I am reminded here of Newman's "Lead, kindly light," particularly its lines:

> I was not ever thus, nor prayed that Thou
> Shouldst lead me on;
> I loved to choose and see my path; but now
> Lead Thou me on!

I am also reminded of Ignatius of Loyola's constant habit of the examen. This was not a regretful looking backward at failure but rather a taking of bearings and a new orientation toward companionship with Jesus.

The point on which we all focus, of course, is the point where we believe God has addressed his Word to us in history. Having a *qibla* is a reminder that we are not simply devoting ourselves to a numinous, utterly transcendent "Real," but to a God who has a Word for us in our historical particularity. For Muslims, that particular historical place where the Word is spoken is Mecca and Medina. Christian prayer has its *qibla* in slightly different ways: it became a custom to orient churches toward the east so that the congregation would pray toward the rising sun as symbol of the resurrection and of the awaited return of the Christ. In the Roman Catholic Church people argue about which way the priest is facing during the Eucharist—he is said to be "facing the people" or to "have his back to the people"—but surely the point is that both celebrant and congregation are focused on our *qibla*, our orientation point, the Eucharist we are celebrating in obedience to the command of the one who told us to remember him by breaking the bread and sharing the cup. Christ is our *qibla*, because his self-sacrifice is the point at which, in the Christian understanding, the divine Word is most clearly expressed in our human history.[2]

The Muslim ritual prayer itself is carried out for the most part in silence, its physical rhythms measured by the praise of God—*takbīr*. It is not a dialogue between a leader and a congregation, as much Christian ritual is, and it is not reliant on clergy. It is very obvious in Muslim worship that those who participate are not spectators but worshippers. In many Christian liturgies we too often witness a move away from the assembly as co-celebrants toward the assembly as audience. This can happen even in situations where there is a great deal of involvement of the people in various liturgical ministries, rendering the worship truly beautiful. It can lead to a sense of having "the cast" on the sanctuary and "the audience" in the pews—especially when we, as it were, "roll the credits" at the end of the liturgy and give a round of applause to the choir, the organist, the cantor, the liturgy committee, and so on.

Even when one person is praying it alone, the *ṣalāt* is physically dramatic, and in large assemblies it is strikingly expressive of a profound communal solidarity in faith. The postures are physically demanding, and in spite of their boldness they do not seem to cause self-consciousness, as witness the almost casual way in which a lone Muslim might pray even in apparently very unpromising surroundings. All the world, we are reminded in a ḥadīth, is a mosque, a place appropriate to the worship of God. And there is nothing more pressing, no power that cannot wait its turn for our attention behind the God who claims it. Not only that, but all the world is itself at prayer. According to the Qur'ān, as Dheen Mohamed reminds us in his chapter in this volume, all of creation knows its *ṣalāt* and is performing it constantly (24:41). Our own prayer is of a piece with the rest of creation. This will recall to the Christian mind, perhaps, the canticle of the three young men in the fiery furnace in the Book of Daniel 3:51–90 or Psalm 19.

The robust gestures of Muslim prayer and the expressiveness of its postures are often in contrast with many Christian rituals in which movement and gesture have been reduced to an embarrassed minimum, the involvement of the body sacrificed to an ever greater reliance on words to substitute for and explain symbols that have now become so vestigial that they can no longer speak for themselves.

With the possible exception of the Friday sermon, Muslim worship is nonclerical. The obligation to perform this ritual five times a day is incumbent upon the individual whether there is a community and a leader or not. One witnesses among those Muslims who fulfill the obligation a striking sense of individual responsibility even if the time and place are less than ideal. The imām (literally, "the person in front") is the facilitator of the community's common worship in the most minimal way. Virtually anyone who knows what he is doing can perform the role. He performs the same actions as the other worshippers and says the same words, just setting the pace and giving the audible cues for those ranged behind him.

In my own Roman Catholic tradition, the decline in the number of men who feel called to the celibacy currently required for ordination to the priesthood has brought about an increase in the number of communities that are taking responsibility (I was almost going to say "that are forced to take responsibility") for their own life of common worship. Nevertheless, there is still a sense that such responsibility is exceptional rather than fundamental; and it could scarcely be considered obligatory: no priest, no Mass, therefore no obligation. How different a sense one gets from a Muslim for whom constant attention throughout the day to time and to space is required for maintaining the ritual prayer. To an outside observer, a day rhythmed by the moments of prayer—to say nothing of the many other actions and attitudes adopted by observant Muslims in their daily life—looks like a kind of monasticism. But did not the Prophet famously say that there is no monasticism (*ruhbāniyya*) in Islam? Monasticism, the Qurʾān tells us, is something that Christians developed for themselves (57:27). It was not laid on them as an obligation by God. However, that is not the basis on which it is criticized. The basis of God's censure was the fact that those who had created the monastic way of life had not observed it properly. *Ruhbāniyya* could perhaps lead to a kind of farming out of one's religious responsibility. Many of the desert ascetics of the Qurʾān's time were spiritual athletes of a high order, and of course the danger of such athleticism is that it becomes an elite and specialized calling to which the rest of us are merely spectators—a kind of spiritual Olympics. Ordinary believers can be led to understand that their relationship with God has been contracted out, as it were, to the experts; they end up, the Qurʾān tells us, "partnering" those experts with God (9:31), and some Muslims claim that the same sin has befallen their own community. True Christian monasticism, like the ordinary observances of Muslim daily life, does not rely on prowess but on simple fidelity and regularity—regularity in its literal sense of observance of a rule.

Since we have allowed gender to raise its head here, let me acknowledge how striking it is to see the robust masculinity of Muslim public prayer. One realizes straight away that the *ṣalāt* is a political act in the broadest and most positive sense of that word. It is an act of the *polis*, the citizenry together; so to participate in prayer, particularly the *jumʿā* prayer, is to take one's place in public life. Is this why, I wonder, it is so intriguing to a Christian to see two or three college-age students going matter-of-factly to the mosque together for *ṣalāt* in the course of their normal day? For many Christians a visit to a church out of hours (or even on a Sunday) might seem to be a public demonstration (perhaps edifying, maybe puzzling, perhaps even unwelcome) of an interior life that would normally be kept private. One can't help but applaud this lively sense of the connection between our life of faith, our orientation to God in prayer, and our public political responsibility.

At the same time, the relegation of women to a position out of sight—where they will not prove an immodest distraction to the ever-susceptible male—offers a dramatic demonstration of a de facto exclusion from public life. Even though the obligation to pray is also incumbent on women, one witnesses a hesitancy to allow the same connection between faith and public life in their case. As a Roman Catholic, I'm hardly in a position to throw stones here. Seeing such exclusion in an unfamiliar setting alerts me further to the ways in which women are excluded in so many ways from worship in my tradition, even more so *de facto* than might be required *de jure*. In most parts of the world the involvement of women in the liturgical ministries currently open to them lags well behind the law that allows it. And even more striking in both our traditions than the exclusion, or at least dissuasion, from full participation in worship is the resistance to women's leadership and governance.

Before I dig myself in too deep here, let me change the subject to memory and remembering, terms central to both our traditions of prayer. In Reza Shah-Kazemi's chapter in this volume we are offered a wonderful presentation of the theme of *dhikr*. For a Christian, the Muslim notion of *dhikr* bears many echoes. The Eucharist, our central act of worship, is explicitly an act of recalling (*anamnesis*), and not simply the recalling of information. It is a reliving, an entering once more into the reality of those events of Christ's death and resurrection. It is also a prayer for God to remember us, and thus a mutual remembering in which we count on God's promise spoken through the prophet Isaiah (49:15) that even though, heaven forbid, a nursing mother forget her baby at the breast, God will not abandon us.

The mutuality of remembering is also closely related to a mutuality of hearing, *samaʿ*. Our scriptures, although of course they underline God as a speaker of the Word, repeatedly remind us that God is also a listener: he hears the cry of the poor, the prayer of the just, the blood of the slain Abel crying out for justice; and God quotes against us the things he has heard us say. Yet God has less need to listen than we do, and we risk so filling our prayer with our empty-headed words that we are unable to hear the Word addressed to us. It is the Word addressed to us that, we believe each in our own way, creates us and recreates or saves us.

The words of *ṣalāt* are by and large Qurʾānic words; that is to say that for the believer they are God's words. Perhaps paradoxically, it is the Word that has been given to us, not the one that we imagine we have produced or invented, that is our appropriate response to God. So many of the practices of Muslim prayer remind us that it is the divine Word given to us that is our point of contact, our way of return to the God who speaks. God's Word draws us to God's self. By resonating with the sound, the energy of God's speech, particularly what God says of God's self, the believer is brought near to God. For Christians, of course, the Word is expressed in our history in flesh and blood rather than in words. Our resonating with the Word will be, as Archbishop Rowan put it in his reflection in this volume on his own practice of prayer, an allowing ourselves to be drawn into "the stream of self-giving that flows from Jesus to the Father."

Now for a few comments on Muslims and Christians praying together. John, in his first letter, asks his Christian readers rather pointedly how we can claim to love the God we cannot see when we do not love the brother or sister we do see (1 John 4:20–21). A disunited worship will always be an incomplete worship because it bespeaks an as-yet imperfect love. A united worship is an objective we have still to work toward.

It may be that in this connection between love of the other and the true worship of God lies the answer to our difficulty about common prayer. Recognition of the creature will draw us to worship the creator, so we begin with that recognition—perhaps in ritualized form but even more basically and more importantly in non-ritual activity, which might eventually find its way into ritual and explicit worship. Rather than thinking that if we could worship in common we would come to love one another, I am suggesting that we should pursue first the ordinary experience of a deepening affection and respect; then a desire for and sense of common worship will naturally emerge from that.

Let me offer an example. Some years ago, when I was teaching in Rome, I was at a seminar in Istanbul. One of my Muslim students was also there, and she invited me and two other professors (who are rabbis) and the wife of one of them to visit her family. We sat under the trees outside the small summer house on the Anatolian side of the Bosphorus, picking cherries and mulberries from the branches above our heads as we chatted using the various languages we could manage to muster between the eight of us. It was unavoidable that we would talk about religion at least part of the time because the father of the family was a retired high school religion teacher. Never having had a rabbi in his house before—let alone two at once—he could not miss the opportunity to ask about various things that had puzzled him over the years. The honest courtesy of the inquiries, the warmth of the hospitality, and the unostentatious care taken to ensure that the meal could be readily shared by all combined to make the evening truly memorable. At the end of the meal the father invited the three Jews present to pray the grace. Then my student asked me to sing the Taizé Magnificat that is used after meals in the community where she lived in Rome. The family followed this with their own prayer in Arabic. For all of us, it was a moment of profound gratitude for a rare glimpse of unity among believers. However, it was a moment long prepared by studying together, by simple contacts in the university, by years spent by all parties in trying to understand the tradition of another. That small unrehearsed "liturgical" moment, which seemed so perfectly to express the reality of our friendship as believers of related but diverse traditions, was the goal toward which we strive, not the point from which we begin. We could sense in one another at the end of that evening a genuine desire to worship and to give thanks. It was, in the literal sense of the word, "eucharistic."

If our interreligious worship is to have any sense as praise and thanksgiving, then it probably has to come after the simple living and working together in which we discover a motive for gratitude and a desire to praise the God who made all this and brought us together in human solidarity.

The simplicity and dramatic directness of Muslim ritual prayer and its eloquent embodying of humble submission to God are surely attractive to the Christian. As Dheen Mohamed reminds us in his chapter, the Muslim worshipper is the *ʿabd*, the "servant" or "slave," whose worship is the humble acknowledgment of human submission to God. Yet, as he notes, there is also an essential element of intimacy open to the believer. The doctrine of loving intimacy, as expounded for example by Aḥmad al-Ghazālī (brother of the more famous theologian Abū Ḥāmid al-Ghazālī) and other Persian Sufis and poets, presents a rather different view from some more common views based on the master–servant relation between God and the believer. In the master–servant relation the human being is always the servant and God is always the Master. One wills and commands while the other is obliged to obey. In the lover–beloved relation, however, the positions of the lover and the beloved are not fixed. The love relation is reciprocal. At times the human being is the lover while God is the Beloved, and at times God is the Lover while the creature is God's beloved. Sufis appeal for justification to the words of Qur'ān 5:54: "God loves them, and they love him." They have taught that God's love for the human person precedes our love for God, and if it were not for the fact that God had favored humanity by his primordial love, mercy, and compassion, humanity could never have loved God and his creatures.[3]

Ultimately for a Christian, worship must take its tone also from Jesus's declaration that we are no longer slaves but friends, that we are guests whose feet he will wash, or from Paul's insight that we are the adopted daughters and sons of the household, that we are prodigals whose confessions of unworthiness are cut short by a Father who wants to embrace us and celebrate our return. It is something we need to be reminded of again and again, since, as George Herbert puts it in his poem "Love," our souls draw back, "guilty of dust and sin." We do come into God's presence, but we prefer to remain shamefaced servants rather than accept that we are honored guests worthy to be there. When it comes to worship, the Christian must hear the final lines of that haunting poem:

> "You must sit down," says Love, "and taste my meat."
> So I did sit and eat.

Notes

1. Kenneth Cragg, *Islam and the Muslim* (Milton Keynes, UK: Open University Press, 1978), 7.

2. Here I am thinking in particular of two moments in the New Testament. The first is the word of Jesus in John's Gospel (19:30) as he dies on the cross: τετέλεσται ("it is accomplished"). In his dying, the Word has entered most fully into the human condition; the incarnation of the Word is complete. Pilate had said more than he realized when he brought the scourged Jesus out to the crowd and said, "Behold the man!" (19:5). The other moment is the hymn in Paul's letter to the Philippians (2:6–11) in which the reason for Jesus's exaltation is precisely that he humbled himself even to the point of being crucified. It is for this that God gives him the name above all names, God's own name, the unpronounceable יהוה. See Daniel A. Madigan, "Particularity, Universality and Finality: Insights from the Gospel of John," in *Communicating the Word*, ed. David Marshall, 14–25 (Washington, DC: Georgetown University Press, 2011).

3. Nasrollah Pourjavady, "The Sufi Way of Love and Peace," in *Voices of Islam*, eds. Vincent J. Cornell, Virginia Gray Henry-Blakemore, and Omid Safi, 2:157–66 (New York: Praeger Publishers, 2006).

Response

ROWAN WILLIAMS

After the great intellectual and spiritual nourishment of the day, it is a little difficult to boil things down into a few minutes at the end. But I have five words that I have picked up from today's discussion, on each of which I shall offer some brief reflections.

The first word is *friendship*. The point was made this morning that our common ancestor in faith, Abraham, is called "God's friend," and that there is in all our reflection about prayer a crucial and central element of thinking about what it is to be a friend of God. In a text from the Gospel of John (15:12–14) that was referred to today, a friend is one who knows or understands what is going on, as opposed to a slave who does not know what the master is doing or what the master really wants. Friendship, then, is a good place to begin—friendship with God, not to mention friendship with one another.

Friendship is very closely connected with my second word, which is *knowledge*. Prayer is a way of knowing God because, if prayer is rooted in friendship with God, then of course prayer is about knowledge; but this is knowledge as sharing, absorption—not an acquisitive knowledge, a knowledge that seeks to pile up intellectual property. I welcomed very much the question about whether there is an epistemology of the physical in prayer. I think that, as Daniel Madigan said, the answer is that there clearly is. You learn something simply by going through the motions of celebrating Holy Week as a Christian. It was the late, and very great, Russian Orthodox teacher Metropolitan Anthony of Sourozh who said that you begin to understand Orthodoxy in your legs. Anyone who has been to Orthodox services will know exactly what that is about. Knowledge as participation, knowledge as sharing—not acquisitive.

Perhaps that may allow us to understand a little better one other question that came up this morning in the comments made by Dheen Mohamed about modernity and puritanism. Modernity and modern religious puritanism (or fundamentalism) are not the same thing. But what they do have in common is an impatience with traditional means of knowledge. They both have a view of knowledge that is essentially about accumulating or acquiring rather than participating or absorbing. Prayerful knowing, I would say, sets itself both against modern consumerist culture and against a false and impatient primitivist religion that seeks quick answers with which to reproach other people.

To speak of knowledge in this nonacquisitive way takes us back to another word that was mentioned this morning as a possible area of tension or disagreement between us, and I am not sure that it is. That is the word *desire*—which is my third word. Reza Shah-Kazemi quoted the wonderful threefold typology of prayer from Imām ʿAlī, beginning with desire: the prayer of the merchant.[1] There are very similar texts in Christianity that talk about the mercantile attitude to prayer. But this clearly is about a desire that is, precisely, acquisitive. It is a desire that wants to gain a particular goal for the self, whereas one of the fascinating features of Christian reflection on prayer—and I would be very interested to see what corresponds to this in the Islamic world—is a fresh account of desire that sees it as more and more letting go of the acquisitive, the selfish, more and more simply the opening up to what is to be given. That naked desire—not for anything in particular, any goal in particular, any future in particular—but sheer openness to the real, to the true; and, therefore, a desire which always expands and is never fulfilled, never met—a constant, undying thirst for the real, the true, the divine. And it is at that level, I think, that there is a convergence between what we have heard from Islamic sources, and what we find in Christianity, and what we find also in the Buddhist critique of craving. To grow spiritually, for the Buddhist, is to grow beyond desire in the sense of craving. And yet it is still a radical nakedness or openness to what is true or what is real.

My fourth word is *protest*. Desire, in the sense that I have mentioned, means openness. Openness means trust, an absolute confidence that, when you have opened your heart, your soul, your selfhood, your body, to God, God honors his promise to be there for and with you. And if God honors his promise, is it then possible to think of having the confidence simply to let the words of protest, doubt, trouble rise to the surface of the mind because we trust that God can absorb them? It is not that Jewish or Christian prayer rebels against the idea of submission to God—in the Psalms, say, or the writings of Martin Luther. I would much rather say that submission is seen as something which can be a process. And in that process, we may need to find the words of discontent, of bewilderment, of anger, and allow them to arise in order that our submission may be the more full.

George Herbert perhaps deserves one more reference today. His great poem "The Collar" begins with an outspoken cry of protest against God: "I struck the board, and cried, 'No more. . . .'" The poem begins by saying "I will have no more to do with God!" Through the poem, Herbert explains why he is disillusioned, angry with God, the God who, he feels, has let him down. And at the end of the poem comes the perfect resolution of submission:

> . . . as I raved and grew more fierce and wild
> At every word,
> Methought I heard one calling, *Child!*
> And I replied My *Lord*.

Submission is there, but it is a submission that is achieved; it has taken time.

Perhaps that has a little to do with my fifth word, which is *unity*. Unity, we have discovered today, is a very complex notion. We have looked at it from a number of points of view. We began with some very profound reflections from Reza Shah-Kazemi on *tawḥīd* as the fundamental category in which to understand prayer and everything else. And precisely because of its fundamental nature, we are reminded that to speak of the unity of God is never to speak of the unity of one thing. God is not one as an object is one—with an edge around it. God's oneness is different.

We spoke not only of the unity of God but also of our potential for unity with God. However, what *is* our unity with God? What is the unity we seek? Certainly not to be one *thing* with God, which is literally not thinkable. It would not make sense to think of us being one thing with God, not only because we are created and God is not but also because God is not "a thing." So what is the nature of that unity that we move or grow into? This is neither the unity of one thing nor simply a unity of distant agreement or consonance—as if we wave at a distance across the cosmos and agree that we have basically the same ideas, God and ourselves. It has to be more than that, and it has to be different from being one thing.

I shall resist the temptation to respond at length to what Caner Dagli said about the doctrine of the Trinity and the nature of fatherhood, but I think some of what Christians would want to say in this connection is that we are looking in our language about the Trinity for a way of speaking about divine unity that is neither the unity of one *thing* nor simply the unity of *agreement*. Rather, Trinitarian language is a way of speaking that has an ontology to it that our words will always fall short of, but our words remind us that we have to say more than anything else we would ever say about any other sort of unity. This is why, in the *Mystical Theology* of Pseudo-Dionysius, one of the great classics of Christian mysticism, we read that God is not one and He is not three—relativizing all of the concepts of number that we might want to bring to that question.

So in today's discussions we have been taken very deep. We have had some excellent questions from the floor, as well as some excellent papers to stimulate our thinking and our praying. I want to express the warmest possible thanks to our speakers today, and to all of you who have come to participate in the discussion, who have given your time and energy and attention very generously today, and have contributed so greatly to the common understanding that we seek in this seminar.

Notes

This is a lightly edited version of the comments made at the end of the day of lectures that began the Qatar seminar on May 17, 2011. Some of the comments refer to points made by participants that are not included in the lectures published in this volume but were their unscripted responses to questions. Recordings of the question-and-answer sessions following the lectures are available at http://berkleycenter.georgetown.edu/resources/networks/building_ebridges.

1. Imām 'Alī's threefold typology: worship based on desire, that of the merchants (*al-tujjār*); worship based on fear, that of the enslaved (*al-ʿabīd*); and worship based on gratitude, that of the liberated (*al-aḥrār*).

PART II

Prayer and Scripture

The Lord's Prayer

SUSAN EASTMAN

Matthew 6:5–15

[5]And whenever you pray, do not be like the hypocrites; for they love to stand and pray in the synagogues and at the street corners, so that they may be seen by others. Truly I tell you, they have received their reward. [6]But whenever you pray, go into your room and shut the door and pray to your Father who is in secret; and your Father who sees in secret will reward you.

[7]When you are praying, do not heap up empty phrases as the Gentiles do; for they think that they will be heard because of their many words. [8]Do not be like them, for your Father knows what you need before you ask him.

[9]Pray then in this way:
Our Father in heaven,
hallowed be your name.
[10]Your kingdom come.
Your will be done,
on earth as it is in heaven.
[11]Give us this day our daily bread.
[12]And forgive us our debts,
as we also have forgiven our debtors.
[13]And do not bring us to the time of trial,
but rescue us from the evil one.

[14]For if you forgive others their trespasses, your heavenly Father will also forgive you; [15]but if you do not forgive others, neither will your Father forgive your trespasses.

Luke 11:1–13

[1]He was praying in a certain place, and after he had finished, one of his disciples said to him, "Lord, teach us to pray, as John taught his disciples." [2]He said to them, "When you pray, say:

Father, hallowed be your name.
Your kingdom come.
3Give us each day our daily bread.
4And forgive us our sins,
for we ourselves forgive everyone indebted to us.
And do not bring us to the time of trial."

5And he said to them, "Suppose one of you has a friend, and you go to him at
midnight and say to him, 'Friend, lend me three loaves of bread; 6for a friend of
mine has arrived, and I have nothing to set before him.' 7And he answers from
within, 'Do not bother me; the door has already been locked, and my children
are with me in bed; I cannot get up and give you anything.' 8I tell you, even
though he will not get up and give him anything because he is his friend, at least
because of his persistence he will get up and give him whatever he needs.

9"So I say to you, Ask, and it will be given to you; search, and you will find;
knock, and the door will be opened for you. 10For everyone who asks receives, and
everyone who searches finds, and for everyone who knocks, the door will be
opened. 11Is there anyone among you who, if your child asks for a fish, will give a
snake instead of a fish? 12Or if the child asks for an egg, will give a scorpion? 13If
you then, who are evil, know how to give good gifts to your children, how much
more will the heavenly Father give the Holy Spirit to those who ask him!"

Introduction

> Words only have meaning in the stream of life.
>
> Ludwig Wittgenstein

The Viennese philosopher Ludwig Wittgenstein's comments about language suggest that *what* words mean and *how* they mean can be abstracted from neither those who speak nor those who hear. This resistance to abstraction is surely true of the words of prayer in Jesus's teaching; that teaching is embedded in his own life, and it directs us both to the lives of those who pray and to the faithfulness of God who hears.

In the introduction to the Lord's Prayer in Matthew's gospel (6:5–8), Jesus contrasts two ways of praying by comparing the assumptions embedded in them about what makes prayer efficacious. Those who he holds up as a negative example assume that the abundance of their words, and perhaps their eloquence and intensity, make them effective. They are mistaken, however, because it is not the words themselves but their recipients who give them significance; when prayer is directed primarily at impressing human auditors, the prayer goes no further. Those who "love to stand and pray in the synagogues and at the street corners, so that they may be seen by others

. . . have received their reward" (6:5). Don't be like that, says Jesus; God does not need your words because God already knows what you need. In other words, the effectiveness of prayer lies not in the one who speaks but in the one who hears: God "who sees in secret" is the hidden "audience" who makes the words of prayer efficacious.

And what does it mean for prayer to be "effective"? It is not that prayer gets God to do something for us, says Jesus, for God already knows what we need. Rather, prayer is simply communication, or communion, between God and humanity. It is entrance into the presence of God. As such, it is a participation in the divine life of endlessly generative love. The words of prayer make sense and reach their proper end in the "stream of life" that proceeds from God, ends in God, and is embodied in Jesus as God's communication with the world. Jesus is identified early in Matthew as "Emmanuel, God with us" (1:23) because he is both "son of David, son of Abraham" (1:1) and generated by the Holy Spirit indwelling Mary (1:20). That is, the name Emmanuel has been prepared by the revelatory history of God's dealings with Israel, and before that, God's creation of the world. God as revealed to Moses is the creator—"I am that I am"—and the merciful redeemer who delivers from bondage and accompanies Israel in the wilderness. "Emmanuel" names this history and anticipates the deepened, embodied enactment of God's solidarity with all humanity in the death and resurrection of Jesus. But Jesus is also the embodied enactment of human response to God; crying out to God in anguish and surrender as he faces his impending arrest, torture, and execution, Jesus as Emmanuel joins fully with humanity's dereliction. Hereafter every desperate cry to God bespeaks the divine solidarity with every human being at the null point of betrayal, abandonment, and death.

So God is the auditor who makes prayer effective, and through Jesus Christ God also joins with the one who prays. It is as Emmanuel that Jesus teaches the pattern of prayer that Christian tradition calls "the Lord's Prayer." Indeed, the structure of Matthew's gospel, which alternates narrative and discourse, tells us that his life and his teaching on prayer cannot be separated but are mutually illuminating. This means quite simply that if we want to understand prayer as Jesus taught it, we need to attend to the whole of Jesus's life and ministry from start to finish—and the end is yet to come. But such attention also exposes the particulars of our personal and corporate "stream of life" to God's judgment, forgiveness, and transformation.

The Lord's Prayer

The gospels give us two versions of the Lord's Prayer: a brief set of petitions, in Luke 11:2–4, and a longer edition of the same petitions, in Matthew

6:9–13. Both are in the context of Jesus's instructions to his disciples, although the setting differs. In Luke Jesus responds to a specific request from his followers: "Lord, teach us to pray," and he adds a parable and teaching to encourage persistence in prayer. In Matthew, the prayer is part of a much longer series of instructions that in the immediate context reclaim devotional practices of alms-giving, prayer, and fasting from self-serving forms of public piety. The existence of different settings and versions of the prayer in the gospels demonstrates that prayer occurs in a variety of ways. At the same time, the common thread in both the accounts is Jesus himself as the speaker of the words. This common thread is important because abstracted from Jesus's own life and wielded on their own, the very words of Jesus's prayer—"father," "kingdom," "will," "on earth as in heaven"—can be deployed in manipulative, oppressive, and even violent ways.

In what follows I will focus on the form of the prayer in the gospel of Matthew because it has been most influential in Christian liturgical usage and because it includes and expands the shorter version found in Luke. The prayer has two parts, each including three petitions. The first part focuses on God's honor and reign, and the second focuses on human need. As we shall see, the third petition, "your will be done," forms the heart of the prayer by summing up the hallowing of God's name and yearning for God's kingdom, and by situating the petitions concerning human need in terms of surrender to God. The entire prayer is addressed to God as "our Father in heaven."[1]

Scholars debate whether the prayer is oriented primarily to the future or to the present. Is the prayer for the coming of God's kingdom primarily concerned with the hidden presence of the kingdom now, or the future Day of the Lord? Is the prayer for bread a petition for daily bread now, or for a share in the eschatological banquet? Is the prayer for forgiveness in the present day-to-day existence, or for mercy at the Last Judgment? Does deliverance from evil concern protection from evildoing now, or preservation from apostasy and final destruction at the Last Day?

To my mind, these are false dichotomies, similar to misleading distinctions between concrete concerns, such as physical sustenance and freedom from debt and the quality of our spiritual life. Our physical needs and the economy of our corporate life intimately affect our relationship with God and one another, and vice versa. Similarly, the eschatological hope of God's final kingdom is the basis for a transformed life in the present. Thus the Lord's Prayer expresses and confers a bifocal vision that simultaneously sees both the "near" horizon of present and concrete human experience, and the "far" horizon of the future reign of God.

Although a thorough exploration of the content of the Lord's Prayer is not possible here, I will offer some brief thoughts about central issues that arise in seeking not only to understand it but also to pray it: the naming of God as "our Father"; the coming of God's kingdom; surrender to God's will; bread, debt, and the economy of God; and deliverance from evil.

Our Father

What does it mean to call God "father"? Perhaps equally important, what does it *not* mean to call God "father"? We note first the occurrence of this language in Jewish sources, where it signifies God's particular care for the people of God. Several times in the Old Testament God is named as the father of Israel. For example, Deuteronomy 32:6 chides Israel: "Do you thus repay the LORD, O foolish and senseless people? Is not he your father, who created you, who made you and established you?" Isaiah directs a petition to God: "For you are our father, though Abraham does not know us and Israel does not acknowledge us; you, O LORD, are our father; our Redeemer from of old is your name" (Isa. 63:16).[2] In the *Hymns* from the Jewish monastic community at Qumran, contemporaneous with Jesus, we hear a petition to God as both father and mother: "For my mother did not know me, and my father abandoned me to you. Because you are a father to all the sons of your truth. In them you rejoice, like one full of gentleness for her child, and like a wet-nurse, you clutch to your chest all your creatures" (1QH 9). Slightly later Jewish prayers address God as "Our father! Our king!" (ascribed first to Rabbi Akiba, *Ta-anit* 25b), surely drawing on ancient practices of calling kings by the term "father."[3] Taken together, this terminology for God evokes images of power, protection, deliverance, and supreme authority.

What of Jesus's use of this paternal language, which occurs far more frequently in the New Testament than in the Old Testament? Several clues in Matthew's gospel point us in helpful directions. First, from the beginning of the gospel, Jesus is identified as having a special relationship to God as "father," both fulfilling and exceeding that of Israel with God. For instance, his childhood exile in Egypt fulfills Hosea 11:1: "Out of Egypt have I called my son" (Matt. 2:15). When he is baptized, and again at the Transfiguration, a voice from heaven identifies him as "my beloved son" (Matt. 3:17; 17:5).

Second, Jesus prays to God as "father" and invites his followers to do the same. In Mark's version of the garden of Gethsemane, Jesus prays "Abba, father" (Mk. 14:36), using the intimate term for "father" in Aramaic. The apostle Paul knows this form of address to God, and Paul depicts the Spirit of God dwelling within us and moving us also to call out, "Abba, father!" (Rom. 8:15; Gal. 4:6). Notably, "the Spirit of God" (Rom. 8:14) is also called "the Spirit of his Son," which God sends into our hearts (Gal. 4:6). Here the invocation of God as "Abba, father" is a divinely generated participation in the inner life of divine love.

Third, Jesus imposes qualifications on the paternal metaphor, which limit its use in human relationships. He teaches his disciples to think of God as their "heavenly father," or "father in heaven" (e.g., Matt. 5:16; 6:1, 9, 15, 32; 7:11, 21; 10:32; 12:50). The qualification draws a sharp distinction between the paternal metaphor for God and all earthly "fathers," whether metaphorical or biological. He also calls God "your father in secret," or "your father who sees in secret" (6:4, 6, 8). In each case, the designation for God subverts ostentatious acts of public devotion, such as alms-giving, fasting, and prayer itself as a means of self-promotion (6:1–18). The secret Father does not authorize self-promotion over the interests of others. Finally, the perfection of God precisely as "heavenly father" is demonstrated by mercy shown without partiality, for the "evil and the good," the "just and the unjust." Perfection is not demonstrated by one's moral superiority and judgment of others but by something quite different—God's all-merciful love for all people, who are all sinners. Hence, the most "perfect" and complete expression of one's own identity as a "son" of this heavenly "father" is love for one's enemies (5:43–48). This divine "father" does not exclude anyone from mercy.

Fourth, Jesus's distinction between the heavenly "father" and all biological families of origin takes shape throughout his ministry. When he calls James and John, they leave their boat and their father and follow him (4:22). Jesus warns that his coming will "set a man against his father, and a daughter against her mother, and a daughter-in-law against her mother-in-law" (10:35), and requires a loyalty and love that exceeds that between parents and children (10:37). Indeed, when his own mother and brothers come seeking him, Jesus points rather to the disciples and says, "Here is my family! Whoever does the will of my father in heaven is my brother and sister and mother" (12:46–50). This redefinition of family relationships culminates in a drastic reordering of human hierarchies: "But you are not to be called rabbi, for you have one teacher, and you are all students. And call no one your father on earth, for you have one father—the one in heaven. Nor are you to be called instructors, for you have one instructor, the Messiah. The greatest among you will be your servant. All who exalt themselves will be humbled, and all who humble themselves will be exalted" (23:8–12).

It is clear that calling God "our father" places one in a new relational matrix with everyone else, in which there is no room for claims to superiority. That is, there can be only one "father" to whom all other claims of authority are subordinate. In this way Jesus's fatherly language for God subverts any oppressive human relationships that it may wrongly be deployed to support. All of this suggests that the use of paternal language for God to oppress or exclude people has no warrant in Jesus's own practice. Nonetheless, insofar as "words have meaning in the stream of life," our particular experiences of human fathers do enter into the words of prayer as well. Clearly the paternal language of scripture has been used to exclude and oppress, and as such its use not only directs our attention to God but also exposes the wrongs that wound the body of Christ. This is why paternal metaphors for God—indeed, all familial metaphors in the life of faith—are both powerful and dangerous: powerful because they evoke the foundational experiences of human identity; dangerous for the same reason.

The First Three Petitions: Honoring God

Drawn into the relationship of Jesus with God as "father," the supplicant now focuses all attention on God. Insofar as God's name is hallowed through the extension of the divine rule throughout the earth, the first three petitions are tightly interwoven. "Hallowed" is in the passive voice, suggesting God as the one who sanctifies the divine name. Indeed, who else can truly make anything holy? Similarly, in John 12:28 Jesus prays, "Father, glorify your name." The petition echoes the prophetic promise in Ezekiel 26:33: "I will sanctify my great name," and is similar to an early version of the traditional Jewish prayer, the Kaddish:

> Exalted and hallowed be his great name, in the world which he created according to his will.
> May he let his kingdom rule in your lifetimes and in your days and in the lifetime of the whole house of Israel, speedily and soon.
> Praised be his great name from eternity to eternity.
> And to this say: Amen.[4]

The prayer that God's will be done on earth as in heaven simply amplifies the prayer for the coming of God's kingdom because the full performance of God's will on earth would indeed signify the complete reign of God. On the one hand, the kingdom already has come on the scene in Jesus's own presence and actions. His arrival is announced by John the Baptist and by his own preaching: "Repent, for the kingdom of heaven has come near" (3:2; 4:17). This kingdom, which is Jesus's enactment of God's rule on earth, may be recognized by the signs through which Jesus confirms his identity to John the Baptist: "the blind receive their sight, the lame walk, the lepers are cleansed, the deaf hear, the dead are raised, and the poor have good news brought to them" (11:5). On the other hand, to pray "your kingdom come" is to acknowledge that, as Martin Buber put it, "we still live in an unredeemed world."[5] Therefore, the announcement of the coming rule of God is always a call to repentance in the face of God's judgment: the meek do not yet inherit the earth; the poor are forgotten; death still reigns. To pray "your kingdom come" is to inculcate discomfort with the status quo. Because the awesome judgment of God overrides all human judgment and stands over the church as well as the world, the prayer also teaches the believing community to suspend judgment of others, to keep its doors open to the stranger, to know itself as sinful and yet forgiven, and above all to witness to the redemption accomplished through Christ's death and resurrection.

In the present, such an eschatological orientation is expressed through the prayer "your will be done." This is the heart of the Lord's Prayer, which Jesus himself prayed when he faced impending arrest and death:

> He took with him Peter and the two sons of Zebedee, and began to be grieved and agitated. Then he said to them, "I am deeply grieved, even to death; remain here, and stay awake with me." And going a little farther, he threw himself on the ground and prayed, "My Father, if it is possible, let this cup pass from me; yet not what I want but what you want." Then he came to the disciples and found them sleeping; and he said to Peter, "So, could you not stay awake with me one hour? Stay awake and pray that you may not come into the time of trial; the spirit indeed is willing, but the flesh is weak." Again he went away for the second time and prayed, "My Father, if this cannot pass unless I drink it, your will be done." (26:37–42)

Such prayer is very far from an identification of the kingdom of heaven with the church on earth, let alone with our own limited and inevitably self-serving ideas of what the kingdom should look like. Rather, it is a prayer of surrender. It expresses Jesus's desire and then surrenders it to God. As such it hallows God's name, enacts the kingly reign of God, and places all other human needs within the domain of God's will.

The Last Three Petitions: Asking for Help

Under the heading "your will be done," Jesus teaches the disciples to ask for basic human needs: bread, forgiveness, protection from evil. Each of these needs can be interpreted in spiritual terms, and each also has concrete practical significance: the spiritual and the concrete go together, and it is well not to get too abstract in prayer here.

Bread. The word that modifies bread in this petition may mean "daily," or "for tomorrow," or "necessary," leading to a wealth of interpretations. A prayer for daily bread reminds us that each day we live only through the sheer gift of God, just as the Israelites in the wilderness lived daily only through the gift of manna from heaven (Ex. 16). Furthermore, just as that daily gift entailed a prohibition against taking more than one needed, so the prayer for daily bread is a reminder not to hoard God's provision but rather to take only what is necessary and thereby live in continual reliance on God. And since the one teaching this prayer is Jesus, whose meals with sinners shocked the "righteous," perhaps the prayer for "our" bread reminds us who our fellow feasters are—all who are hungry and in need (11:9).

At the same time, as a petition for bread for tomorrow the prayer points forward to the eschatological banquet that Jesus himself anticipated even as he ate his last supper with his disciples (26:17–30). Thus, centuries of interpreters have seen in this prayer also a petition to share in the Eucharistic meal, which is both a remembrance of Jesus's last supper and a foretaste of the heavenly banquet. As a supplication for both present and future, literal and metaphorical "bread," this prayer inculcates practical reliance on God for concrete daily needs and cultivates a hunger for God's liberating provision for all people. As long as some are still hungry, both physically and spiritually, the kingdom has not arrived; blessed are those who hunger and thirst for righteousness, says Jesus (Lk. 6:21; Matt. 5:6).

FORGIVENESS. Significantly longer and breaking the rhythm of the prayer, the petition for forgiveness receives special emphasis in Jesus's teaching. Immediately following the Lord's Prayer (6:14–15), Jesus explains the petition. Later in Matthew's gospel, he again emphasizes forgiveness in his teaching about life in the community of faith (18:15–35). There Jesus's promise to his disciples that he will be with them "wherever two or three are gathered in my name" (18:20) is preceded by exhortations to reconciliation within the Christian fellowship (18:15–19) and followed by insistence on limitless forgiveness (18:21–22). The presence of Christ is incommensurate with backbiting, resentment, grudges, and hostility, instead calling for confession and mutual forbearance.

As with bread, so with forgiveness: there is a concrete component to this petition. The language of "debts" and "debtors" evokes economic relationships and the dynamics of power that are always present in such relationships. A person, institution, or nation to whom money is owed is in a position of power over the debtor. Conversely, to owe someone else, whether the debt is financial or otherwise, is to lose freedom in relationship to them. Debt becomes a form of slavery. In this light, the relinquishment of another's debt is also a relinquishment of power because it moves one from an almost God-like position of control over others to a position of equal indebtedness to the Lord from whom everything comes. Such liberation from the complicated dynamics of debt would indeed be a partial instantiation of the kingdom of God.[6]

Nonetheless, precisely because of the power dynamics implicit in all human relationships, things are not so simple. Rightly or wrongly, moral judgments accrue to the owing of a debt, and there is nothing more insulting to human pride than being "forgiven" precisely because to accept forgiveness is to acknowledge that we need it. There is something in us that would rather be good than be forgiven; we would rather be in the position to grant forgiveness than to receive it. I suspect that this is a significant point of resistance to God exposed by Jesus's insistence that in the matter of forgiveness, giving and receiving cannot be separated. We cannot have one without the other, because the genuine struggle to forgive when one has been deeply wronged paradoxically entails facing one's own inability to forgive, and that leads one into a deeper consideration of the need for divine mercy.[7] This is a complex dynamic that deserves much more exploration than is possible here but perhaps may be a helpful topic for further reflection, particularly insofar as the struggle to give and receive forgiveness may lead us deeper into prayer.

Protection. The Greek word translated "time of trial" also means "temptation," and certainly Jesus viewed temptation as a form of trial or testing. God does not tempt people, but God may allow people to be tempted. This is stated in 1 Corinthians 10:13, where Paul promises, "No testing has overtaken you that is not common to everyone. God is faithful, and he will not let you be tested beyond your strength, but with the testing he will also provide the way out so that you may be able to endure it." So the sense of this petition may be something like that of an ancient Jewish prayer: "Bring me not into the power of sin, and not into the power of guilt, and not into the power of temptation, and not into the power of anything shameful" (*b. Ber.* 60b). That is, the petition for rescue from the evil one interprets the prayer for deliverance from temptation. Here temptation or testing does not originate in oneself, and certainly not in God, but rather comes from an external, malignant, anti-God and antihuman power. Indeed, in the story of Jesus's own temptation in the wilderness (4:1–11), the devil is named as "the tempter" (4:3).

Yet that same story of Jesus's temptation also reminds us that he himself was "led by the Spirit into the wilderness to be tempted by the devil" (4:1). Despite telling his disciples to pray not to be led into temptation, Jesus himself was led into a time of trial—led by the Spirit of God. The paradox seems to tell us that there are some things only Jesus can do; only Jesus can defeat the ancient enemy, the tempter, the evil one. At the beginning of his ministry, he does this proleptically in the wilderness, and at the end of his ministry he does it decisively on the cross, where evil does its worst but cannot destroy him. Here is the ancient idea that even the evil one can be the instrument of God's purposes. Here also is a picture of Jesus doing battle with the evil one on behalf of all human beings, including but not limited to his disciples in the garden of Gethsemane, whose "weak flesh" could not even resist the temptation to sleep while their Master prayed in anguish. No wonder he reminded them: "Stay awake and pray that you may not come into the time of trial; the spirit indeed is willing, but the flesh is weak" (26:41). In other words, only the power and mercy of God can deliver humanity from the power of evil, both in the present time and in the future.

Conclusion

The words of the Lord's Prayer find their meaning in the shape and direction of Jesus's own life, and in Jesus's identity as Emmanuel, God with us. Jesus addresses God as "father" and invites his followers to do the same as members of a new family system. He teaches us to direct our attention first to God's honor, sanctity and rule, and then to human needs for sustenance, forgiveness, and deliverance from evil. His own earnest prayer in the garden of Gethsemane mirrors the prayer he taught and expresses the central movement of his life: surrender to God's will and deliverance from evil for all humanity.

Notes

1. For a helpful discussion of the structure and content of the Lord's Prayer in its context, see Dale Allison, *The Sermon on the Mount: Inspiring the Moral Imagination* (New York: Crossroad, 1999).

2. See also Jeremiah 3:19; 31:9, 20; Hosea 11:1–4; Wisdom 14:3; 3 Maccabees 6:3, 8. For a helpful discussion of the Jewish background of the Lord's prayer, see Jacob Petuchowski and Michael Brocke, ed., *The Lord's Prayer and Jewish Liturgy* (New York: Seabury, 1978).

3. See Simon Lauer, "*Abhinu Malkenu*: Our Father, Our King!" in *The Lord's Prayer and Jewish Liturgy*, ed. Jacob Petuchowski and Michael Brocke, 73–80 (New York: Seabury, 1978); and discussion in Allison, *Sermon on the Mount*, 116–17.

4. Translation from Allison, *Sermon on the Mount*, 121.

5. The quote comes from a letter Buber wrote to a German newspaper in 1926. Quoted in J. L. Martyn, *Theological Issues in the Letters of Paul* (Nashville, TN: Abingdon, 1997), 279.

6. In "The Merciful Economy," Peter Selby offers an insightful analysis of the dynamics of power implicit in debtor relationships. See Alistair McFadyen and Marcel Sarot, ed., *Forgiveness and Truth: Explorations in Contemporary Theology* (Edinburgh: T & T Clark, 2001), 99–118.

7. On this dynamic, see David Self, "Enfolding the Dark," in *Forgiveness and Truth: Explorations in Contemporary Theology*, ed. Alistair McFadyen and Marcel Sarot, 157–63 (Edinburgh: T & T Clark, 2001).

Al-Fātiḥa

RKIA ELRAOUI CORNELL

1 In the Name of God, the Merciful, the Mercy-Giving.
2 Praise be to God, Lord of the Worlds,
3 The Merciful, the Mercy-Giving,
4 Master of the Day of Judgment.
5 You alone do we worship and on You alone do we rely.
6 Guide us to the Straight Way:
7 The way of those upon whom You have bestowed Your favour, not of those who have incurred Your wrath or have been led astray.[1]

One cannot speak about Sūrat al-Fātiḥa without speaking of prayer because the Fātiḥa is used in every act of *al-ṣalāt,* the Muslim formal prayer. Every Muslim who recites her five daily prayers recites the Fātiḥa seventeen times a day. If one prays the Sunna or supererogatory prayers, the number of recitations may be even higher. The Arabic word *fātiḥa* means "opening." The Fātiḥa is an opening for the Qur'ān because it is the first of the Qur'ānic *sūras*. It is also an opening for the ṣalāt prayer because without the Fātiḥa the ṣalāt prayer is not valid. The Prophet Muḥammad said, "One's prayer is invalid if one does not recite the Fātiḥa."[2]

One can omit the *basmala*, the phrase *Bismillāh al-Raḥmān al-Raḥīm* ("In the Name of God, the Merciful, the Mercy-Giving"), from the beginning of the prayer, and one can also omit reciting other parts of the Qur'ān in the prayer, but one cannot omit the Fātiḥa. Symbolically, the Fātiḥa is used to open or inaugurate other acts in Islam as well. It often opens the recitation of Sufi invocations of remembrance or *dhikr*. Muslims also use it to inaugurate other acts, such as journeys, important events, or speeches. The Fātiḥa is so important to Islam that the Prophet Muḥammad said, "By Him in whose hands is my soul, neither in the Torah, the Psalms, the Gospel, nor the Qur'ān was the like of [the Fātiḥa] revealed" (*Tafsīr Ibn Kathīr*).[3] In the Shīʿī

Qur'ān commentary of Abū ʿAlī al-Tabarsī (d. 1154) the Prophet is reported to have said, "One who recites the Fātiḥa will be given as much merit as if he had recited two-thirds of the Qur'ān and as if he had given alms to every man and woman of faith."[4]

Prayer is the means through which the Muslim confirms her vows to God. It is also through prayer that the believer's commitment to God is validated through acts of worship. It is in prayer as well that religious knowledge (*ʿilm*) meets religious practice (*ʿamal*) and the inculcation of virtue (*iḥsān*) takes place. The words of the prayer, whether uttered aloud or silently, bring God and the human being into a binding covenant (*ʿahd*). Prayer helps make tangible the contingent nature of the world and the realization that God is the ultimate Reality (*al-Ḥaqq*). It is in the act of prayer that the mind and the heart together uplift us toward the divine presence and prepare us to meet God. Whether it is recited through the voice or in the mind, in private or in public, the Fātiḥa is the most common form of communication with God and the threshold of knowledge of God. This is why the Fātiḥa is essential to prayer in Islam.

The Fātiḥa appears under many different names in Islamic tradition. As we have seen, it is called al-Fātiḥa because it opens the discourse of the Qur'ān and because it symbolically opens other important acts that are performed by Muslims. Sometimes the Fātiḥa is referred to as *al-Sabʿ al-Mathānī* (literally, The Seven Couplets). This name, which comes from Qur'ān 15:87 ("We have given you [Muḥammad] *al-Sabʿ al-Mathānī* and the Glorious Qur'ān"), is believed to refer to the seven verses of the Fātiḥa. It also refers to the fact that the Fātiḥa—and, hence, each of its verses—is recited a minimum of two times in every prayer. The Fātiḥa is also called *al-Kāfiya* (The Sufficient) because by itself it is sufficient for prayer, and *al-Wāfiya* (The Fulsome) because it always has to be recited in full. Because of its sufficiency for prayer, it is also called al-ṣalāt, after the prayer itself. Sometimes the Fātiḥa is called *Umm al-Kitāb* (Mother of the Book) or *Umm al-Qur'ān* (Mother of the Qur'ān) because many Muslims believe that it contains the essence of the Qur'ānic message. Similarly, it is called al-Asās (the Foundation) because it is foundational for both the ṣalāt prayer and the Qur'ān. Many Muslims additionally believe that the words of the Fātiḥa possess the power of healing. According to one popular tradition, the Prophet Muḥammad said, "The Fātiḥa is a source of healing for every ailment except death."[5] Names that refer to the Fātiḥa's healing properties include *al-Shifā'* (the Healing) and *al-Ruqya* (the Antidote).

Islamic scholars differ over whether the Fātiḥa contains six or seven verses. Whatever the number, the verses of the Fātiḥa constitute an ocean of meaning that overwhelms anyone who tries to comprehend the wisdom that they portray. Although there are common elements to all interpretations of the Fātiḥa, there are as many different versions of its meaning as there are interpreters. Since space is limited, I will briefly discuss each verse of the Fātiḥa, focusing on only one or two of the most important points about each verse.

1. In the Name of God, the Merciful, the Mercy-Giving

The tradition that the Qur'ānic term *al-Sab' al-Mathānī* refers to the Fātiḥa depends on the idea that the first verse of the Fātiḥa consists of the Islamic formula of consecration, the basmala. Without this formula, the Fātiḥa would have only six verses. Not all commentators regard the basmala as part of the Fātiḥa. For example, in regions of the Muslim world that practice Mālikī jurisprudence, the Fātiḥa is recited in the ṣalāt prayer without the basmala. However, even scholars from Mālikī regions tend to view the basmala as part of the Fātiḥa in a de facto sense. For example, the Andalusian Sufi Muḥyiddīn ibn 'Arabī (d. 1240), who saw the Fātiḥa as containing the essential meaning of the Qur'ān, also saw the basmala as the essence of the Fātiḥa and saw the dot under the letter *bā'* in the particle *bi-* which begins the basmala as the essence of the basmala, the Fātiḥa, and the Qur'ān together. This interpretation reflects the Islamic theological concept of *tawḥīd,* the oneness of God, because it focuses the worshipper's attention on God as the single point of origin for all things, including His Word as expressed in the Qur'ān.

Ibn 'Arabī's interpretation of the Fātiḥa should not be dismissed as just another example of mystical "creative license." Rather, it should be understood that his view of the centrality of the Fātiḥa and the basmala together is intimately related to the notion that the Fātiḥa is essential for prayer as a means of communication with God. The basmala precedes every sūra in the Qur'ān except *Sūrat al-Tawba* (9). The words of the basmala recall the compassion and mercy beyond measure that God bestows upon His creation. Access to divine mercy is one of the most important goals of prayer in Islam. The worshipper who is truly conscious of God reciprocates God's mercy by being merciful toward all of God's creatures without discrimination. This is an important aspect of the Islamic *imitatio Dei*, which in Arabic is called *al-takhalluq bi-khulūq Allāh* (literally, "patterning oneself after God's conduct"). The Fātiḥa motivates the worshipper to progress on this virtuous path by recalling God's mercy and goodness. In a tradition that is accepted by Muslims everywhere, the Prophet Muḥammad said: "None of you has believed until he desires for his brother that which he desires for himself" (Bukhari, Muslim, and other Ḥadīth sources).

2. Praise be to God, Lord of the Worlds

This verse expresses the praise that is due to God from His creatures. One of the names of the Fātiḥa is *al-Ḥamd*, "The Act of Praise." In Islam, the noun *al-ḥamd*, which is used to praise God in this verse, is reserved only for God or that which pertains to God, such as the Fātiḥa itself. It is also related to the divine name *al-Ḥamīd*, "The Praiseworthy," which is one of the ninety-nine "Beautiful Names of God" (*Asmāʾ Allāh al-Ḥusnā*) in the Qurʾān. God's worthiness of praise is a token of His majesty. However, the God of the Qurʾān is not an impersonal deity or an arbitrary ruler. Despite the fact that some Muslim theologians have stressed that God is not bound by necessity or have used the exegetical technique of apophasis to describe the incomparable nature of the divine essence, God is not a remote deity who is only to be praised at a distance. Muslims praise God not only because He is incomparably great but also because He is near. As the Qurʾān states, God is nearer to a person than her jugular vein (50:16). Praise for God also acknowledges the fact that God, through divine names such as *al-Qayyūm* (The Sustainer), supports us through the development of our physical and mental abilities. Finally, through names such as *al-Nāfiʿ* (The Beneficial) He provides us with the ability to act as custodians of the Sharīʿa, which regulates our behavior toward Him, our fellow human beings, and the world as a whole.

The phrase "Lord of the Worlds" (*Rabb al-ʿĀlamīn*) alludes to the world beyond human experience. Although some scholars have stated that the term "worlds" refers only to humans or the four rational orders of humans, angels, jinn, and *shayāṭīn* (devils), others assert that it refers both to the human and to the extrahuman realms. The medieval Qurʾān commentator Fakhr al-Dīn al-Rāzī (d. 1209) conceived of the Earth as floating in space and imagined that God could create a thousand worlds bigger and greater than ours, each containing its own earth, sun, and heaven, and even including its own divine throne and footstool.[6]

3. The Merciful, the Mercy-Giving

The meaning of this verse has already been covered in the discussion of the *basmala*. However, it is important to add that the Qurʾān states, "[God] has ordained mercy upon Himself" (*kataba ʿalā nafsihi al-raḥma* [6:12]). This means that God has made it incumbent upon Himself to act mercifully at all times toward His creation. Sūra 55 of the Qurʾān, which is called *al-Raḥmān* (The Merciful), is a reminder of the many undeniable signs of mercy and grace that God has bestowed. The discernment of the truth, the knowledge of the inner nature of things, and the ability to understand and interpret the signs (*āyāt*) of God are only some of the divine favors human beings should never deny. One of the purposes of reciting the Fātiḥa so many times a day is to recall such divine favors and to emulate God's mercy by making mercy incumbent upon us.

4. Master of the Day of Judgment

This verse exalts God's sovereignty. God is both Master of the Day of Judgment and *al-Mālik*—another divine name—the absolute master and agent of the Truth out of which all realities emanate and within which all human acts of inspiration, creativity, and innovation take root. God is the Owner of our souls and the Ruler over our hearts. A statement attributed to the famous Sufi woman Rābiʿa al-ʿAdawīyya (d. 801) furthers our understanding of God's ownership of the heart: "He who truly knows (*al-ʿārif*) asks God to grant him a heart. So [God] grants it to him from Himself. When a person takes possession of the heart, he offers it back to his Lord and Master, so that in [God's] repossession of it he will be protected and will be veiled in its concealment from created things."[7]

Rābiʿa's statement implies that there is immense profit to be found in giving one's heart back to God. This profit is control over the passions and the temptations of the material world. This measure of self-control helps ensure that the accounts of one's deeds that are presented on the Day of Judgment are balanced. The Prophet's companion Abū Ḥurayra stated: "I heard the Messenger of God (may God bless and preserve him) say that God the Exalted said: 'I have divided the prayer between my servant and Me, and my servant shall have what he prays for. When the servant says: "Praise be to God, Lord of the Worlds," God Most High says: "My servant has magnified Me." When the servant says, "Master of the Day of Judgment," God says, "My servant has glorified me. This is my portion and to [my servant] belongs what remains."[8]

5. You alone do we worship and on You alone do we rely

This verse addresses the theology of divine oneness (*tawḥīd*) by singling out God as the focus of our reliance and worship. It again reminds us that only God is worthy of worship and that God, as the Creator of all things, is also the ultimate source of our aid and salvation. The verse also demonstrates the contingent nature of human agency and gives ultimate legitimacy and power to God alone. Under the influence of the recitation of this part of the Fātiḥa, the mind and heart of the worshipper are reminded of the divine realm, where they rejoice in the divine presence. Free from the burdens and cares of the ego, the soul enters a sublime serenity and peace in its encounter with its Maker. This is the station of *tawakkul*, complete and utter reliance on God, which is expressed through our actions and witnessed by the heart. The strong assertion of divine agency in this verse is another reason why the Fātiḥa is considered the essence of prayer.

6. Guide us to the Straight Way

This verse is a supplication. As the previous verse implies, imploring guidance from God also entails acknowledging His Lordship (*rubūbīyya*). In this verse the worshipper calls upon God in the guise of the divine name al-Hādī (the Guide) as the ultimate guide in her spiritual journey. This verse also touches on the subject of *al-ta'dīb al-ilāhī*, the training and education of the worshipper in the life of the virtues through the Divine Word. This concept was very important for the ascetics of early Islam, although it tends to be overlooked in the superficial exteriority of much Islamic practice today. It also relates to the concept of *tawakkul* described in the discussion of the previous verse. Complete reliance on God's guidance is the key to progress in *al-ṣirāṭ al-mustaqīm*, the path of the Spirit. The worshipper seeks divine guidance to live a life of virtue, to be inspired to do good and forbid evil, and most of all to enable her heart to know and love God. Love and knowledge of God are the torches that light the Straight Way. A life of virtue guided by divine light enriches the faith. Toshihiko Izutsu notes that in the context of seventh-century Arabia when the Qur'ān was revealed, *al-ṣirāṭ al-mustaqīm* referred to paths across the desert between distant wells in unfamiliar territory, in which the slightest deviation from the "Straight Way" could lead to missing a well and dying of thirst.[9] The Qur'ān uses this powerful metaphor to stress how great our need for guidance is on our path through life. In another well-known verse the Qur'ān states: "Whomsoever God will, He makes him go astray; and whomsoever He will, He sets him on a straight path" (6:39).

7. The way of those upon whom You have bestowed Your favour, not of those who have incurred Your wrath or have been led astray

As indicated in the discussion of the previous verse, God is our guide toward the life-giving well of spiritual sustenance. Guidance is one of God's greatest bounties, dispensed upon those whom He chooses. In the present verse the worshipper petitions God to include her among those whom God chooses to guide. In opposition to guidance stands misguidance, the path of those who miss the life-giving wells in the desert of existence because their hearts are blind to God and faith. Those who deny God are blinded by their own passions and egos and miss the signs of God that will guide them to salvation. As this verse implies, the sincere worshipper must avoid following such people lest their misguidance lead her astray.[10]

Despite its brevity, the Fātiḥa sums up the message of the Qur'ān, which embodies the Islamic faith as a whole. In conclusion, one may summarize the Fātiḥa by noting the importance of three key concepts. These concepts are Divinity (*ulūhīyya*), Lordship (*rubūbīyya*), and Limitless Mercy (*raḥmānīyya*). The key to these concepts can be found in the fifth verse of the Fātiḥa. In the phrase *Iyyāka naʿbudū* (Only you do we worship), the concept of *ulūhīyya* or divinity emerges as we look toward God as the one true Divinity. The same phrase also recalls the concept of *rubūbīyya* or Lordship, since the worthiness of God for worship ultimately depends on His exalted status as Lord of All Things. The *raḥmānīyya* or Limitless Mercy of God is expressed in the phrase *Iyyāka nastaʿīn* (On You alone do we rely). The complete reliance on God that is signified by the concept of *tawakkul* depends on the assurance that God will keep His promise and that the needs of all that He creates will be fulfilled.

In accordance with the meaning of the Fātiḥa it is customary for Muslims to end religious addresses such as this essay with an invocation like the following: "Praise be to God in His Oneness and on Him alone we rely" (*al-Ḥamdullilāhi Waḥdahu wa bihi nastaʿīn*).

Notes

1. All translations from the Qur'ān and other Arabic sources are my own.
2. Tirmidhī, *Mawāqit*, 116; and Ibn Ḥanbal, 2:428; see also Abdul Ḥamid Siddiqi trans., *Imam Muslim's Ṣaḥīḥ Muslim* (New Delhi: Kitab Bhavan, 1978), 1:214 (ḥadīth 771).
3. Mahmoud Ayoub, *The Qur'an and Its Interpreters*, vol. 1 (Albany: State University of New York Press, 1984), 43.
4. Ibid.
5. Ibid., 44.
6. Ibid., 48.
7. ʿAbd al-Mālik ibn Muḥammad al-Kharkūshī, *Tahdhīb al-Asrār*, ed. Bassām Muḥammad Barūd (Abu Dhabi: al-Majmaʿ al-Thaqafī, 1999), 53.
8. See, for example, Siddiqi, *Ṣaḥīḥ Muslim* (ḥadīth 775), 215–16.

9. Toshihiko Izutsu, *God and Man in the Koran: Semantics of the Koranic Weltanschauung* (Salem, NH: Ayer Company Publishers, 1987), 144–45.

10. In the Qur'ān, the verb "to disbelieve" is *kafara*, which literally means "to deny" or "to cover up." This verb is used in two ways: the most general form of *kafara* refers to the denial of God's commands; the noun form of the verb is *kufr*. In this latter sense *kufr* is best translated as "disobedience" and can apply to both Muslims and non-Muslims alike. The second form of *kafara* refers to the denial of the theological truth of God's oneness; in this sense *kufr* is best translated as "disbelief" and applies primarily to polytheists and Christians (because of the doctrines of Christology and the Trinity). According to the Qur'ān, both senses of *kafara* involve the abrogation of the human being's responsibility to God. The Qur'ān states: "It is [God] who made you vicegerents (*khalā'ifa*) on Earth. If one rejects [God's command] the consequences of his unbelief are upon him (*fa man kafara fa-ʿalayhi kufruhu*); the unbelief of those who deny God only increases their abhorrence to the Lord. Truly the denial of the unbelievers only adds to their despair" (35:36).

Prayer in the Spirit in Romans 8

PHILIP SEDDON

Romans 8

1There is therefore now no condemnation for those who are in Christ Jesus. 2For
the law of the Spirit of life in Christ Jesus has set you free from the law of sin and
of death. 3For God has done what the law, weakened by the flesh, could not do:
by sending his own Son in the likeness of sinful flesh, and to deal with sin, he
condemned sin in the flesh, 4so that the just requirement of the law might be
fulfilled in us, who walk not according to the flesh but according to the Spirit.
5For those who live according to the flesh set their minds on the things of the
flesh, but those who live according to the Spirit set their minds on the things of
the Spirit. 6To set the mind on the flesh is death, but to set the mind on the Spirit
is life and peace. 7For this reason the mind that is set on the flesh is hostile to
God; it does not submit to God's law—indeed it cannot, 8and those who are in
the flesh cannot please God.

9But you are not in the flesh; you are in the Spirit, since the Spirit of God
dwells in you. Anyone who does not have the Spirit of Christ does not belong to
him. 10But if Christ is in you, though the body is dead because of sin, the Spirit is
life because of righteousness. 11If the Spirit of him who raised Jesus from the dead
dwells in you, he who raised Christ from the dead will give life to your mortal
bodies also through his Spirit that dwells in you.

12So then, brothers and sisters, we are debtors, not to the flesh, to live according to the flesh—13for if you live according to the flesh, you will die; but if by the
Spirit you put to death the deeds of the body, you will live. 14For all who are led
by the Spirit of God are children of God. 15For you did not receive a spirit of
slavery to fall back into fear, but you have received a spirit of adoption. When we
cry, "Abba! Father!" 16it is that very Spirit bearing witness with our spirit that we
are children of God, 17and if children, then heirs, heirs of God and joint heirs
with Christ—if, in fact, we suffer with him so that we may also be glorified with
him.

18I consider that the sufferings of this present time are not worth comparing
with the glory about to be revealed to us. 19For the creation waits with eager

longing for the revealing of the children of God; [20]for the creation was subjected to futility, not of its own will but by the will of the one who subjected it, in hope [21]that the creation itself will be set free from its bondage to decay and will obtain the freedom of the glory of the children of God. [22]We know that the whole creation has been groaning in labour pains until now; [23]and not only the creation, but we ourselves, who have the first fruits of the Spirit, groan inwardly while we wait for adoption, the redemption of our bodies. [24]For in hope we were saved. Now hope that is seen is not hope. For who hopes for what is seen? [25]But if we hope for what we do not see, we wait for it with patience.

[26]Likewise the Spirit helps us in our weakness; for we do not know how to pray as we ought, but that very Spirit intercedes with sighs too deep for words. [27]And God, who searches the heart, knows what is the mind of the Spirit, because the Spirit intercedes for the saints according to the will of God.

[28]We know that all things work together for good for those who love God, who are called according to his purpose. [29]For those whom he foreknew he also predestined to be conformed to the image of his Son, in order that he might be the firstborn within a large family. [30]And those whom he predestined he also called; and those whom he called he also justified; and those whom he justified he also glorified.

[31]What then are we to say about these things? If God is for us, who is against us? [32]He who did not withhold his own Son, but gave him up for all of us, will he not with him also give us everything else? [33]Who will bring any charge against God's elect? It is God who justifies. [34]Who is to condemn? It is Christ Jesus, who died, yes, who was raised, who is at the right hand of God, who indeed intercedes for us. [35]Who will separate us from the love of Christ? Will hardship, or distress, or persecution, or famine, or nakedness, or peril, or sword? [36]As it is written,

"For your sake we are being killed all day long;
we are accounted as sheep to be slaughtered."

[37]No, in all these things we are more than conquerors through him who loved us. [38]For I am convinced that neither death, nor life, nor angels, nor rulers, nor things present, nor things to come, nor powers, [39]nor height, nor depth, nor anything else in all creation, will be able to separate us from the love of God in Christ Jesus our Lord.

Christian Prayer

Christian prayer derives from many sources: Jesus's own prayer ("Abba, Father"), the prayer he gave the disciples (the Lord's Prayer), his final prayer before his death in John 17 (the High-Priestly Prayer), and the hymns of praise in the book of Revelation, as well as many passages in the New Testament letters, quite apart from its immense debt to the Old Testament. I have chosen to examine chapter 8 in St Paul's Letter to the Romans in order to explore how deeply Christian prayer is rooted in the relationship between Jesus, the Spirit, and the Father. I will first offer an overview of the chapter as a whole, mentioning the analyses offered by a number of scholars; then, in the rest of this essay, starting at the section titled "The Place of Prayer in Romans 8," I will focus on the verses that are most directly relevant to our theme of prayer, namely 12–17 and 18–27.

It is true that in terms of the dialogue in which we are engaged, serious questions may be raised concerning the "proto-Trinitarian" theology that emerges in this chapter and that is bound up with these earliest, deepest, and most intimate aspects of Christian prayer. It feels equally important to share what is most fundamental and precious to each of our traditions. For Christians, this is "holy ground"—a place of encounter with the living God: transcendent, immanent, beyond, and within.

The Place of Romans 8 in the Letter as a Whole

I offer two points of orientation, one large-scale, the other smaller-scale. First, Romans 8 concludes the first half of St Paul's stunning Letter to the Romans.[1] Whichever analysis of the letter we follow, Romans 8 forms the climax of the argument concerning the centrality of the revelation of Jesus the Messiah ("Jesus Christ") for Jew and Gentile alike (1:14,16, 2:9–10, 9:24). There are three genres of analysis, each of which has its appeal:

- Scriptural: If we follow Charles Cranfield's proposal that chapters 1–8 are an argument shaped round Habakkuk 2:4:[2] "the one who is righteous by faith shall live" (1:17, NRSV footnote), then in chapters 1–4 Paul addresses the first part of the text from Habakkuk ("the one who is righteous by faith") and Romans 8 concludes chapters 5–8, in which Paul addresses the second part of the text ("shall live").[3]

- Theological: If we follow Ernst Käsemann's outline, shaped around "The Righteousness of God," which is God's gift and demand (Ger.: *Gabe* and *Aufgabe*), chapter 8 is the conclusion of section 4, "The Righteousness of Faith as a Reality of Eschatological Freedom," and chapter 8 is subtitled "Man in the Freedom of the Spirit."[4]

- Structural-Rhetorical: If we follow Robert Jewett's structural-rhetorical analysis, chapter 8 concludes "The Second Proof (*Probatio*): Life in Christ as a New System of Honor That Replaces the Quest for Status

> through Conformity to the Law" (5:1–8:39), each of the four Proofs arguing Paul's "Thesis about the Gospel as the Powerful Embodiment of the Righteousness of God."[5]

Second, chapter 8 also offers the last of a series of section headings and conclusions within chapters 5–8, with variants on the phrase "through our Lord Jesus Christ" (5:1, 11, 21; 6:23; 7:25; 8:39). These repetitions are an intentional rhetorical structuring device (*inclusio*), that implicitly conveys both the early Christian conviction that, for Jewish and non-Jewish (Gentile) readers alike, there is only one God and one Lord (3:29; see also 1 Cor. 8:6[6]), and that the Greek name for God in the Septuagint—*Kurios*—can be used for Jesus, the Messiah of Israel, to indicate his divine status and identity.[7]

Analysis of Romans 8

Despite the division of Romans 8 into seven paragraphs in the version presented at the head of this essay (NRSV), it is wiser to divide it into four sections:

(a) 1–11, which form the conclusion to Paul's argument in chapter 7 concerning the ambiguity of the Jewish Torah, and of its inability to bring the life it promised, while also introducing the new topic: "life."[8]

(b) 12–17, which build on the opening section to expound the "ministry of the Spirit" in terms of our adoption into God's family (8:15).

(c) 18–30, which use the word "glory" as an *inclusio* (18, 30) to focus on the future destiny of both creation itself and those in whom the Spirit intercedes (8:19–20, 26).

(d) 31–39, which act as a peroration both to Romans 8 and to the first eight chapters of Romans to portray the immensity of God's gift of "his own Son" (8:32) and the promise of our inseparability from "the love of Christ" (8:35, 39).[9]

We should note in passing that the two key points where details of prayer are mentioned occur in parallel in sections (b) and (c), the first focusing on adoption in Christ (v. 15) and the second focusing on the internal assistance of the Spirit (vs. 26–27) immediately after a repeated mention of—in this case, future—"adoption" in v. 23.

Doublets and Triplets

This, then, is the cosmic canvas against which Paul expounds a double theological correlation: the macrocosmic groaning of creation (8:22) and the human microcosmic groaning in prayer of those who receive "the first fruits of the Spirit" (8:23). Christian prayer takes place within the context of the restoration of the whole creation, exemplified in verses 1–17 in the two foundational gifts of Jesus and the Spirit:

- The resurrection of Jesus from the dead. As so often in Paul's letters, 8:11 is a hinge verse that at once concludes the first section (1–11) and opens the door to the second (12–17). With deliberate variation, Paul describes God twice in the same verse as "the One who raised Jesus from the dead . . . the One who raised Christ from the dead." This virtually constitutes Paul's definition of God (see 4:17); his use here of the past tense is both striking and fundamental to all early Christian testimony (1 Cor. 15:4, Rom. 4:25, 1 Pet. 1:3). He also frames this verse with an *inclusio* of "indwelling": "if Christ is in you" (v. 10) . . . "If the Spirit . . . dwells in you" . . . (v. 11) . . . "his Spirit that dwells in you" (v. 11). As soon as Paul speaks of the resurrection, he speaks of Jesus/Christ and the Spirit. Resurrection is first outer and historical, then inner and personal.

- Adoption into the family of God by the Holy Spirit—"the spirit of adoption"—through the outpouring of the gift of the Spirit.[10] "When we cry, 'Abba! Father!' it is that very Spirit bearing witness with our spirit that we are children of God" (8:15). To be in Christ, or to be indwelt by Christ, is to be an heir with Christ (v. 17) to demonstrate to creation God's purposes for its own restoration.

Verses 18 and following then constitute the first of a "double triplet." In the first triplet, the word creation (*ktisis*, the cosmos as created order) is triply personalized, very likely with an internal chiasm of future-past-future (a-b-a):[11]

- "*Creation* waits" with eager longing for the revealing of the sons of God (v. 19)—a *future* look toward the fulfilment of creation;

- "The *creation* was subjected to futility" (v. 20)—a look *backward* to Genesis 3:17–20; and

- "The *creation* itself will be set free from its bondage to decay" (v. 21)—a second *future* look toward its final emancipation from its inevitable entropy.

Verse 8:22 is then another hinge verse, where a fourth use of "creation" simultaneously introduces the first occurrence of the key word of the second triplet: "groans" (*stenazei*). "The whole *creation* has been *groaning* in labour pains until now."[12] This does not mean, as is often assumed, that creation is and always has been in a permanent state of groaning into which we ourselves are now drawn, but that the creation that has been groaning up until this present moment in the labor pains of what Hans Urs von Balthasar calls a "millennial pregnancy" has now given birth to the first fruits of its own future harvest, namely Jesus, whom God raised from the dead.[13]

The second triplet of "groaning" then follows, in turn offering a concentric reversal of the order of components of the previous verses: the order of the Spirit—believers—creation in verses 14–19 now in verses 20–23 becomes creation—we ourselves—the Spirit.

- The whole of creation has been *groaning* in labor pains up till this present moment (v. 22), the moment of Christ's resurrection, destroying the process of entropy.

- *We ourselves* . . . groan inwardly (v. 23).

- *The Spirit*, too, intercedes alongside us with inarticulate groanings (my translation of *stenagmois alalētois*) (v. 26).

The Place of Prayer in Romans 8

With this introductory overview in place, we can now turn our attention to the proper topic of this essay: prayer in Romans 8. Certainly, throughout the New Testament Christian prayer demonstrates its constant indebtedness to its Jewish heritage. In Romans 8, however, it is located more specifically within those earthquake events that distinguish Christian faith from Jewish faith than in almost any other letter by St Paul. It is grounded theologically in the resurrection of Jesus, and in the new awareness of what would come to be called the Trinitarian activity of God as Father, Son, and Spirit; and it is grounded temporally in being revealed as primarily forward-looking—anticipating the restoration of all things in Christ.

Within these two foundational events of the Resurrection and gift of the Spirit, let me highlight three key facets: immensity, intimacy, and intensity.

First, there is an immensity involved. Paul grounds Christian prayer in the resurrection of Jesus (8:11)[14]—the resurrection which (re-)creates the future and is the sign of the new creation. So Christians can pray for that which is humanly impossible but which is possible for God, for it is God who has brought about the resurrection of Jesus from the dead and has begun to establish God's rule—the Kingdom of God—on earth. For Christians, the status quo does not equate to the will of God; too often, the status quo is that which God does *not* will, and which is to be overcome through what some traditions of prayer called "prevailing prayer": prayer that longs to see God making his presence known in lives—by the love of God "that has been poured into our heart through the Holy Spirit that has been given to us" (5:5).[15]

If prayer is based on the resurrection and the consequent restoration and renewal of creation, then it is linked to both cosmic and personal renewal. That is why prayer is so frequently linked with prayer for healing and the forgiveness of sins in the Christian tradition—not so much forgiveness for particular individual sins but the total, unequivocal proclamation of the obliteration of sins that derives from the death of Jesus on the Cross, as anticipated in Micah 7:19: "You will cast all our sins into the depths of the sea."[16] Forgiveness flows from the sacrifice of the Cross; healing from the power of the resurrection.

A famous example here is the work of Jackie Pullinger in the Old City of Hong Kong. Through a very specific charismatic ministry of prayer and healing, especially of long-term drug addicts, lives of enormous numbers of people were turned round.[17] In an area that would normally be out of bounds to most people, Jackie Pullinger—like St. Paul himself (1 Cor. 6:9–11; Gal. 3:2–5)—prayed the power of the resurrection into broken bodies, as Romans 8:11 makes explicit, bringing forgiveness and healing.[18]

Second, there is intimacy (8:15–16). Christian prayer takes place in the free space of God's presence. It flows out of the new relationship established with God through "the spirit of adoption" (8:15).[19] We pray as those who have been drawn into the closest relationship of love with God. We are given the privilege of praying to God as "Father," "dear Father," as Jesus did. Drawn by the Spirit into the person of Jesus, we do not simply pray *to* the Trinity but *within* the intimate mutual love of the Trinity; the Holy Spirit makes our prayers part of Jesus's. As we are caught up into at least some experience of the resurrection of Jesus, so we enter Jesus's own trust and experience of the Father's love. As Tom Wright says, "Christians will find themselves prompted by the Spirit to call God 'Father,' and to use the Aramaic word that, according to Mark 14:36, Jesus himself used in his prayer in Gethsemane (and, by implication, at other times as well). . . . It was a way . . . of making Jesus' prayers one's own, and hence of sharing the sonship of Jesus."[20]

I add two other points of interest. The first is that Paul's language here most likely *predates* St. Mark's Gospel account of Jesus's final confrontation with God and death. More importantly, this prayer is thus part of Jesus's own preparation for his death and then resurrection; it was in *Gethsemane*, the night before his crucifixion, that Jesus addressed God as "Abba, Father." These two precious words therefore combine intimacy with the call to an unlimited obedient vocation and invite us to identify with Jesus in his journey to the Cross.[21]

Third, we find a profound *intensity*. Christian prayer is the work of the Holy Spirit in us. Verses 26–27 clearly highlight the origin of our praying in God; the Spirit prays God's prayers in us. James Dunn uses the nice phrase "Spirit Speech" of the way in which both the Son and the Spirit are found operating in this chapter in the context of prayer and Christian identity.[22]

And yet these verses contain some surprises, given the previous focus on the divine origin of prayer, for Paul immediately turns the tables by radically juxtaposing human frailty alongside divine power. Accordingly, frailty is not the opposite of power but the form in which God's power comes close. The Spirit of intimate unity is also the Spirit of deepest weakness. Paul's exposition sets a series of three further points like jewels in a ring.

First, the element of weakness, frailty, and ignorance ("in our weakness . . . we do not know"; v. 26) truly is a huge contrast with the joyful practice of the presence of the resurrection. However, it is not merely a concession to our human weakness; it is also a statement of the priority of God's prayers. Frailty is not the opposite but the requisite of power, even—especially—within our redeemed existence. God comes alongside us in the Person of the Holy Spirit to pray the prayers God wants in us. The admission of inadequacy allows God to provide: the Spirit who enables us to call God "Abba! Father!" gives us prayers not created by the distortions of our own ego.

Second, this tender sense of limitation has already been foreshadowed by another triplet of waiting (itself a triplet in vs. 19, 23, 25), patience, and hope. Note the careful pattern:

> . . . a spirit of adoption (15)
> hope (20)
> . . . we wait for adoption (23)
> hope . . . hope . . . hope . . . hopes . . . hope (24–25)

Following a sensitive interlacing of present privilege (15, 23) and future anticipation (20, 24–25), Paul stresses with considerable forcefulness in a quite unique pair of verses that there is and always will be that which we have not seen (contrast 1 Cor. 2:9–10) and for which we must wait "with patience" (the highlighted final words of v. 25). Hope is not optimism but the certainty of faith, looking at what we cannot see but by which we live. It is constitutive. I like Käsemann's subtitle for the section 8:18–30: "Being (Ger.: *Sein*) in the Spirit as Standing in Hope."[23]

Third, the Spirit specifically intercedes by way of a double inarticulate groaning: *for* us and *with* us. In verse 26, the double compound verb *hyperentungchanei* indicates that the Spirit intercedes on our behalf to make up for our ignorance. Then, in verse 27, the verb *entungchanei* explains that the Spirit intercedes "for us," "on our behalf" on the basis of God's will, that is, the Spirit enables us to pray God's prayers because the Spirit not only knows the depths of our hearts better than we do ourselves but also expresses God's mind as we pray (8:27). Verse 32 also reveals that Jesus, too, is engaged in that ministry of intercession "for us" at the place of supreme authority ("the right hand of God"); indeed, it is "Christ Jesus who died, yes, who was raised" (8:11) who is *The* Intercessor. So the Cross is God's own place and shape of Intercession—a thought also found in Hebrews 7:25 but ultimately derived from Isaiah 53:12: "he bore the sin of many, and made intercession for the transgressors."

But what is this "groaning"? Some take the term to refer to a "charismatic" expression of the inarticulate sounds of some kind of spiritual language, and there is plenty to support this point of view.[24] Others take it to refer more generally to eruptions and yearnings of a more primal and psychological kind, perhaps even like the babblings and gurglings of infant speech resurfacing in adult longings for God in prayer given by God. Then, too, Christian tradition repeatedly emphasizes the prayer of tears, tears that wash the soul clean, tears that express repentance and compunction, tears for being overwhelmed by God's love, tears of joy and sorrow, tears that express the ever-deeper longing of the heart for God that is itself God's gift.[25]

As a particular instance of this, we can see the entire following section of chapters 9–11 of Romans as Paul's agonized intercession for his own people, Israel. Building on the work of my student Kwang Ho Chung,[26] we observe "the great sorrow and unceasing anguish in [Paul's] heart" (9:2), his willingness to be *anathema* to God if that could bring about Israel's repentance (9:3), and "[his] heart's desire and prayer to God for them . . . that they may be saved" (10:1). The three chapters would then be an extended illustration of the way in which believers in Christ are themselves caught up into the groaning of the Spirit (8:26), "in hope" (8:24–25) "that the creation itself will be set free from its bondage to decay and will obtain the freedom of the glory of the children of God (8:21)."

These interlinked groanings are what therefore constitute the depths of Christian prayer. Arising out of creation's own prior groaning, they are given by the Spirit precisely as evidence of the power of the resurrection working in those through whom God is praying his prayers. The "new creation" of the first believers in Jesus becomes the laboratory in which the whole creation can discern its own ultimate destiny and renewal—as if creation is awaiting its own equivalent experience of the death and resurrection of Jesus. So prayer is praying not simply *with* the drift of creation but with the drift of the Creator who has begun to bring into being a new creation; and praying *against* the drift of the creation, which is still determined by frustration and futility. Not that Christians are exempt from frustration and futility—far from it; but they view it under the sign of redemption. They are drawn into a renewed groaning precisely as they join Jesus's triumphal procession, as he draws the creation out of death while descending into death and draws Adam and Eve out "with a strong hand and an outstretched arm": (Ps. 136:12, Jer. 32:21). Eastern Orthodox icons of the Anastasis (the resurrection of Jesus) combine that descent into Hell and resurrection in an unforgettably life-giving way.

I return, finally, before concluding, to a further triplet of themes that I have touched on in order to highlight the fact that, in our prayer and intercession, the creation for which we pray, and which we are, stands under the promise of glory through the twin vocations of our suffering and God's love. As we indwell Christ and the Spirit indwells us, we are drawn more deeply both into the future of creation (18–30) and also into its, God's, and our heart as illuminated on the Cross (8:32).

1. "The glory about to be revealed" (8:18). The destination of this chapter is "glory." Creation will obtain the freedom of the glory of the children of God (21); those whom God justifies he also glorifies (30). The creation that was drawn unwittingly into the sin of Adam, and reveals the same frustration as humanity does, now that it sees that the new Adam—Jesus—has come and reversed the irreversible process of corruption, decay and death, looks forward again even more excitedly for the fulfilment of that "freedom" in its own being. It is "on tenterhooks," craning its neck forward, waiting with outstretched longing for the final revelation of God's triumph (19).

   The word "glory" (17, 18, 21, 30) depicts the solidity, the weighty brilliance of God, the shining uncreated light of his presence. And that same Spirit who has already begun to draw creation out of its futility, out of the frustration of its entropy, its inherent bias toward declination, is interceding within the people of Jesus so that we may be drawn with it into its own re-creation, and with it find our destiny. Intercession is both personal and cosmic in scale. Even as we do not see the glory about to be revealed, we intercede for it with breaking hearts because it is held in the promise of glory, which is Christ.

2. The second word follows on: *sufferings* (*ta pathēmata*). "Sufferings" in verse 18 explicitly introduces that section, and the final peroration of the chapter ends (35–38) with two lists of potential sufferings—one of seven and one of nine specific threats (35, 38–39). It is not just a generality of nuisances, as we might imagine, but a list of recidivist oppositional powers and potencies. Even as Paul stresses the incommensurability of our sufferings when put alongside future glory, the list of destructive powers shows that Paul was well aware of the cost of following Jesus.

3. But the very context in which Paul speaks of suffering is also the place where Paul speaks three times about "the *love* of God": verses 35, 37, and 39. Introducing the first list of questions and objections, Paul says that, if God is for us (31–32), and if Jesus is interceding for us (34), then there is nothing to fear and no one can separate us from the love of God (35). This is then the word-field that features three times in this rhetorical and Christological conclusion: the love of God—"in Christ Jesus our Lord" (8:39):

> 8:35 "Who will separate us from the love of God?";
> 8:37 "We are more than conquerors through the One who loves us"; and
> 8:39 "the love of God in Christ Jesus our Lord."[27]

Here, again, the verb and cognate noun for "love" in Greek occur slightly more in this section of Romans than in any other.[28] It is as if to say that love, self-sacrificing love, is the reality in which everything else is held together because that is what God has demonstrated to be the case: resurrection and forgiveness; adoption into and intimacy within God's family; the weakness, ignorance, and inarticulate groaning of our intercessions; and the glory, sufferings, and the love of God.

This underlines the conviction that love is the heart of prayer, and that prayer is the incarnation of love. It is a form of the expression of love for another person, or community, or world, that is at this moment of my—or our—praying being held under the sign of the glory of the resurrection and offered back to God in the same way as it was given by God and received by us in prayer.

Conclusion

For Christians, the central aspect of prayer is the set of divine-human relationships that underlie it. The language of Romans 8:15–16 is amazingly close to phraseology Paul used some seven to ten years earlier in Galatians 4:4–6; and it is as if those thoughts still strike him as a miracle of experience and expression. He is saying that the One and only God in whom Christians believe has revealed unknown aspects of his identity, as demonstrated in his generosity in "not withholding" "his own Son" (8:32—a reference back to the sacrifice of Isaac in Genesis 22[29]) and then raising him from the dead (8:11, 34). And he has sown the seeds of the later more fully developed doctrine of the Trinity, of what we could call the Deep God, whose love surpasses knowledge (Eph. 3:19), that is to say, of that reciprocal relationship of mutual self-giving and self-outpouring that so characterizes developed Trinitarian thought. That is the deepest and richest location of Christian prayer.

Notes

1. Ernst Käsemann, *Commentary on Romans* (London: SCM, 1980), x; see also the two-volume commentaries of both C. E. B. Cranfield and James D. G. Dunn. Cranfield: *A Critical and Exegetical Commentary on the Epistle to the Romans*, vol. I: Romans I–VIII (Edinburgh: T&T Clark, 1975); vol. 2: Romans IX–XVI (Edinburgh: T&T Clark, 1979); Dunn: *Word Biblical Commentary*, vol. 38A, *Romans 1–8*; vol. 38B, *Romans 9–16* (Dallas: Word Books, 1988); see also Peter Stuhlmacher, *Paul's Letter to the Romans. A Commentary*, "Part One: The Righteousness of God for Jews and Gentiles"; and "Part Two: The Righteousness of God for Israel" (Edinburgh: T&T Clark, 1994), vii and 33–141; N. T. Wright, Outline of Romans, "The Letter to the Romans," in *The New Interpreter's Bible*, vol. 10 (Nashville, TN: Abingdon, 2002), 410–11; Bruce J. Malina and John J. Pilch, *Social-Science Commentary on the Letters of Paul* (Minneapolis, MN: Fortress Press, 2006), 220; and Peter Oakes, *Reading Romans in Pompeii: Paul's Letter at Ground Level* (Minneapolis, MN: Fortress Press, 2009), vi and 152–59.

2. Technically this takes the form of an extended *pēsher* interpretation, such as was widely used at Qumran, and which analyzed each component part of an existing text for its contemporary interpretation.

3. In strong support of this reading is the fact that both the noun *zōē* (life) and the verb *zaō* (I live) each occur overwhelmingly in chapters 5–8 (1:17: "The one who is righteous (chs. 1–3) by faith (chs. 4–7) *will live* (chs. 5–8)": *zōē* appears sixteen times in these chapters (roughly four times per chapter) and only five elsewhere; *zaō* appears

eleven times in chapters 5–8 (four times in chapter 6, twice in chapter 7, and five times in chapter 8), with the verb only appearing subsequently eight times.

4. Käsemann, *Commentary on Romans*, x and 212–52.

5. Robert Jewett, *Romans. A Commentary* (Minneapolis, MN: Fortress, 2007), vii–viii, 344, and 474–554. Christopher Bryan is the only commentator known to me who does not follow this customary division of the letter at the end of chapter 8 but with great skill views the entire section 5:1–11:36 as a single unit: "Demonstration and Defense (5:1–11:36): Peace with God through Christ." Bryan, *A Preface to Romans. Notes on the Epistle in Its Literary and Cultural Setting* (New York: OUP, 2000), x and 120.

6. This text is shaped by the Jewish *Shᵉmaʿ* (Deuteronomy 6:4–5), and, thus, by aligning Jesus ("one Lord, Jesus Christ") with God ("one God, the Father") fundamentally reasserts the unassailable Oneness of God. See Richard Bauckham, *Jesus and the God of Israel: "God Crucified" and Other Studies on the New Testament's Christology of Divine Identity* (Grand Rapids, MI: 2008), 26–31. I also welcome N. T. Wright's parallel study of 1 Corinthians 8 in *The Climax of the Covenant: Christ and the Law in Pauline Theology* (London: T&T Clark, 1991), and his language of "Christological monotheism," especially 132 and following.

7. There is currently a wealth of research on the nature of Jesus's "divine identity." See Andrew D. Clarke and Bruce W. Winter, *One God, One Lord: Christianity in a World of Religious Pluralism* (Grand Rapids, MI: Baker, 1993); Larry Hurtado, *Lord Jesus Christ: Devotion to Jesus in Earliest Christianity* (Grand Rapids, MI: Eerdmans, 2003); Bauckham, *Jesus and the God of Israel*; and James D. G. Dunn, *Did the First Christians Worship Jesus? The New Testament Evidence* (London: SPCK, 2010). See also, most recently, Chris Tilling, *Paul's Divine Christology* (Tübingen: Mohr Siebeck, 2012).

8. Wright, "Letter to the Romans," 410, 573–90; see also Käsemann, *Commentary on Romans*, x and 212–52.

9. See Jewett, *Romans*, 532.

10. The Spirit is mentioned some twenty-one times in this chapter, compared with only nine in the rest of the letter.

11. J. Ramsey Michaels argues strongly that *ktisis* should be translated "creature," rather than "creation," and that "Romans 8:21 is an affirmation of the bodily resurrection of believers, no more and no less." Michaels, "The Redemption of Our Body: The Riddle of Romans 8:19–22," in *Romans and the People of God: Essays in Honor of Gordon D. Fee on the Occasion of His 65th Birthday*, ed. Sven K. Soderlund and N. T. Wright, 92–114 (Grand Rapids, MI: Eerdmans, 1999), 93. But it seems to me that the scope of the whole chapter, not least as it heads toward the final peroration in 8:31–39, clearly focuses on the largest possible scale of God's activity in response to the cosmic scale and effect of Adam's sin—namely, the cosmos—already established as the sphere of God's promise to Abraham in 4:13, "that he would inherit the world."

12. The Greek for "until now" is "*achri tou nun*." Paul here uses the key word for "now," the strong temporal and theological import of which was already established in 3:21 (there: *nuni*) as "'the time of salvation begun through Christ' . . . the eschatological situation which has 'already now' begun." W. Radl, art. *nun*, in *Exegetical Dictionary of the New Testament*, ed. Horst Balz and Gerhard Schneider (Grand Rapids, MI: Eerdmans, 1991), 2:480.

13. Hans Urs von Balthasar, *The Glory of the Lord. A Theological Aesthetics*, vol. 1, *Seeing the Form*, trans. Erasmo Leiva-Merikakis, ed. Joseph Fessio, SJ, and John Riches (Edinburgh: T&T Clark, 1982), 537.

14. It is the merit of the recent study of J. R. Daniel Kirk, *Unlocking Romans: Resurrection and the Justification of God* (Grand Rapids, MI: Eerdmans, 2008), to have recognized the crucial significance of this topic in the study of Romans. Specifically, chapter 7 investigates Romans 8:12–39 under the title "Resurrection and New Creation."

15. See Roy Godwin and Dave Roberts, *The Grace Outpouring. Blessing Others through Prayer* (Eastbourne, UK: Kingsway Communications, 2008).

16. N. T. Wright, *Jesus and the Victory of God: Christian Origins and the Question of God*, vol. 2 (London: SPCK, 1996), 268–74, 432–37.

17. Jackie Pullinger, *Chasing the Dragon* (London: Hodder & Stoughton, 2006 [1986]).

18. See Eugene Peterson, *Practise Resurrection: A Conversation on Growing up in Christ* (Grand Rapids, MI: Eerdmans, 2010). In *Unlocking Romans*, Kirk nicely develops the appropriate subtitle of "Resurrection Hermeneutics in 8:12–30" (138–53).

19. A personal example of the power of this language of adoption comes from Mark Stibbe, who openly shares his own experience of human adoption and the way that illuminates our own generous adoption and incorporation by God into his own life. Mark Stibbe, *From Orphans to Heirs: Celebrating our Spiritual Adoption*, 2nd rev. ed. (London: Bible Reading Fellowship, 2005).

20. Wright, "Letter to the Romans," 593.

21. The use of the simple "Father" in Luke's version of the Lord's Prayer (Lk. 11:2) is not out of kilter with this. However, the use of the petition for the coming of God's Kingdom there differs from its usage here in that the Lord's Prayer was given for use during Jesus's lifetime ("Thy Kingdom come") while the event of the resurrection demonstrates that Kingdom as having now "come in power" (Mark 9:1).

22. James D. G. Dunn, "Spirit Speech: Reflections on Romans 8:12–27," in *Romans and the People of God: Essays in Honor of Gordon D. Fee on the Occasion of His 65th Birthday*, ed. Sven K. Soderlund and N. T. Wright, 82–91 (Grand Rapids, MI: 1999).

23. Käsemann, *Commentary on Romans*, x and 229–45.

24. Ibid., 241.

25. See especially Evagrius Ponticus, "Chapters on Prayer: 153 Texts," in *The Philokalia: The Complete Text*, 5 vol., ed. G. E. H. Palmer and Philip Sherrard (London: Faber and Faber, 1979–99), 1:55–71. See also the narrative of St. Silouan praying for Nicholas in Anthony Bloom, *School for Prayer* (Libra, London, 1970), 74–75, as good an illustration of the movement of intercession as I know.

26. Kwang Ho Chung, *Paul's Prayer and Mission: A Study of the Significance of Prayer in Paul's Missionary Theology and Praxis, and Its Contemporary Relevance*. Unpublished ThD thesis, University of Birmingham, 2004. See especially "The terminology: 'groaning' and 'travail,'" 103–5; "The eschatological suffering of creation (Rom. 8:19)," 105–6, "The eschatological-cosmological feminine groaning of creation (Rom 8:22)," 109–14, and "The groaning of the Christians and the Holy Spirit (Rom 8:23–27)," 114–18.

27. Note here, too, as in the verses on hope, the chiastic arrangement with love as noun, verb, and noun.

28. The verb *agapaō* occurs five times: in 8:28 and 37; in 9:13; and twice in 9:25. The noun *agapē* occurs four times: in 5:5 and 5:8; and then in 8:35 and 39. Thus, Romans 8

is the chapter with the single greatest concentration of the noun and verb "love." The fact that this is also the heart of the letter structurally and theologically gains strength by being linked with the theme of prayer. In turn, the triple appearance of the word group in the peroration of 8:31–39 (v. 35, noun; v. 37, verb; v. 39, noun) indicates its importance in terms of both the destiny of creation (eschatology) and the identity of "Christ Jesus our Lord" (Christology). As a term, "love" only occurs in chapters 5 and 8 (both the Romans 9 occurrences are in Old Testament quotations), and then chapters 12–15.

29. Much discussed in New Testament theology—not least since the Second World War—the *Akedah* (lit. "binding") is the Jewish term for this primal covenant-grounding event. See the commentaries, e.g. Dunn, *Romans 1–8*, 501; Wright, "The Letter to the Romans", 610–11; and Jewett, *Romans*, 536–37, and literature cited in Jewett. Note in particular Jewett's reference to the article by the German Jewish scholar H. J. Schoeps, which initiated a large and continuing discussion on this passage: Hans Joachim Schoeps, "The Sacrifice of Isaac in Paul's Theology," *Journal of Biblical Literature* 65 (1946): 385–92.

In Reverence of the Almighty

Understanding Prayer and Worship in Qur'ān 3:190–94 and 29:45

ASMA AFSARUDDIN

Qur'ān 3:190–94

> 190Indeed in the creation of the heavens and the earth and the alternation of night and day are signs for those endowed with understanding.
>
> 191These are they who remember God standing and sitting, and [reclining] on their sides, and reflect on the creation of the heavens and the earth, [and they say]—"Our Lord, You have not created this in vain; glory be to you! And protect us from the torment of the Fire.
>
> 192Our Lord, the one whom You cause to enter the Fire has been abased; indeed the wrong-doers have no helpers.
>
> 193Our Lord, we have heard a caller summon to faith—'Believe in your Lord!'—and we have believed, O our Lord; forgive us our sins; expiate our evil deeds, and make us die as one of the righteous.
>
> 194Our Lord, grant us what You have promised us through your messengers, abase us not on the Day of Judgment; You do not break your pledge."

Qur'ān 29:45

> Recite what has been revealed to you of the Book and carry out prayer, for prayer protects from lewdness and reprehensible deeds; indeed the remembrance of God is greater; and God is knowledgeable of what you do.[1]

The passage that opens this essay (3:190–94) is among the most significant clusters of verses in the Qur'ān concerned with prayer and supplication in its various forms. The second passage (29:45) is another important verse on this theme, emphasizing different elements of establishing a personal relationship with God through worship and reflection. In this essay I discuss these verses, drawing selectively on exegetical and pious edificatory literature through the centuries.

Qur'ān 3:190–94

These verses occur in the third sūra, which was revealed during the early Medinan period, very likely during the third and fourth years after the *hijra*. This was a time when the life and practices of the Muslim community were becoming more regulated due to the increasingly frequent revelations concerning the specifics of devotional practices, among other matters. Al-Ṭabarī (d. 923), the famous exegete of the late ninth and early tenth century, explicates these verses at some length; a brief synopsis of his comments is offered here. He glosses the Arabic expression *ūlī 'l-albāb* as referring to "those who possess understanding and rationality" (*dhū lubb wa-ʿaql*), and who are thereby aware that everything on earth is a paean to the might and generosity of God, the One Who created everything and provides for humans. The *ūlī 'l-albāb* are also conflated with those who remember God (*al-dhākirīn allāh*) standing, sitting, and reclining—that is to say, both in formal and informal prayer. This was the opinion of the early Muslim authority Ibn Jurayj (d. 767), who added the recitation of the Qur'ān as one of the activities indicated in this all-encompassing description of the various postures of worship. Another early authority, Qatāda b. Diʿāma (d. 736), commented that the verse essentially refers to every situation in an individual's life during which he or she remembers God, whether in easy times or during periods of hardship.[2]

The remaining verses underscore the accountability of human beings to God and exhort humans to be mindful of the reward and punishment that await us in the Hereafter. The *ūlī 'l-albāb* are aware that the heavens and the earth were not created in vain and that their existence points to their Creator, inviting reflection on the part of humans as to the purpose of creation. According to al-Ṭabarī, the "caller" summoning to faith (v. 193) is none other than the Qur'ān, even though he acknowledges that other scholars, such as Ibn Zayd (d. 798) and Ibn Jurayj, have understood it to be a reference to the Prophet Muḥammad. Al-Ṭabarī defends his understanding by pointing to the fact that not every human being could have been summoned by the Prophet, but the Qur'ān as a book fulfils that role. Reflection on the words and message of the Qur'ān is clearly part of prayer and worship for the believer.

What does the Qur'ān summon to? Al-Ṭabarī, now addressing God directly, comments that it summons "to belief in You; to affirmation of Your existence; to following Your Messenger, and obeying him in what he has commanded us to do and avoiding what he has forbidden according to what You revealed to him." Prayer offers an opportunity to believers to do just that—to affirm their faith in the presence of God and to implore Him to blot out their sins so they are not disgraced on the Day of Judgment and so that God may grant them absolution for their evil deeds. In prayerful supplication, the believer entreats the Almighty to "erase them [evil deeds] by Your grace and mercy upon us [*bi-faḍlika wa-raḥmatika iyyānā*], and gather us to You in the company of the righteous and resurrect us with them."[3]

The thirteenth-century exegete al-Rāzī (d. 1210) understands this cluster of verses to encode a holistic understanding of human worship of God (*al-ʿubūdiyya*). Verse 190 is understood to refer to "the consummate lordship" (*kamāl al-rubūbiyya*) of God, while verse 191 refers to "the consummate worshipfulness" (*kamāl al-ʿubūdiyya*) of humans. The latter verse refers to three interlocking, all-encompassing, and ceaseless forms of worship: affirmation in one's heart of faith in God; attestation to it by means of the tongue, and the physical accomplishment of righteous deeds.[4]

Similar to al-Ṭabarī, al-Rāzī understands the summoner to God in verse 193 as a reference to the Qur'ān, for while not everyone may have heard the Prophet, all have heard and comprehended the Qur'ān. This verse significantly identifies what one should ask of God in personal supplication (*duʿāʾ*): forgiveness of one's sins; renunciation of bad deeds; and being counted among the righteous after death. According to many exegetes, persistence and excess in personal entreaties directed to God are commendable practices (*mandūb*).[5]

Qur'ān 29:45

This verse occurs in sūra 29, known as "the Spider" (*al-ʿAnkabūt*), widely regarded as a late Meccan or very early Medinan revelation, during a time of increasing persecution of Muslims at the hands of the pagan Arabs. Prayer is clearly enjoined here as an important part of being resolute in one's faith and enduring the hardships that came one's way by seeking strength and solace in the remembrance of God.

Al-Ṭabarī indicates that the exegetes had differed among themselves on the meaning of the critical Arabic word *al-ṣalāt*, usually translated into English as "prayer," mentioned in this verse. For example, the well-known Companion ʿAbd Allāh b. ʿUmar was of the opinion that *al-ṣalāt* refers to "the Qur'ān which is recited in mosques," while another famous Companion Ibn ʿAbbās, maintained that it refers to the daily prayers that protect one from disobeying God. Ibn ʿAbbās further comments that if one's prayers do not restrain the self from inclining to evil, then such prayers only increase the distance between the individual and God. The Companion ʿAbd Allāh b. Masʿūd similarly stressed that even if one was given to frequent prayer, if one did not refrain from wrongdoing and obey God, then prayer was of no benefit to the individual.[6] Al-Ṭabarī himself prefers the commentary of those who understood *al-ṣalāt* specifically as the daily required prayers, fidelity to which protects the worshiper from committing fornication and other acts of disobedience to God.[7]

As for "the remembrance of God" (*dhikr allāh*), al-Ṭabarī records a significant exchange between the two Companions ʿAbd Allāh Ibn Rabīʿa and Ibn ʿAbbās. When the latter queried the former as to the meaning of this phrase, the former glossed it as "the praising, glorification, and exaltation of God during prayer; the recitation of the Qur'ān, and the like." Ibn ʿAbbās responded by saying that the phrase in his understanding indicated that the mention of God's revealed commandments and prohibitions by the believer constituted the greater *dhikr*—that is, "greater than your mention/remembrance of Him."[8] We may discern in this discussion a tension between a more dogmatic or legalistic explanation of the key Arabic terms "*ṣalāt*" and "*dhikr*", as evident in Ibn ʿAbbas's comments, and a more expansive and spiritualized understanding of the same, as exemplified by Ibn Rabīʿa's remarks. According to this latter more expansive understanding, the formal prayer is one of many important components of the locution *dhikr allāh*, which holistically includes any and every act—mental, spiritual, and physical—that fosters the remembrance of God.

Al-Rāzī in the thirteenth century echoes much of al-Ṭabarī's commentary in his exegesis of this verse, which need not be repeated here. He adds that the verse emphasizes that prayer must be offered in sincere remembrance of God and not for public show of piety (*al-riyā'*). When the worshiper continues to pray and prostrate before God, he grows in closeness to Him, as promised in another Qur'ānic verse, 96:19—"Prostrate and draw closer!" It is this resulting closeness with God that prevents the believer from disobeying Him and violating His commandments.[9] As for *dhikr*, al-Rāzī says it includes both the recitation of the Qur'ān and performance of prayers since both lead to complete magnification of God through the tongue and the heart. The elative *akbar* ("greater") is used to indicate that praise of God surpasses any other kind of praise directed by humans at any other being—for example, their forefathers. God, in any case, is the only one possessed of greatness (*al-kibar*).[10]

Al-Ghazālī's Exegesis of *Dhikr*

Even from this relatively brief discussion of two key passages dealing with prayer, it is obvious that *dhikr* is the more capacious, umbrella term that includes diverse forms of worship, including recitation of the Qur'ān and formal prayer. In his magisterial work *Iḥyā' 'ulūm al-dīn*, al-Ghazālī (d. 1111) deals with a cluster of Qur'ānic verses that deal with *dhikr*, including the verses we discussed earlier. This broader comparison of a larger pool of verses yields the following observations on his part.

First, *dhikr* implies that believers pray anywhere and everywhere, at any time and indeed at all times; or as Ibn 'Abbās phrased it, "at night and day, on land and sea, while journeying or at home, in richness and in poverty, in sickness or in health; in secret or in public." This situation is in contrast to those who only feign belief, for example, the hypocrites of Medina (*al-munāfiqūn*), who are described in Qur'ān 4:142 as "scarcely remembering God." It is also in contrast to "the negligent" (*al-ghāfilūn*), who are described in Qur'ān 7:105 as failing to remember God in private and in silence and to acknowledge him in the deepest recesses of their hearts. Furthermore, *dhikr* is a reciprocal activity between God and humans, according to Qur'ān 2:152, in which God addresses humans thus: "Remember Me and I will remember you."[11]

These and other Qur'ānic verses stressing the importance of *dhikr* are bolstered by ḥadīths and other kinds of reports that similarly extol this pious activity. In one such ḥadīth, the Prophet is pointedly asked, "Which action is the best?" He replied, "That you face death while your tongue is still moist from uttering the name of God the Exalted."[12] Another nonprophetic report contains a rebuke for those who would let the material benefits of this world distract them from the constant worship of God. The report emanates from the Companion Abū Ḥurayra, who entered the marketplace in Medina and addressed the people there: "I see you are gathered here while the inheritance (*mīrāth*) of the Messenger of God, peace and blessings be upon him, are being divided in the mosque!' " At that the people abandoned their transactions and hurried off to the mosque, where they found no physical evidence of the inheritance. They complained to Abū Ḥurayra about having been misled by him. He asked them what they had seen instead. They replied that they had seen people mentioning the name of God and reciting the Qur'ān, at which Abu Ḥūrayra exclaimed that that was indeed the inheritance of the Prophet![13]

This report is included in the section on "the excellences of *dhikr* sessions." In the Sufi mystical tradition in which al-Ghazālī became deeply immersed, prayer as encapsulated in the capacious term "*dhikr*" is regarded as a constant mode of interaction between God and humans through various acts of devotion and consecration. The telos of dhikr is the meeting with God in the next world: one who wishes to meet Him, God will meet him willingly; one who would eschew such a meeting, God will also shun him, says al-Ghazālī.[14] The constant, prayerful remembrance of God in this world prepares us for that final encounter in the Hereafter, the joyful culmination of the one earthly relationship that takes precedence over all others.

Notes

1. Translations from the Qur'ān and other Arabic sources are my own.
2. Al-Ṭabarī, *Jāmiʿ al-bayān fī tafsīr al-Qur'ān* (Beirut: Dār al-kutub al-ʿilmiyya, 1997), 3:550–51.
3. Ibid., 3:552–54.
4. Al-Rāzī, *al-Tafsīr al-kabīr* (Beirut: Dār Iḥyā' al-Turāth al-ʿArabī, 1999), 3:458–59.
5. Ibid., 3:467.
6. Al-Ṭabarī, *Jāmiʿ*, 3:144–45. Other authorities also hold this position.
7. Ibid.
8. Ibid., 3:145–46.
9. Al-Rāzī, *al-Tafsīr al-kabīr*, 9:60–61.
10. Ibid., 9:62.
11. Al-Ghazālī, *Iḥyā' ʿulūm al-dīn* (Beirut: Dār al-fikr, 1989), 1:350.
12. Ibid., 1:351.
13. Ibid., 1:352.
14. Ibid., 1:360.

PART III

Learning to Pray

Learning to Pray with and in the Christian Tradition

Personal Reflections

LUCY GARDNER

As is to some extent reflected in the collection of personal reflections at the end of this volume, the Christian tradition offers several different accounts of prayer, and there are at least as many different approaches to learning or teaching to pray. In this chapter I do not attempt to provide a map of all of these or a detailed discussion of any of them. By way of introduction, I rehearse some of my formative memories and recollections of learning to pray not to privilege my own experience but in the hope that this might be more informative and palatable than generalized abstraction. Having chosen and collated them, I am struck by how physical and sensual my own memories are; there is something, I think, of the body teaching the spirit to pray.

I also attempt to articulate something of my own underlying understanding of prayer, garnered from my own experience and fed by that rich and varied tradition. In the main body of this essay, I draw out some very general points (both practical and theological) about different aspects of learning (and teaching) to pray in the Christian tradition. But first a few words on the typical occasions and contexts of that learning.

Children in Christian families will usually first learn to pray at home with their families, praying with other family members, hearing, reading, and learning stories and prayers of various biblical characters and the saints. They will also learn in church and in special groups provided for them, often while adults are praying and listening to God's Word in the main Sunday liturgy.

All Christians, including both child and adult converts, will also learn primarily by praying with others at the liturgy, by listening to teaching on prayer in sermons, by reading prayers and about prayers, by engaging in the task of learning to carve out time to pray in their lives, and sometimes by joining a prayer or fellowship group from their congregation. Many retreat centers also offer a wide variety of workshops on prayer—ranging from Bible study to liturgical dance, from Zen techniques to Ignatian approaches, from chanting to icon painting. There are also a lot of leaflets and guides available, ranging from the general and simple to the complex and quite particular.

Some Memories of Learning

Sunday School, 1971: "Hands together, eyes closed and repeat after me." We are sitting cross-legged on the cold, hard, slightly smelly linoleum floor of the school dining hall; the gaps in the tiles leave uncomfortable red marks on our legs. The sun is shining brightly through the wall of metal-framed windows to my left, sending out broadening shafts of light in which the dust whirls around us. I bow my head and close my eyes, screw them up tight, squeeze my fingers and the palms of my hands together, pointing upward, my forefingers touched to my lips. The darkness is warm, mysterious, and comforting. The adult voice reads a formal prayer from a book of children's prayers. I leave the world I can sense around me and try to see, to hear, to feel more, something else. I'm trying to understand the unfamiliar words; trying to catch something of what they point to, something of the true meaning of the world that you can't see with your eyes but have to find somewhere inside; reaching out to the heart and the edges of the universe with my mind's eye and my heart, tentatively longing.

Prayer Book Evensong, 1975: We're sitting in the mixed but sedate surroundings of a lively evangelical Anglican Church looking to modernize some aspects of worship. I've never seen the words, no one has ever taught them to me, but we are reciting and singing the service, ancient words inviting me into an ancient community; familiarly strange words laden with layer upon layer of meaning inviting me into a living, breathing understanding of the world; supple, resonant rhythms inviting me into a set of sinuous relationships; mysterious, ordinary words that beckon as an invitation but that also seep into me, becoming part of who I am and how I think, changing me. Not everyone's eyes are closed all the time. People move and stand together, but when some kneel, others sit.

Fellowship Group Prayers, 1980: Horribly anxious, distracted, squirming, heart pounding in my ears. We're sitting on uncomfortable chairs in a circle, praying in turns; no one has to say anything (they say), but somehow there is pressure to speak; I feel I must find words that will sound worthy, that will show that I'm thinking the right thoughts, desiring the right things, that I have understood the discussion. But nearly everything that has been said about the Bible reading seems to me to have missed the point, to have sprung off onto a familiar, favorite theme to do with the intensity of belief, simplifying the difficult words, ignoring the complex structure of the text, plundering it for supposed treasure and somehow rubbishing it, forcing it to be trite. "Help!" I cry inside, "help me to say something, something truthful; help me to pray in a way that might be helpful; perhaps I should say nothing?"

Prayer before the Sacrament, 1994: Sat on this bench by myself for the first time. Stillness. Resting. Breathing. Resting in this place, in this time, before this beautiful, devastating wonder. Bright sun, high up; here and now bathed in refreshingly cool shade. Eyes closed, head bowed, hands in my lap facing upward, hair hanging before my face, legs and feet side by side. No words; just watching, listening. My inward eye traces the contours of the small white disc hidden in the heavy metal box draped in a rather tatty veil, wondering at the figure of the glorified crucified One who holds it out to me; tenderly, tentatively, thankfully exploring with my inner senses what this is, how this can be. Waiting.

Praying with my Children, from 1998: Our bedtime prayers still begin: "Dear God, Thank you . . ." Everyone contributes reasons to be grateful—the beautiful world, friends, ice cream, dressing up. "Sorry when we spoil your world, especially . . ." Memories of our recent failings follow. "Please forgive us; please help us to say sorry, and please help us to forgive each other; please help us to do your will. Please also. . . ." We each add our petitions for loved ones, for personal desires, for local or global situations, for the sick, the needy . . . "Amen." This structured personal free-form prayer is invariably followed by reciting familiar prayers of the Church: the Lord's Prayer, the Nunc Dimittis,[1] the Grace,[2] and some concluding responses: "The Lord be with you." "And also with you." "Let us bless the Lord." "Thanks be to God." Our eyes are not often closed; we do not always put our hands together; we are often in the dark or the half light. We make the sign of the cross at the beginning of the Nunc Dimittis and during the Grace. And always I have marveled at my children's ability to pray: the beautiful things they have to say; their matter-of-fact combination of wonder and concern; their uncomplicated appreciation of the complex; their ability to trust and worship God. I have learned much with them, and continue to do so even now as I learn to pray with (and for!) a teenage son who is not sure what to believe at all.

The Many-Sided Contradictions of Prayer

Prayer is how and when we address God. It is our deliberate attention to God, but it is also our instinctive attitude toward God. In prayer we get to know God, but we also get to know ourselves. Prayer is part of the duty we owe God, what we are supposed to offer; but prayer is also whatever we happen or decide to offer God. We often try to be someone we are not in prayer, and are afraid of showing our true selves. This is rather foolish, since God knows everything. Prayer is a bold act; to address God at all is unnerving. And yet it seems that we are made for prayer. The Christian tradition teaches that we are created for praise and union with God. Prayer is both natural and impossible; we cannot do it by ourselves.

Prayer is about our total attention and the direction of our whole life. It can be grand and sweeping, meticulously composed and choreographed. But it can also be fleeting, small spontaneous gestures, fragments of recitation, thoughts left hardly formed, feelings directed before we are aware we have them. Prayer has to do with the overarching themes of existence and the petty details of everyday life in equal measure. Prayer is intensely personal—my prayer is always "my" prayer and never anyone else's; even when I pray someone else's prayer, I make it my own. And yet prayer is also always communal and corporate. It is an activity we share with countless other human beings, but Christians also always pray with the whole Church. My prayers are always offered with and for others, on earth and in heaven, even when I am alone in my room.

Prayer can be spoken or silent; still or frantic; individual or corporate; joyful or grieving; exciting or boring. Prayer can be sometimes more mental and sometimes more physical, but always both. During prayer, our eyes can be open or closed; we can stand or lie prostrate; we can sit or kneel; we can walk or dance. Our hands can be held together, closed in tight fists, wrapped around our foreheads, thumbing their way over prayer beads, or opened wide; they can be laid on the floor, they can hang by our sides, they can be held in our laps or raised above our heads. We can face each other, the earth, the sun, the east, the sky, a candle, or an icon.

Learning to Pray—Some Undertows

Prayer in the Christian tradition is and can be many things. Like many things we value, prayer is at once hugely rich and complex but also always shockingly simple. Learning to pray includes a growing understanding and acceptance of the coexistence of this complexity and simplicity. Since there is no one way to pray in the Christian tradition, there is no one way to learn to pray, and so learning to pray can be learning to do some very different, perhaps apparently contradictory, things. It is the common direction, the shared intention, of these varied activities—our turning to God—that makes them our attempts at prayer. It is a shared relation to Christ—usually praying to the Father, in Christ's name, empowered by the Spirit—that will make them Christian attempts at prayer. And in the Christian tradition there is an important sense in which we shall only ever be trying to pray because it is God who completes the offering; it will only ever be the arrival of our attempts in something like God's reception that will turn our attempts into prayer. For Christians, prayer is God-given not just in the sense that God lays down the basis or the order for us to pray, not just in the sense that God has given us some words to pray, not just in the sense that God appears to have made us "spiritual," "praying" creatures, but also in the sense that, while each prayer is what we offer to God, it is always also something that God gives to us.

Hearing and reading about different ways of praying will form an important part of learning to pray, but they are not enough. Even though prayer is a unique activity unlike any other, in many ways learning to pray is much like learning to do anything else. Just as I can only learn to write by writing, so I can only learn to pray by praying. Indeed, I can only begin to learn to pray when I am prepared to begin to *try* to pray, and to accept the mistakes, failures, humiliation, and frustration that trying will almost inevitably include. Reflecting on and discussing my experiences with others will also form an important part of my learning. But my prayer will always have to be *my* prayer in order to be prayer, in order to be the offering that I make, in much the same way as my writing will need to become unique to me in order to be my writing and not mere pastiche.

Similarly, I shall only learn to pray if I have the motivation to do so. This may be the positive motivation of a desire of some kind—I want to pray, or I understand I ought to, or believe it will do me good. But there can also be the more negative motivation of a fear of some kind—I'm afraid of disappointing someone, of failing in my duty, of being punished. However, despite the many analogies to other types of learning, there are some key distinguishing features to note about learning (and therefore also about teaching) to pray in the Christian tradition.

For Christians, prayer is never simply a human activity. Prayer is always also God's work in us; we have to have the initial desire and make the start, but God has always already invited and instructed us, will always support and sustain us, and will always complete our prayer. Learning to pray, therefore, is not just me learning to do something; it is always learning to allow God to do something. Moreover, for Christians, prayer is in some sense something that God is already doing without us, in the eternal expression of the Word, in the conversation and movement that already exist between the Father, the Son, and the Spirit. We are created, redeemed, and sanctified by and from within that divine activity. For Christians, prayer is made possible by Christ's prayer. We are called to pray with him and in his name, empowered by the Holy Spirit. Our prayer is not merely our conversation with God but our participation in a divine, eternal conversation that is itself identical with the divine life. Learning to pray in the Christian tradition is learning to participate, learning to join in. Sin prevents us, so learning to pray is always also learning to seek and accept God's assistance.

Another important aspect of prayer is learning to grow quiet and still. This is a strange form of "activity." It is about stopping our general busyness, about learning to do nothing and allow God to work in us. It seems strange, therefore, counterproductive even, that we end up focusing on our activity, learning words and actions and practices to help us to do nothing. Learning to pray is learning to stop, which many of us find difficult, and it seems counterintuitive to address this by learning things to do. Similarly, since the heart of prayer is about the inner, spiritual life, it can sometimes seem extremely odd, misleading even, to focus on the apparently "external" and "physical" aspects of prayer as the means to this when we often experience them as obstacles and distractions.

But for all that the "externals" might help us learn to pray, it is doubtful whether I can be *forced* to pray, for without me turning myself to God (however imperfectly or weakly willed), any putative prayer will in fact only be other human actions. I think ultimately I could only ever be forced to *appear* to pray, but I can sadly imagine situations in which this might happen (just as I can also imagine true prayer in fact emerging in desperation out of such a trauma). Learning or teaching to pray requires us to attend to the difference between encouragement and coercion. "Going through the motions" of prayer might be helpful and even necessary, but it cannot always (if ever) produce prayer.

Another distinctive aspect of prayer, then, is that it is a form of pedagogy. In prayer we are called to learn a variety of things: honesty and truth, humility and confidence, how to train our desires and to have our desires trained, how to surrender ourselves and everything to God, how to abandon ourselves to God's good providence. We learn to take appropriate responsibility for ourselves and for others; we learn to receive and grant forgiveness; we have to learn to be loved and to love. We grow in faith and hope; we surrender ourselves and yet also receive our true identities. We learn endless patience alongside an impatient desire for justice. And we have to unlearn things we have misunderstood. Learning to pray, then, is in some sense always learning to learn.

At the same time, my experience of praying with children suggests that when we are learning to pray we are in some sense often, if not always, trying to relearn something that we have somehow forgotten. We are born learning, inquisitive creatures; we were created to pray. Learning is what we do "naturally"; how strange to have to learn to do it again. It is in prayer that we learn to be like little children who can wonder and praise and trust and have faith and for whom the Kingdom of Heaven is accessible. When we pray with children, when we learn to pray with others, it is not always at all clear who is doing the teaching and who is doing the learning. Always when we pray—even when we are supposed to be teaching others to pray—we are only learning to pray, learning to be the learning, praying creatures that God made us, and ultimately it is God who is doing the teaching.

Learning to Pray—Places to Begin

Prayer is made of many elements; different approaches to learning to pray start from and highlight different facets and combine similar components in different ways. I trace here a crude taxonomy across two pairs of different aspects of prayer—words and silence; spontaneous impulse and regulated habit. The sketch is not comprehensive, but each of these aspects has a place in a mature life of Christian prayer. Importantly, any one of them can be the mode of someone's "first steps" in prayer. Prayer should not—cannot—be reduced to any one of its dimensions; growing in prayer means finding an appropriate combination of its many different aspects.

Prayer as Words

Once the initial decision to pray has been made, it will almost always include some verbalization. For the vast majority of Christians, whatever their age, learning to pray means first of all learning some of the church's prayers, and the Lord's Prayer in particular. Christian prayers come from various sources (scripture, the liturgy, prayer books, the writings of the saints). These shared words unite us to other Christians, whether we pray them alone or in a group. Appointed words provide a structure to each prayer session and to the experience of prayer over time. Words learned from others can help us to explore different approaches to God. They help us learn "what" and "how" to pray. We will often pray them without fully understanding them; as we pray, our understanding grows and we make them more and more our own. Their repetition becomes part of the fabric of our lives; their insights and attitudes become part of our mental furniture, even part of our breathing. Learning these prayers is like gathering a treasure store on which I can draw for the rest of my life.

Words are also important in Christian prayer because the relationship and conversation with God is always fed and directed by attention to God's words entrusted to scripture. The church's liturgy and prayer services draw heavily on biblical language and imagery, and for many Christians a significant part of their daily prayer is spent reading, thinking, and praying on appointed sections of God's Word. Learning to pray, then, includes learning to read scripture and to pray with and through it.

But prayer can also be nonscripted; prayer can be my own words, what I want to say now. This might be adaptations of prayers I already know, or it might be entirely free-form, especially as I struggle to understand, or pour out my longings, or intercede for those in difficulty. For some people and groups of Christians, extemporary prayer is the "normal" form of prayer (even if individual prayer sessions become montages of words already spoken) while for others it remains a rather odd form of prayer. Nevertheless, learning to pray always includes discovering my own voice in prayer.

Prayer as Impulse and Inclination

Whether we are considering someone's "first ever" prayer, or the emergence of prayer in a particular situation, prayer often begins *before* the conscious decision to try to pray. Prayer can start as a sudden, involuntary exclamation or feeling, or it can grow slowly out of a gradual awareness of a certain directedness of my thoughts. In either case, the focus of the prayer, the sense of its addressee, can be quite vague and hesitant ("something," "someone") or it can be dramatic and certain (the voice of God calling, a vision of Christ welcoming). Those who want to learn to pray have probably already started even if they are not aware of it themselves.

Learning to pray, then, includes discovering and exploring this initial impulse or inclination, refining and cultivating it, allowing it to grow into a fundamental aspect of life and our response to the world. Learning to pray involves moving from innate prayer to conscious prayer but then from conscious prayer "back" to prayer that is a constant activity as unconscious as my heartbeat. It also requires me to explore and work through the full range of my responses to God—and not just the ones I am proud of—adoration, confession, thanksgiving, supplication, yes, but also interrogation, exasperation, outpourings, and confusion as well as inconsequential conversation. As we grow in prayer, the range and the depth of our responses grow as they become ever more fully a part of our life. Different responses will dominate in different situations as we travel through life. Helping others learn to pray is not just about telling them what they ought to think and say. It requires a variety of activities (not just talking) in which people can discover and explore their own responses to the world, their own intuitive sense of God, the basic shape of their fundamental predispositions, and how they are already praying.

Prayer as Regular Rhythm

In order to grow in prayer, in order for prayer to become a full part of our lives, in order for our prayer to become at first conscious and then thoroughly instinctive, we need to give it regular space and time to grow and take hold in us. Throughout the Christian tradition, those who want to come to Christ, those who want to learn to pray, have been advised to set aside regular time in the day and the week for prayer of different kinds, in groups and alone. There are no universally prescribed times for prayer; we need to learn to make time for prayer, not just hope to "find time." Just as the athlete or musician must work hard and regularly to become proficient in their art, so must those who want to pray. This is particularly important in overcoming the many difficulties people can face in trying to pray, be that a sense of inadequacy, various distractions, or the experience of "dryness" (having nothing to say, or enjoying no sense of "response").

Many programs and suggestions can be made, but only those that are possible will in fact be adhered to; a certain realism is necessary, and better-than-impossible ideals. Weekly prayer on Sundays with other Christians coming together to celebrate the resurrection, to share in fellowship with Christ in Word and Sacrament, and to pray for the world forms the normal cornerstone of Christian prayer life; indeed, the Eucharist (our participation in Christ's offering of himself and our receipt of its benefits, enabled by the Holy Spirit) forms the pattern for all Christian prayer. Other traditional common times for prayer (alone or in groups, but always with the whole church) include first thing in the morning and last thing at night, as well as in grace before meals. Some people find this easy, the necessity is obvious to them, perhaps because they do not have much spontaneous prayer, or they know their lives are otherwise messy and they would forget. For others establishing a regular pattern is a continual struggle; perhaps this type of habitual prayer seems alien and cold, or their lives and perhaps their minds are just too chaotic.

Having a regular pattern of prayer is in some sense "giving time to God." The repeated witness of those who pray regularly, however, is that at some stage this giving flips: prayer time becomes time that God gives me, just as prayer itself becomes not so much what *I* am giving God as what *God* is giving me (and time is one of those gifts as much as any spiritual grace or consolation). This change in outlook probably needs to be experienced more than willed. Helping others learn to pray includes helping them to establish a pattern in which prayer can become habitual.

Prayer as Silence

Many Christians (pastors and congregations alike) have been suspicious of the aspect of prayer as silence, for silence can cover many different things, some of which may not be prayer or Christian at all. Traditionally, silence has been the preserve of the "virtuosi." More recently, however, there has been a rediscovery of silent prayer as an essential element of all Christian prayer, both communal and individual, and several studies suggest that most of us, even children, are perfectly capable of at least "stilling" and learning to meditate.

Silent prayer can just mean prayer that is not noisy. It can be another name for mental prayer, words spoken only inwardly. But it can also mean nonverbal prayer, prayer in or with images, emotions, gestures, or body movements—not necessarily trying to "say" anything at all but being part of our attempts to direct ourselves toward God and to allow God to direct us. Silent prayer may be listening prayer, prayer that is waiting to hear a Word from God.

But silent, contemplative prayer can also be far less "active" than all of these, a watching and a waiting on God that is not watching or waiting "for" anything; an intentional attempt to experience oneself as creature before Creator, as redeemed before Redeemer; a focused "nondoing," a type of "resting" or "breathing" in God, an active passivity, a passive activity. Although this type of prayer is often somewhere people arrive after much praying, occasionally this silent waiting is where someone will begin, and here the Quakers offer a significant witness. Learning to pray and helping others to pray should therefore include explorations of various physical and mental preparations (attention to posture and breathing, laying aside distracting thoughts) that can help us learn to pray nonverbally and assist us in reaching the still point in which we can just "be" before God, allowing God to make and remake us.

Concluding Thought: Prayer and Reward—The Puzzle of "Motivation"

Prayer will not begin without some desire to pray, but why pray? The physical, mental, and psychological "benefits" of prayer—greater calmness, better health—can be significant, and we should be alive to these, but the Christian tradition suggests that we do not (and should not) pray just because it is "good" for us. Similarly, the "rewards" of prayer are tremendous—a release from our guilt, a discovery of our true selves, union with God—but again, we do not pray simply in order to "win" these. We do not even pray simply because we are instructed to do so, although we are. Prayer, I want to suggest, can in one sense have no "ulterior" motive because prayer is both the means and the end; it can give us nothing more than it is: a transformative relation with God. In an important sense, prayer doesn't "get us anywhere," although it also changes everything. Ultimately our prayers will only become true prayer when we pray because of who and what God is and because of who and what we are. How strange, then, that our prayer will also in fact have only begun because of who and what we are and because of who and what God is.

Notes

1. This is the traditional Night Prayer canticle of the Church, the song the aged Simeon sang when Christ was presented at the Temple, "Lord, now lettest Thou Thy servant depart in peace, according to Thy word. For mine eyes have seen Thy salvation which Thou hast prepared before the face of all people, to be a light to lighten the Gentiles, and to be the glory of Thy people Israel." Followed by the traditional Christian doxology: "Glory be to the Father, and to the Son and to the Holy Ghost, as it was in the beginning, is now and ever shall be, world without end, Amen."

2. This common prayer is used to complete communal worship or close other meetings, comprising Paul's words in II Corinthians 13:14: "May the grace of our Lord Jesus Christ, the love of God and the fellowship of the Holy Spirit be with us all, evermore. Amen."

Sources

Balthasar, Hans Urs von. *Prayer*, translated by Graham Harrison (San Francisco: St Ignatius Press, 1986).

———. *Unless You Become Like This Child*, translated by Erasmo Leiva-Merikakis (San Francisco: St Ignatius Press, 1991).

Beckett, Sister Wendy. *Sister Wendy Beckett on Prayer* (London: Continuum, 2006).

Byrne, Lavinia. *Original Prayer* (London: SPCK, 2008).

———, ed. *The Hidden Tradition* (London: SPCK, 1991).

Catechism of the Catholic Church (London: Geoffrey Chapman, 1994), §§2558–2864.

Daniélou, Jean. *Prayer: The Mission of the Church*, translated by David Louis Schindler (Edinburgh, UK: T&T Clark, 1996).

Davison, Andrew, Andrew Nunn, and Toby Wright, eds. *Lift up Your Hearts* (London: SPCK, 2010).

Dupré, Louis, and Don Saliers, eds. *Christian Spirituality: Post-Reformation and Modern* (New York: Crossroad, 1989).

Jenson, Robert. *Systematic Theology*, vol. 2, *The Works of God* (Oxford: Oxford University Press, 1999).

McCabe, Herbert. *God Matters* (London: Geoffrey Chapman, 1987; repr. 2000) (especially chapters on sacraments and prayer).

Nye, Rebecca. *Children's Spirituality: What It Is and Why It Matters* (London: Church House Publishing, 2009).

Richards, Ann, and Peter Privett. *Through the Eyes of a Child* (London: Church House Publishing, 2009).

Stonehouse, Catherine, and Scottie May. *Listening to Children on the Spiritual Journey* (Grand Rapids, MI: Baker Academic, 2010).

Learning to Pray as a Muslim

The Foundational Stage

IBRAHIM MOGRA

In this brief essay I present my observations and experiences of learning and teaching prayer in Islam. As my focus is on the practical side of learning and teaching to pray at the foundational level, I will say little about the theology and philosophy of prayer in Islam. I will also make very limited use of the Qur'ān to support my observations, presenting my understanding of only a small sample of verses relevant to the subject of prayer.

Most Muslims generally understand and approach prayer in two ways: *ṣalāt* and *du'ā'*. *Ṣalāt* refers to the ritual prayers five times a day and on some other occasions while *du'ā'* refers to supplication.

Ṣalāt is prayer as ritual worship. In performing ṣalāt the Muslim is praying to God Who says, "And I did not create the jinn and mankind except to worship me" (Qur'ān 51:56).[1] The worship of God through this ritual prayer helps one to become righteous: "Indeed, prayer (*ṣalāt*) prevents from obscenity and evil and the remembrance of God is the greatest" (29:45). Muslims therefore feel a sense of duty to pray as obedience to God and as a way of achieving piety and protection from evil and most importantly as a way of remembering Him (*dhikr*). Reward is promised for those who pray, and there are warnings of punishments for those who do not.

Ṣalāt gives the individual an opportunity to be with God and in His presence. We all like to be in the company of our loved ones, our family, and friends as much as we can. Five times a day, prayer gives Muslims the opportunity to be with their most beloved. We are encouraged when standing before Him to be humble and attentive, to give up for a short while our attachment to all worldly matters. Indeed, we are to cast worldly concerns away as we make the gesture when raising our hands to our ears at the beginning of the prayer declaring "God is the greatest." We seek to visualize God being there before us as we worship Him, trying to achieve the level of *iḥsān*, the perfection in the worship of God that is required of us. Jibrīl (the angel Gabriel) asked the Messenger of God, "O Muḥammad, what is *iḥsān*?" He said, "That you worship God as though you see Him. And if you do not see Him then indeed He sees you" (Muslim, *Ṣaḥīḥ*). Those who are not focused in their prayer are warned: "So woe to the worshippers, those who are neglectful of their prayer" (107:4–5).

Duʿāʾ refers to prayer as invocation and supplication to God. Such prayer has been encouraged by God, as in the following verse: "And when my servants ask you concerning me then I am close to them. I answer the prayer (*duʿāʾ*) of the supplicant when He calls me" (2:186). The ritual prayers and supplications collectively are seen as the remembrance (*dhikr*) of God. He says, "Remember me and I shall remember you" (2:152). The Qurʾān declares, "Those who believe, and whose hearts find contentment in the remembrance of God, indeed in the remembrance of God do hearts find contentment" (13:28).

Supplication is also a way of thanking God for His blessings and asking for help and the fulfillment of one's needs. It is the expression of one's utter helplessness and total dependence on Him. The purpose of the human being's creation is to worship God. Muḥammad (peace be upon him) said, "Supplication is the essence of worship" (al-Tirmidhī, *Sunan*). He also said, "Supplication is worship" (ibid.).

Supplications give a person the opportunity to communicate with God in a very personal and private way. There is assurance of God's acceptance each time, so Muslims are encouraged to pray after every good deed with full faith in God's acceptance. As the Qurʾān declares: "Pray to me and I will answer you" (40:60).

In light of all these understandings, Muslim families start teaching their children prayer from a very early age. The first word an infant is taught is "*Allāh*," God's proper name in Arabic. This is soon followed by learning the *Kalima*: "There is none worthy of worship except God; Muḥammad is God's messenger." Soon these are followed by al-Fātiḥa (1:1–7) and the many daily supplications to be said on different occasions, such as before and after a meal, before and after using the bathroom, before going to sleep and upon waking up, when putting on clothes, when getting into a car, and so on. All these supplications are learned in Arabic even by non-Arabic speakers, but they also learn and understand their meanings in their mother tongue. All Muslims are encouraged to say these supplications by being reminded of the virtues, benefits, and rewards that come from praying. These supplications also help Muslims to live in the regular, if not constant, remembrance of God as they busy themselves with day-to-day things.

The ritual *ṣalāt* prayers are learned by younger children when they observe their older family members praying or when they accompany their parents to a mosque for congregational prayers. As there are certain differences in some of the postures in prayer for males and for females, it is amusing to see male children sometimes praying like females and vice versa.

More structured teaching and learning of prayer takes place outside the home in some of the Indian subcontinental communities in the United Kingdom. These communities have set up a *madrasa* system in which classes are held every weekday in the evenings after school. The word *madrasa* (pl. *madāris*) means a place of learning or school. It can refer either to an institution of higher education as in most Muslim countries, or to a Muslim elementary school called a *maktab* (pl. *makātib*). The words *madrasa* and *maktab* are sometimes used interchangeably. In Britain, whenever the word *madrasa* is used, it usually refers to supplementary evening schools that are carrying out the role of a *maktab* in the true sense of the word. A vast majority of these madāris or makātib are located within the mosque or are attached to the mosque complex. A growing number of Muslims are also holding these classes in government schools, public buildings, and other community premises. A smaller number also run classes privately in their homes. A few classes are also held in church halls. Classes usually run for two hours. Every madrasa follows a curriculum and a syllabus, with children progressing every year after sitting exams. Children usually study from the age of four or five until fourteen or fifteen, with very few staying on for another year. Syllabi are structured in such a way that all the key essentials are taught before the pupil leaves. There is a diverse methodology that is implemented by these institutions, and each has its own flavor in terms of the school of law, tradition, and culture of the communities whose children attend these classes.

During the early years, the children are taught the prayers they should say when doing normal day-to-day things, for example, the prayer said before taking a meal. The teacher begins by explaining that food is a gift from God, explains how it grows and is prepared, how it helps to nourish people, and so on. Once the children understand what a wonderful gift food is, the teacher then continues to remind them of the need to pray to God and to thank Him for it. The children are then taught the Arabic formulation of the prayer, which is also explained to them in English. The same is done with the prayers to say before and after using the toilet. The children are reminded that God has enabled them to remove waste from their bodies to remain healthy and that they should therefore thank Him by saying the prayer. The same is done for prayers at bedtime and waking up. The teacher explains the creation of night and day and the gift of sleep and then teaches the relevant prayers. The same method is used for every occasion when a prayer is to be said. In teaching all these prayers the teacher ensures that the children fully understand why, when, and how they must pray and, most importantly, to whom they must pray. The children are regularly tested on their ability to say these prayers in Arabic readings and are also asked to explain the meanings in English. They are encouraged to say these prayers every day and are rewarded by the teachers for their achievements.

The ritual ṣalāt prayers are taught formally, usually from the age of seven. The children first learn how to perform the ritual ablution (*wuḍūʾ*) in preparation for prayer. They start with the theory and then learn it in practice, sitting at a tap and washing while the teacher supervises them. The next step is learning the names of the five daily prayers and the times when they are to be performed. The times between which the prayers are to be performed are explained, and children are taught how to work them out. They are then taught the call to prayer (*adhān*) and the second call to begin the prayer (*iqāma*). Using diagrams and practical demonstrations, the teacher helps the children learn the different postures of standing, bowing, and prostrating. Each child is observed by the other children in class and they are encouraged to learn in this manner. By the age of ten they will have been taught all the rules of prayer and would be expected to offer them regularly. Prayer becomes obligatory from the age of puberty. The pupils are reminded of their duty to God and are encouraged to express their love for Him by praying regularly. When prayer times fall within the madrasa time, the older pupils are given the opportunity to lead the congregational prayer with their teacher and classmates.

The adult population is also taught the same things either as a refresher course or as a beginner's course for those who did not learn prayer for any reasons. In addition to everything else, they are also encouraged to wake up in the latter part of the night and offer *tahajjud* prayers in order to deepen their relationship with God and increase their level of sincerity. They are taught the deeper meanings of prayer and encouraged to search for a meaningful attachment with prayer that can lead to greater heights of spirituality.

Another aspect of duʿāʾ is that of asking God's forgiveness for one's sins. Muslims are taught to pray for forgiveness for themselves and their loved ones, especially for those who have died.

Muslims are taught how to ask God for all their needs through prayer. Such prayers do not have to be said in Arabic. Many non-Arabic-speaking Muslims do use Arabic prayers, but it is important for them to understand what they are praying for. It is often better to pray in one's own language and thereby fully understand what one is praying for than to use Arabic formulations without any understanding. The great danger of praying without understanding is that it can become a simple daily routine, a lifeless prayer, not from the heart and without yearning.

Muslims are taught to ask for all the good things of this world and of the Hereafter. They learn to pray for others as a sense of duty but also because this hastens and increases the chances of the acceptance of one's prayer. Muslims will often ask fellow Muslims to pray for them.

Muslims are taught that in order for their prayers to be accepted and answered by God, they have to ensure that their earnings are all lawful and acquired in a legal way. It is taught that an unlawful livelihood results in prayers going unanswered.

Part of teaching prayers also includes the teaching of the Qur'ān because reciting it is regarded as an important form of worship. Many non-Arabic-speaking Muslims also learn how to recite the Arabic script, though not necessarily to understand it. For example, my mother recites a portion of the Qur'ān every day but has to use a translation to understand the meanings. Muslims are taught that to recite the words of the Qur'ān is virtuous, to recite them with understanding is more virtuous, and to recite them with understanding and to practice them is most virtuous. Many memorize the often-repeated chapters of the Qur'ān, which they recite as part of their daily recitation (*tilāwa*).

Muslims are also taught to say prayers for the remembrance of God (*adhkār*, plural of *dhikr*) and to send greetings and salutations (*ṣalawāt*) upon Muḥammad and God's messengers. Many use set forms of these *adhkār* every day, thus purifying their hearts and growing in their love for God and Muḥammad.

I conclude with a wise saying of Shaykh Dr. Abdul Hayy Arifi (1898–1986), a prominent Indian scholar and renowned saint of the Sunni tradition: "Does there exist any problem that cannot be solved through *du'ā'*? How can there, when *du'ā'* is a request made to Allah for the removal of problems and there is no problem on earth whose removal is beyond His ability?"

Note

1. Translations from the Qur'ān are my own.

Growing in Prayer as a Christian

TIMOTHY WRIGHT

For me, prayer is a love affair in which words, gestures, and memory all come into play. I have read many books on prayer; most of them offered me little help. Why? Not because their authors are insincere, nor because their authors have not had considerable experience, but because a love affair by definition is unique. My love affair will not be yours, nor yours mine. "Pray as you can, not as you ought" is a wise saying. I particularly like the phrase "love affair" because it emphasizes that this relationship is unique and special; its human equivalent is also unique and special but in an altogether different way.

In this reflection I want to develop this notion of "prayer as love affair" under three themes: first, a general summary of what I mean by the love affair of prayer; second, a short summary of some techniques of praying; and third, a brief outline of the four "pillars" that create the framework of my daily prayer.

What do I mean when I call prayer a love affair with God? If my faith is to be an essential part of my spiritual life as breathing is for my physical life, then faith must be present every second of my day. God is my Lover who wills me to be, grants me the faith to see the divine hand at each second—however ordinary, however painful, however exhilarating. From another perspective, life makes no sense if my Divine Lover is either forgotten or excluded.

Let me put it another way. Because I am created in the image and likeness of God, and since God is love, then I am by definition already in love with God. In prayer I express my loving response to my Divine Lover. Over time I realize this love can be expressed as an act of thanksgiving, a request for urgent help, an action encouraged by family or friends. My life expresses this love affair, reflecting my desire for ever closer intimacy with God. Without that intention, my prayer remains one activity among many of daily life: duties of living are one thing; praying is another.

To realize my intention I have to do two things: first, be ever more aware of God's presence through daily engagement with the divine Word "spoken" in the inspired scriptures; and, second, to "hear" that divine Word in all the events, duties, activities, discussions of daily life. If the Word has found intimacy in my heart, so my heart will express that divine Word during the day—not as homily, but as the smile I bring, the endurance I show, the kindnesses I offer, and, above all, the reverence with which I listen to the "other," whoever he or she may be. In this way my prayer enlarges the mutual love between us, with the Divine Lover an enthusiastic participant at every moment. I will face both temptations that distract me and revelations that remind me of my Divine Lover. This is the pattern of human living and praying. But unchecked temptations weaken commitment and cause the divine love affair to fade.

To counter such weakening there are "reminders" of the Divine Lover; for example, a pause in activities to express thanks or a quick request for help are ways of turning to the Divine Lover at moments of joy or sorrow. The beauty of the countryside may suddenly strike us, or the generous action of the driver in front who allows us to park evokes a word of thanks, or the sight of a helpless person sitting by the road jolts us to remember that they too are an important sign of the presence of God. These reminders cause us to stop and remember that "I am who I am" because of the Divine Lover, and this invites us to a silent reflection, or a word of praise, or a gesture of love. The love affair with God relies on this memory. God is always near; occasionally we should acknowledge "God is here." That is the essential element in prayer. It will, I suggest, echo strongly with the Muslim view.

There are different techniques in prayer. Many people speak about their difficulties in praying, often arising during formal prayer. A common complaint of believers is that when they sit down to meditate, or are present in a service in church, their minds wander and they find it difficult to concentrate. My response is to assure them that what they experience is precisely the experience of everyone who tries to pray. Occasionally we have moments of full concentration and are inspired by a word in the service or an insight that arises from a moment of silent prayer. Such moments are gifts; they are not the norm. Some find that difficult to understand, saying, "I have made the effort to be at prayer, but God ignores me." The problem is not God's but ours! Writers on prayer will encourage commitment, recommend we lower our expectations and, perhaps, use books or pictures or beads or music to encourage us to focus. Some practitioners train themselves to keep focused by improving their posture, reading more slowly, or keeping to a timed structure. But whatever the technique, the decision to give time to God is what counts; it carries great merit in the eyes of God, even if, in our perception, it seems as if those eyes have blinked at that moment! Much of life is dull, made up of "must do" tasks; so, too, our relationship with God grows by commitment to the seemingly boring experience of much prayer. As in family life the quality of our love is not expressed simply by our feelings; likewise, in prayer the most important advice is to "never give up" and to allow the Divine Lover to produce solutions on the divine timescale.

I offer a framework for prayer that has four elements: *lectio divina*, silent recollection, a passage from a book of spirituality, and celebration of the Church's official prayer—known to some as the Divine Office. This might sound a task more suited to people—male or female—who are dedicated to a religious vocation. So, before outlining each element of the framework, I will show how it can be practical even for a busy person who has little time.

I would start with a verse from a gospel and follow it with a moment of silence to ponder its importance for that day's agenda. At another moment in the day I would take a page or paragraph from a spiritual book and seek inspiration from it. Finally, at another moment I would express thanks to God for the day using a form of the Official Prayer/Divine Office. Technology allows these texts to be carried easily on a Kindle or an iPad, which may help busy people find time for them, even during the daily commute. This framework of a verse from a gospel, a moment of silence, a moment of pondering a passage from a spiritual book, and thanksgiving by means of a traditional text can be adapted to suit individual needs. It allows variety, which both creates and sustains interest. At the same time, this flexibility invites commitment to the framework, which cultivates one's relationship with the Divine Lover.

Let me now offer a thought on each of these four elements. The first element, *lectio divina*, is distinguished from scriptural study by both method and intention. Scriptural study is reflection on the passages of scripture to better understand what the author is trying to say; the aim is information and the method is reading texts. Lectio divina is pondering the meaning of the Word and seeking its relevance to the life and challenges of that day. They are mutually supportive. The more familiar I become with the characters and sayings of the inspired Word, the more able I am to identify the presence of God. If prayer is a love affair, then the scriptures show me the Lover addressing me, and each day the relationship becomes more intimate. The divine message penetrates deeply into me, building the relationship of love. Books offer many methods of lectio divina; perhaps the simplest is simply pondering a passage from scripture. Over time that pondering produces intimacy and generates conversion.

The second element is finding moments of silence during the day or night. In silence we can find stillness, which allows reflection and opens up opportunities for inspiration, promptings of the Divine Lover. We begin with prayer, sitting in silence, perhaps slowly repeating a favorite word or phrase, allowing the mind to be still, the body to be quiet, and the focus to be on God the Lover. Such prayer is vulnerable because the human body is not trained for stillness and the mind takes time to settle. Each discovers the way that suits. The purpose is love. The Lover is always intimate; the intention is ever deeper intimacy, sometimes revealed, always desired, and never fully satisfied. The length of time given to it is not as important as the regularity with which it is practiced; ten minutes a day is better than sixty minutes once a week. The effectiveness of these moments is never easily evaluated, but dogged determination to keep at it brings rich rewards—in ways not planned, at times not expected, but always affirming and encouraging, as one would expect from a Lover who loves without limit and unconditionally.

The third element is to be inspired by the writings of prayerful men and women, either contemporary or from the Christian spiritual tradition. To read a little each day provides a source of instruction, affirmation, and challenge. This keeps the ups and downs of the relationship with the Divine Lover in perspective. This library is huge, so if the text you have chosen is not to your liking, find another. Some authors describe their experiences of prayer. Others speak of their relationship with God. Yet others again describe the problems they faced. All can be both reassuring and challenging. Many offer an insight into their journey into an ever deeper awareness of the presence of God in their lives. Some were written in the early years of Christianity, others yesterday, but all convey their author's enthusiasm for God. Their experiences help us face our negative attitudes and encourage us to persevere to the goal of shared union with our Divine Lover.

The fourth element is the Divine Office, the daily cycle of formal prayer offered in different ways by the Christian churches. I write from the Roman Catholic monastic tradition, for which the Divine Office defines the structure of our day, beginning in the early morning, while still dark, and then at particular moments during the day, dawn, midday, sunset, and at night before retiring. Once the preserve of monastic men and women, it is now encouraged for all Christians. It is published in easy-to-manage forms, even as an e-book. This formal prayer has three functions: first, to remember and give thanks to God; second, to encourage Christians to make holy different moments of the day; and third, to pray for all those millions of people who desperately need the support of God but have no one to pray for them. Of these Offices, the two most important are at dawn and dusk, moments when we appreciate creation as the daylight arrives and give thanks for the day as dusk proceeds to night. One of the simplest forms of the Divine Office is produced by my confreres in St. John's Collegeville. Called *Give Us This Day* (Liturgical Press), it comes out monthly and is available in electronic form. In addition to the order for daily prayer (morning and evening), each issue includes prayers and readings for daily Mass and a reflection on scripture for each day plus other helpful essays. Such resources also are offered from other Christian traditions.

These four "pillars"—*lectio divina*, silent prayer, reading of a book of spirituality, and elements of the Divine Office—provide the framework within which the relationship with the Divine Lover can mature and develop. Prayer—once part of one's daily life—changes with time and, typically, becomes simpler and more intimate with age and practice. To these four pillars of daily prayer as relationship with the Divine Lover, some will add a fifth: regular participation at Eucharist—the memory in liturgical form of the salvation achieved by Jesus Christ and relived in the sacrament. Some, for good reasons, may not include this in their life of prayer or participate only occasionally. The framework offered here, together with the encouragement to remember that each moment is lived in the presence of the Divine Lover, provides a way to the intimacy and union believers so deeply desire.

Growing in Prayer as a Muslim

Reflections and Lessons of a Struggler

TIMOTHY J. GIANOTTI

I OFTEN REFLECT THAT the prayer-related growth we most need within the Muslim community is like a hidden treasure buried beneath or within the religious obligation. I say "obligation" here because prayer is often presented and taught as a duty, as something we owe God, rather than as a way God—in the infinite mercy and love we believe God extends to us—has opened for us to approach and come close to the One who is the ultimate goal of all our longing and unrest. So in my community teaching and in my own self-coaching, I try to engender the sense that prayer is a most welcome and precious opportunity to respond to God's invitation, sounded in the depths of our being as well as in the explicit teachings of the Qur'ān and the legacy of our beloved Prophet, may God's blessings be ever upon him and his family.

Before we forge ahead with this discussion, I must frankly acknowledge that the topic of growing in prayer presents unusual challenges for the scholar in me. While tempted to approach this theoretically and professionally and with a sense of academic competence, I quickly realize that I cannot embark upon this subject without a full admission that the author writes as one who struggles greatly with prayer and who desperately seeks to grow in prayer. Of course, this admission betrays the perspective that prayer is something we do rather than something God does within us, a perspective that dominates the way we Muslims are taught to view prayer. As we will see in this very selective survey of Muslim discussions of prayer, however, filtered as they are through my own experience and understanding, growing in prayer seems to mean, among other things, a letting go of the somewhat materialistic notion that prayer is the product of the worshipper. That said, there is no question in the sources (as well as within my experience) that personal growth in prayer seems to begin with personal struggle—born of a deep, personal desire for a closer walk with God. This desire is itself a gift, of course, and so we again are faced at the outset with the ambiguity of prayer being both an act of the Creator and an act of the creature.

Another ambiguity arises when we speak of prayer as an act of worship as opposed to a process. In the first case, when prayer is understood strictly in terms of duty and as an obligatory act of worship, growing in prayer might, for a Muslim, mean mastering the forms of prayer, memorizing various Arabic supplications and litanies, getting into a better habit of praying with regularity, and becoming more adept at focusing the mind and more fully attending to the act of worship when we are in it. In this sense, growing in prayer is fairly straightforward and can to some extent be quantitatively measured and monitored. Growth in all of these areas is, of course, highly beneficial and meritorious, but I do not think such growth can be separated from the larger religious project of growing as a God-centered, moral being, remembering God with greater frequency and intensity, and, in doing so, infusing everything one does with the love and obedience that we associate with acts of worship. In the prophetic vocabulary, this means making an explicit and permanent connection between our *islām*—our embodied act of surrendering—and our *iḥsān*—the psycho-spiritual and moral "beautification" of our dispositions and our actions in God. In other words, the act of worship, which dwells in the realm of the embodied dimension of the faith (*al-islām*), must enter into a state of constant communion with the transforming, spiritual awareness of standing within the theatre of God's ever-presence (*al-iḥsān*). When this link is made, prayer remains an "act," but an act that reflects a much larger process by which that closer walk with God becomes increasingly real, increasingly intimate, and increasingly transfiguring for the practitioner of prayer. Of course, when taken in this expanded and all-inclusive sense, the idea of growing in prayer becomes much more demanding and more difficult to measure.

In what follows, I will reflect upon seven lessons that, from my perspective as a scholar, a religious teacher, and "a kneeler in training,"[1] are essential for any Muslim who seeks to grow his or her prayer life. Because I am presenting these lessons first and foremost to myself, I often frame these lessons in the language of the first person.

Lesson 1: Growing in prayer involves tests and difficulties. I have to want it and be willing to work for it.

Insofar as prayer forms the core of the religious life, the Qur'ān states quite powerfully that it necessarily involves difficulty and testing. We are to be tested in prayer, and we are meant to struggle in prayer as in the entirety of our religious life. This difficulty seems to be part of a divinely ordained test that is designed to awaken struggle within the truly devoted, a struggle or striving that promises to open the door of God's blessing. So the first word of advice given to the aspiring practitioner of prayer (and given first and foremost to myself) is to embrace the hardship; struggle and strive for God, and God will help you.

In the following *āyāt* (verses) from the Qur'ānic chapter of "the Spider" (*sūrat al-ʿAnkabūt*), we see that struggling is a promise that contains a promise; difficulty and struggle will definitely come to those who seek God, and divine help will come if and when we embrace the test, the difficulty, the struggle.

> Do the people reckon that they shall be left alone [after saying] "We believe" and that they will not be tested? We certainly tested those [who came] before them, and [thus] God most certainly knows those who are true and those who are false. Whosoever hopes to meet God [let him/her know that] God's appointed time is surely coming; He is the [all] Hearing, the [all] Knowing. . . . And whosoever strives [to meet God], truly he strives for [the betterment of] his own soul. Verily God has no need of [anything within] the worlds [of creation]. (29:2–3; 5–6)[2]

Then, as if by design, the ray of hope—the promise of Divine help—comes at the very end of the *sūra*: " [As for] those who strive for Us, We shall surely guide them [along] Our paths. God is indeed with the doers of beautiful deeds" (29:69).

This theme of necessary personal struggle is corroborated and expanded upon by many later Muslim sources. For example, an anonymous thirteenth-century Persian author wrote, "No one can reach Him through performing good works, but no one has ever reached Him without them."[3] The ambiguity of this personal effort does not escape the anonymous author, who states just prior to this, "whoever supposes he can reach God through other than God has been deceived."[4] So who is striving to do the work of prayer? Is it the supplicant or God working through the supplicant? Is there a meaningful difference?

A few centuries earlier the extremely influential Sunni theologian-jurist-mystic Abū Ḥāmid al-Ghazālī taught that the prayerful goal of remembering God incessantly in the heart begins with "a laborious effort to turn our thought, mind and concern toward God and the Hereafter. It thus aims to reverse the tide of our whole character and to turn our central concern from this world, with which we have been familiar, to the Hereafter, with which we so far have no experience."[5] It is important to note here that "Hereafter" need not be understood as a time and place other than the here and now;

indeed, in al-Ghazālī's "psycho-cosmology," this world and the next world are contemporaneous, and human beings exist in both simultaneously, even though most are unaware of their otherworldly existence until after death.[6] For al-Ghazālī, then, "heaven" and "hell" are experiential realities that correspond to our own spiritual stations, mental states, and worldly attachments.[7]

Thus, it is safe to say that the process of prayer involves reorienting our perspective—indeed our consciousness—from an unspeakably cluttered, world-centered or ego-centered view to an unfragmented, Hereafter-centered (or theocentric) perspective. In the words of one Prophetic tradition, this process entails "shunning the abode of delusion and turning toward the abode of everlasting life."[8] It also seems well established that this reorientation does not come without difficulty and great effort. Growing in prayerful living thus means engaging in that effort and embracing that difficulty as something God-given, just as the desire to pray must be seen as a gift from God, who longs for us just as we long for God.

Lesson 2: I must make my prayer personal.

Because the formal Islamic act of prayer involves memorized Arabic supplications and the recitation of memorized Arabic verses or "signs" (*āyāt*) from the Qur'ān, it is vitally important for the worshipper-in-training to work toward a point of understanding and even "feeling" the individual words and verses involved—even if the worshipper knows no other Arabic. Achieving such a point of understanding need not mean one's memorization of a particular translation; rather, it means allowing oneself to feel and experience the meanings in a way that becomes intensely personal. This is also true for the various postures involved in prayer: the worshipper should listen to her body in the act of prayer and strive to "hear" the whispered mysteries of each movement and posture. This intimate personalization of the words and movements helps us to experience prayer as an intensely personal, intimate moment of communion, or at least communication, with our Lord, who has promised—right in the prayer—that "God hears the one who praises Him."

Lesson 3: The quality of my prayer has to be given priority over the quantity of prayer cycles or length of recitation. Sometimes, less is more.

We can sometimes be swept away by the somewhat disturbingly widespread, popular emphasis upon the quantity of prayers and the rewards that many believe come from quantitative performance. The antidote for this religious materialism is the teaching of our spiritual sages regarding the necessity of mental presence (*ḥudūr al-qalb*) or mindfulness in prayer and humility or lowliness (*khushūʿ*) in prayer. In his *Book of Knowledge*, al-Ghazālī describes this mindfulness as a state in which "the heart is empty of everything other than that which the person has undertaken and concerning which he is speaking. Awareness must be joined with word and deed, and thoughts must not wander in other than these two. When the person's thought leaves aside everything but what he is busy with, when his heart remembers [*dhikr*] what he is concerned with, and when he is heedless of everything else, then he has actualized the presence of the heart."[9]

Regarding the sense of humility or lowliness in prayer, the thirteenth-century mystic-poet Jalāl al-Dīn Rūmī gives bold expression to this when he imaginatively captures a moment when God is reprimanding Moses, who has been theologically critical of a shepherd's simple and rather anthropomorphic prayer. In Rūmī's account, God reveals the shocking news that the words spoken by worshippers are of little or no concern to God, who rather looks "inside at the humility," at the brokenness, at the lowliness, at the spiritual poverty that acknowledges one's desperate need for God. God is not interested in phraseology, Rūmī says, but wants "burning, burning."[10]

One of the ways in which we grow in prayer, then, is by getting in touch with our longing, our burning, and understanding that this burning is nothing other than God calling us to prayer. Only then, in the words of Rūmī, can we "be friends" with our burning and approach God with a sincere awareness of our need for God. This awareness, driven by our longing and harnessed by our rapt attention and mindfulness to the prayer as we utter and enact it, can make a single cycle of prayer more efficacious than a thousand cycles performed with partial awareness or no awareness at all.

Lesson 4: Growing in prayer means making my entire life a theatre of remembrance.

Addressing the very common and constant challenge of keeping one's mind and heart fixed upon God in the act of ritual prayer, al-Ghazālī and others advise an interconnected hierarchy of remembrances: remembering in the first instance that one is conversing with God in prayer; (if that by itself does not work) remembering with gratitude everything bestowed upon one by God (including the knowledge of how to pray and the promise that "God hears those who praise Him"); remembering one's own poverty and great need of God; and remembering one's imminent death and one's great vulnerability and peril before God.[11] All these "lesser" remembrances are taught with the hope of training the servant to be mindful of God and fixed upon God in the act of ritual worship. We thus find that the practical pedagogy of prayer often employs such a hierarchy of remembrances as helpful supports for the higher goal of being absolutely mindful of the Hereafter and God. While al-Ghazālī makes reference to an ultimate level of prayer where all such supports fall away, the supports are treated as essential, potentially lifesaving practices for seekers in the earlier stages of formation and possibly even for selected moments in the prayer lives of more cultivated and advanced practitioners.

The wider, more generic religious consciousness of which prayer is a part can also be cultivated and sustained by such techniques, including a comprehensive remapping of one's daily experience of the world. This remapping is similar to the practice of allegorical exegesis (*al-ta'wīl*), whereby literal meanings are "turned" toward allegorical referents that are believed to be the true foci of the words and images of particular passages. In reflecting upon this aspect of al-Ghazālī's teachings, Kojiro Nakamura notes that "to those whose sole concern is the Hereafter, everything in this world can be a reminder of, and a lesson in preparation for, the eschatological events."[12] Therefore, if one wants to be such a person, one must train the mind to see things as such people do. Reminders of Hell and Paradise are everywhere, and so the mind is continually turning its perceptions and experiences of this world to the anticipated visions and experiences of the Hereafter. For example, extreme heat and hunger and thirst all conjure images of separation from God (Hell), whereas moments of ease and shade and satiation conjure images and foretastes of the gardens of the blessed. In both cases God is remembered, and the ultimate concern of one's existence is placed before one's eyes. One's sojourn through this world effectively becomes inseparable from one's eschatological journey into the next world; the "here" and the "hereafter" converge.

Frequent supplication, Qur'ānic study and recitation, oral recitation (also *dhikr*) of mantra-like Qur'ānic verses or divine names, and *nashīd* hymns and *qasīda* poems celebrating God or memorializing the virtues of the Prophet all support this mental reorientation and help make it more stable and permanent. The daily exercises of a supplicant seeking to grow in prayer, then, involve a combination of all of these, in addition to the five times daily prayer, so they all can be considered "prayer" in a sense. Of course, the saturation of the senses with tokens of remembrance also aids in this reorientation, and this is why we see, even at the very popular level, calligraphic representations of Qur'ānic verses and phrases in homes, shops, taxis, buses, on jewelry, and so on. We can also hear verbal "remembrance" in our linguistic conditioning, which turns everyday, mundane exchanges into moments of remembrance, such as when we are asked about our condition and automatically say *al-hamdu li'llāh* (praise be to God), or when we declare an intention to do something and follow it with the pious caveat *in shā' Allāh* (if God wills).

As I write and mention these everyday aids to Divine remembrance and their possible impact, memories of weathered taxi drivers firing up even more weathered vehicles assert themselves; I sit next to them again as they turn their key and breathe out, "I bear witness that there is no god but God and that Muhammad is the messenger of God." In such moments, I have observed that remembrance is no less natural than breathing, and I wonder if this is the point. I wonder: if "prayer" is the proper word for the act of reorienting of our consciousness from a world-centered or ego-centered state to a theocentric or Hereafter-centered state, is it possible to separate such aids to prayer from prayer itself?

Another way to speak of the process of prayer within our traditions is to speak of cultivating an ongoing "friendship" or intimate companionship with God. In a modest but evocative chapter titled "Friendship with God in al-Ghazali and Aquinas," David Burrell writes that al-Ghazālī

> presupposes that God's love can bring creatures to a greater and greater proximity to the Creator. The point of encounter is the human heart, and the Divine action is invariably described as "removing the veil from one's heart, in order that one can see with one's heart, to be elevated to God's own self along with those who are already near to God." The progressive stations are then described as successive unveilings of the heart, and the dynamic is summarized as follows: "in this way the love of God for His servants brings them closer to Himself, removing their negligences and sins from them by purifying their inner self (*bāṭin*) from the filth of this world. God removes the veil from their hearts, in such a way as they contemplate what they see in their hearts." He proceeds to distinguish this transforming love of God from the servants' response, which consists in "the desire which animates them to seize hold of the perfection which they lack." There lies the lack of symmetry in the two loves: while God's love is transforming, ours seeks transformation; yet the dynamic of "the way" is to bring us to the point where our response is a perfect reflection of God's initiating love: "the one who has entered into intimacy with God is one who acts with the very action of God."[13]

In this ever-deepening friendship, we become increasingly aware that our desire for God—for happiness, completion, fulfillment, perfection—is a response to God's love, and then we turn to the practice of prayer (and the prayerful life) as a way God has opened for us to progress toward that goal.

In intimate friendship, God's love and our response become the inseparable partners of an eternal dance; this is perhaps Rūmī's intention when he writes, "lovers pray constantly."[14] Our anonymous thirteenth-century mystic adds, "Until now, the lover travelled by means of the Beloved, but from now on, the Beloved will travel in the lover."[15]

Lesson 5: My prayer is never complete until and unless it indiscriminately reaches out in mercy to the needy in my midst. To grow in prayer thus means to grow in mercy and in active response to the needs around me.

If we do not personalize and engage ourselves deeply in the process of prayer, we run into the danger of falsifying, betraying, or belying our religion. Thus, prayer is only transformative if we go beyond treating it as a duty, if we begin to listen to what God is saying to us when we say our prayer. Again, turning to the Qur'ān, we read: "Have you seen the one who falsifies religion? That is the one who treats the orphan harshly and does not urge [others] to feed the destitute. So woe to the worshippers who are heedless of their prayers, those who are seen [to be performing acts of piety], while withholding basic assistance [to those in need]" (107:1–7).

Lesson 6: There is no meaningful difference between growing in prayer and simply growing as a moral and religious person.

Prayer is what and who I am as well as what I do. There is thus no difference within the religious context between the perfection of oneself and the perfection of prayer. Al-Ghazālī reminds us that some of the inner virtues associated with the gradual perfection of prayer include longing, humility, gratitude, thinking well of God, unconditional praise, hope, pleasure with whatever God decrees, a sense of servitude to God, and total trust in God's generosity in which supplication eventually disappears. This culminates in the highest stage of remembrance (*dhikr*) and affirmation of Divine unity (*al-tawḥīd*), a state in which one sees only God.[16] While al-Ghazālī does not see this stage as a substantive union between Creator and creature, this stage is nevertheless, according to him, a momentary experience of perceived union (*waḥdat al-shuhūd*), thus the very pinnacle of prayer in Islam.

Reflecting upon this, our aforementioned anonymous thirteenth-century Persian mystic writes, "You won't become Him, but if you strive, you will find a place where your you-ness will leave."[17] Prayer is thus as much about who and what we are as it is about what we do; or—as is better said in the company of the mystics and sages of prayer in Islam—prayer is what God works in us and through us. The more effaced we become before God and the more God's attributes become manifest within us, the more perfect our prayer becomes. Here our spiritual poverty or personal emptiness in prayer becomes the sine qua non of experiencing or manifesting the fullness of God's presence.

Lesson 7: The end of prayer.

For al-Ghazālī, the ultimate end or goal of prayer is contemplative: reaching a state wherein the worshipper is completely absorbed in God. As we saw earlier, this "unitive state" is not believed by al-Ghazālī to be substantive or ontological; rather, it is a state in which the servant sees only God without any remembrance of self. This "forgetting" of self is, for him and others within the mystical traditions of Islam, the pinnacle of remembrance (*dhikr*), but it is not easy to attain. In order to enter into such a contemplative state, he explains that a worshipper must become completely detached from everyone and everything connected to the world and be able to behold everything with equanimity, wherein existence and nonexistence are the same. It must be granted here that the cultivation of such a state may not be possible or even advisable for worshippers fully engaged in the world, but it nevertheless stands as the ultimate end of the process we have here described as prayer. In al-Ghazālī's words,

> Then, let him seclude himself in a *zāwiya* [a small Sufi shrine or center for spiritual education and prayer], devoting himself to the religious duties, both obligatory and supererogatory, and then sit with the heart empty and the attention concentrated, without scattering his thought by reciting the Qur'ān, nor by considering its meaning, nor by reading the books on Tradition, nor by anything else. Rather, let him see to it that nothing but God enters his mind. Then, as he sits in solitude, let him keep on saying continuously with his tongue, "Allāh (God), God" and keep his heart attentive until he comes to a state in which his effort to move his tongue drops off and it looks as if the word flows on his tongue [all by itself]. Then, let him persevere in this until any trace of motion is removed from his tongue and he finds his heart persevering in the *dhikr*. Then, let him still persevere in this until the image of the word, its letters and its shape are effaced from his heart and there remains the idea of the word alone in the heart, clinging to it, as if it is glued to the heart, without separating from it.[18]

If one remains and perseveres in this state, he says, one will experience the "light of Truth" shining in the heart, an experience that is both, according to him, noetic and transient even though it may endure for some time and even though its impact upon the seeker may be indelible for eternity. The end of prayerful remembrance is thus the inner annihilation of the vessel of remembrance and transfiguration of that vessel and all it contains. Perhaps for this reason, we find references in the Islamic traditions to great mystics, such as al-Ḥallāj, who reportedly experienced difficulty coming out of this unitive state in order to perform the obligatory prayers, which require a conscious recognition of the separateness of the worshipper and the worshipped. That said, after experiencing such a unitive experience, the prayer mat becomes a radically different place where the worshipper joins God as "God bears witness that there is no god but He" (3:18).

Notes

1. I take this beautiful phrase from the diaries of Etty Hillesum, a relatively unsung Jewish spiritual luminary whose life ended tragically and brutally in 1943, in the Nazi concentration camp at Auschwitz. See *An Interrupted Life: The Diaries and Letters of Etty Hillesum 1941–1943* (New York: Owl Books, Henry Holt & Co, 1996), 74.

2. Throughout this essay, all renderings of Qur'ānic passages are my own.

3. From the anonymous treatise "The Rising Places of Faith," in *Faith and Practice of Islam: Three Thirteenth Century Sufi Texts*, trans. William Chittick (Albany: State University of New York Press, 1992), 57.

4. Ibid.

5. Paraphrased by Kojiro Nakamura in his *Ghazali and Prayer* (Kuala Lumpur: Islamic Book Trust, 2001), 63.

6. See Timothy J. Gianotti, *Al-Ghazālī's Unspeakable Doctrine of the Soul* (Leiden: E. J. Brill, 2001), chapter 5, where I explore the simultaneous "worlds" of the here (*al-dunyā*) and the Hereafter (*al-ākhira*) in some detail. For a more basic introduction to al-Ghazālī's view on this simultaneous or parallel habitation, see chapters on the "Knowledge of Self" and the "Knowledge of the Next World" in his *Alchemy of Happiness*, trans. Claude Field (London: M. E. Sharpe, Inc., 1991), 3–14, 33–43.

7. See al-Ghazālī's *Book of Penitence* (*kitāb al-tawba*), in *Iḥyā' 'ulūm al-dīn* (Beirut: Dār al-Khayr, 1993), 4:260 ff. The same point is made by the previously cited anonymous thirteenth-century mystic, who quotes an unattributed poem that proclaims "paradise and hell are within you" (quoted in "Clarifications for Beginners and Reminders for the Advanced," in Chittick, *Faith and Practice of Islam*, 100).

8. Chittick, *Faith and Practice of Islam*, 82.

9. From al-Ghazālī, *Iḥyā'*, as cited by Chittick in *Faith and Practice of Islam*, 239–40n132.28.

10. See "Moses and the Shepherd" in *The Essential Rumi*, trans. Coleman Barks (Edison, NJ: Castle Books, 1997), 166.

11. Al-Ghazālī closes his famous forty-volume compendium, *Reviving Religious Knowledge*, with an entire book on the importance of the practice of remembering death and

the next world; see Timothy Winter's translation of this book under the title *The Remembrance of Death and the Afterlife* (Cambridge: Islamic Texts Society, 1989).

12. Nakamura, *Ghazali and Prayer*, 64.

13. David B. Burrell, *Friendship and Ways to Truth* (Notre Dame, IN: University of Notre Dame Press, 2000), 79.

14. Rūmī, *Essential Rumi*, 80.

15. "Clarifications for Beginners" in Chittick, *Faith and Practice of Islam*, 84.

16. See Nakamura, *Ghazali and Prayer*, 63–78. For a primary text reference, see al-Ghazālī, "*Kitāb al-tawḥīd wa al-tawakkul*," in *Iḥyāʾ ʿulūm al-dīn*, 118ff.

17. "Clarifications for Beginners" in Chittick, *Faith and Practice of Islam*, 85.

18. Nakamura, *Ghazali and Prayer*, 71.

Conversations in Qatar

LUCINDA MOSHER

Building Bridges seminars are characterized by what Rowan Williams has called "appreciative conversation." The size of these gatherings encourages collegiality; so does the methodology. Seminar participants are assigned to break-out groups. Because the membership of each group is consistent throughout the seminar, it is easy to continue a conversational thread from the previous day. A moderator ensures that everyone may contribute to these conversations; a scribe keeps a journal. So, while rich informal conversation takes place over meals, on the bus, and in the hotel lobby, more formal conversation results during the small-group sessions.

This essay draws from the journals of the four scribes in order to share some of the highlights of the Qatar 2011 conversations on prayer.[1] As is the Building Bridges custom, the "Chatham House Rule" obtains: ideas are unattributed; voices remain anonymous. Vignettes have been organized around three overlapping themes of the conference, thus of this book: scripture and prayer, learning to pray, and growth in prayer. Differences between Christian and Islamic perspectives will be evident, but so will similarities. Differences between coreligionists will also be apparent. Indeed, some participants (Muslim and Christian alike) made observations or assertions that may strike some readers as marginal to the mainstream of their respective traditions. In this way we are reminded of the breadth of the Christian and Islamic traditions.

Prayer and Scripture

Christianity and Islam share the practice of a signature prayer taken from scripture, the Lord's Prayer and the Fātiḥa, which both received detailed consideration. The Fātiḥa is "the basis for everything," one Muslim told his discussion group, "business contracts, whatever. It's also like a *duʿāʾ*—a supplication." The Fātiḥa is the opening of the Qurʾān and the opening of each unit of every performance of *ṣalāt*. A Christian noted Muhammad Abdel Haleem's comment that its "more wide-ranging functions in the social and cultural life of Muslims" flow out of this.[2]

As does every chapter but one of the Qurʾān, the Fātiḥa opens with the *basmala*—the invocation "In the Name of God: the Compassionate, the Merciful" (*bismillāh al-Raḥmān al-Raḥīm*). This formula is precious to Muslims, one explained; "it is repeated all the time!" Reflection on the Fātiḥa's first words, "In the Name of God," led to discussion of how God is named. The Fātiḥa names God three ways: in terms of mercy, lordship, and judgment. Some commentators assert that the meaning of Raḥmān is broad and general, a Muslim noted, whereas that of Raḥīm is more specific. Another suggested that Raḥmān can be seen as referring to God's preexistent mercy whereas Raḥīm refers to God's love; yet another, that these terms point to divine majesty, on the one hand, and beauty, on the other. Conversation would return to the theme of God's Names during discussions of supererogatory forms of prayer.

The last verses of the Fātiḥa—"Guide us to the straight path: the path of those You have blessed, those who incur no anger [or, wrath] and who have not gone astray"—generated considerable discussion. How singular is the straight path? Is it one or many? This is related to the question of pluralism. Indeed, the passage mentions three groups of people, one Muslim pointed out: "those on the right path, those who go astray intentionally, and those who are lost. The right path is in the middle." A Christian asked whether this passage refers to one group or three categories. The Abdel Haleem translation implies one group. Similarly, some wondered whether this passage of the Fātiḥa refers to Islam as a specific historic religion or to an attitude of submission to truth within any religion.

A Christian asked whether it was true that Muslim commentaries generally saw the last lines of the Fātiḥa as a barb thrown at Christians and Jews. Some Muslims acknowledged that some classical commentaries do say this; other commentaries interpret this verse with generosity of spirit. Another Muslim said that, rather than a reference to Jews and Christians, this verse "is usually read as a general reference to those who go past the limit of what is acceptable and those who fall short of their obligations. It is not about blaming others; rather, it is about asking for protection from becoming one of the wrongdoers intentionally or unintentionally."

Turning to the Lord's Prayer, the fact that two versions appear in the New Testament prompted discussion. A Christian explained that the Bible includes four of the various gospels produced by early Christian communities. This gives us four points of view. In the case of the Lord's Prayer, we're given two different contexts; the prayer is embedded differently. Matthew's concern is for avoiding hypocrisy; Luke's is for gift and generosity versus neediness. The imagery is different.

Certain nouns differ in the two versions of the Lord's Prayer—which has led to different English translations in common use: "forgive us our trespasses/sins/debts." In the Greek of the New Testament, it is already a translation since Jesus probably spoke it in Aramaic; many Christians used to recite it in Latin; most now recite it in translation in their vernacular. What, therefore, one Christian asked, does it mean to pass on tradition?

A major difference between the two biblical versions of the Lord's Prayer is in the opening: Matthew has "Our Father"; Luke simply has "Father." Matthew seems to be expanding on Luke's bare bones. A Christian shared an anecdote illustrating a shift in his own attitude and awareness when, during a week of retreat, he found himself shifting from offering his prayers to "Our Father," then simply to "Father" (which made them more personal but isolating), then back to "Our Father." His point was that to pray "Our Father" reminds us that we are in community.

A Muslim asked whether Christians could not simply have prayed to "God" instead. One Christian answered: that would have maintained distance; also, to say "Our" poses a question: "Who are 'we'?" In short, Jesus teaches us to say "Our Father," so Christians do. "Father" will remain in Christian usage, a Muslim admitted, but wondered: why not "Mother"? Actually, several Christians noted, Julian of Norwich uses both; so does Anselm of Canterbury. Julian says that we only know what parental care means because God is already parent.

Interestingly, one Muslim noted that a few ḥadīths indicate the acceptability of Muslim use of the father metaphor for God; however, given the Qur'ān's strong statements about God's not-begetting, most Muslims reject this metaphor entirely. The Christian sense of "Father" cannot be confined to the paternal figure, one Christian insisted, noting that Raḥmān (one of the most-used names of God) is derived from the word for "womb."

A Muslim asked: "Luke says 'as John taught.' Do we know what John taught about prayer? Is the text of the Lord's Prayer similar to a prayer we have from John?" The Christians explained that this "John" is John the Baptist, and that we have little information about his teaching. The implication of this passage is that John had taught his followers to pray in some specific way, and Jesus's followers wanted Jesus to give them some specific guidance of his own.

A Muslim asked what it means for Christians to pray that God not bring them to the time of trial. Is this an eschatological trial? A trial in the here and now? In response, it was noted that "trial" is not the same as "temptation"; one has no control of a trial. Therefore, some thought this petition might be a plea that God not give us more than we can bear. Some saw a parallel question in the petition for "daily bread." Perhaps it might mean don't give us more than we need.

But one verse of the Lord's Prayer translated "save us from the time of trial" has often been rendered "lead us not into temptation." The need for protection is recognized, a Christian explained. "God doesn't tempt people but allows them to be tempted. Satan is the tempter. This is a paradox. Jesus was led into temptation. Jesus did what only he can do: he defeated the tempter." A Muslim asserted that praying to be spared from trials is contrary to Qur'ānic teaching, because the Qur'ān states clearly that everyone will be tested. A believer must expect to be tested all the time.

One group spent some time focusing on the relation between silence and scripture, silence and the Word—particularly the Christian practice known as *lectio divina*. A Muslim asked whether this was more than mere meditative reading of scripture. Lectio divina has four steps, a Christian responded: "Take a passage. Remember a sentence from it. Chew it over. Savor it, until it fills your consciousness." At this point, he explained, the passage provokes a personal response to God. This leads to contemplation, presence—perhaps in silence—because there is no more to say. "In hearing the Word of God through our respective scriptures," one Christian explained, "we understand that these scriptures are 'pointing to God,' but in a mode that goes beyond theology. Lectio divina is a reading or listening for the sake of going beyond words to rejoin that silence. In that silence, we as Christians and Muslims are at one. We can have such an experience when we read each other's scriptures. I understand better my own scripture the more I try to understand the Qur'ān." Silence generates mutual trust, someone commented, which alleviates the need to persuade the other or to defend oneself. "Reading texts together, then sharing in silence; *lectio* plus *contemplatio*—an excellent combination!"

A Muslim noted that there are ḥadīths that reprimand virtuosic Qur'ān recitation of the sort that might draw too much attention to the reciter, instead encouraging contemplative Qur'ān reading—which would be somewhat like *lectio divina*. Another agreed, noting that the Qur'ān itself teaches that reading scripture is all about transformation, new life for the reader; Qur'ān reading is not meant to be an end in itself. A Christian explained that the majority of Christians do not think of their scripture as sent down from heaven, as in the Islamic concept of *tanzīl*. Most Christians see the

Bible "as the Word of God in a derivative sense," he said. "It puts us in touch with the Word made flesh. So, in *lectio divina*, the goal is to make the 'words' disappear." A Muslim responded that on the Islamic side it depends on how one sees the words. A Christian explained further that, in the Ignatian tradition, one puts oneself in the scene. One takes cues from the text, from imagination.

Much discussion focused on the role of memorization of scripture in learning to pray. Some studies claim that when boys, aged ten to eleven, are taken out of grade school for a year or two in order to memorize the Qur'ān, they are much better performers during their remaining school years than their peers who had not been through the memorization (*ḥifẓ*) course. "The recitation of the Qur'ān, far from being a mindless ritual," one Muslim pointed out, "is closely related to spiritual realization in Islam. The recitation displaces the ego and its inner chatter; it replaces it with the theurgic blessings of the revealed Word." A Christian concurred: "Memorization of scripture brings about 'self-forgetting.' You can put yourself aside. Instead of inner chatter, there is an inner music. By putting the divine Word first, we get rid of the noise in our heads; we liberate ourselves from our passions and fantasies." "We can learn from Muslims the importance of learning by heart," another Christian stressed; "we need to recognize the importance of learning such scriptures as the Psalms by heart."

Learning to Pray

In considering how prayer is taught and learned, it was natural that much conversation centered on childhood. Lucy Gardner's paper had emphasized the mother's role in teaching children to pray. Muslims and Christians alike recalled being taught by their family, primarily by rote. Others said they had not learned to pray at home; they had discovered the art of praying later, in some other way. One group appreciated Gardner's balanced approach to the need for training in praying—but not in the sense of developing "spiritual athletes" or "prayer virtuosi." One Muslim insisted that practice is important. One has to know how to turn off the chatter in order to pray—when going into a mosque, for example. Trained responses can be good, suggested one Christian, because the automatic response recalls us. "We then can reflect, even if briefly in a busy day, on what we're really here for." One Muslim recalled being taught to pray but not what to "pray for." That was left for her to discover on her own. The same was the case with the Qur'ān. Parents may teach their children how to read it, she pointed out, but not how to use it. Learning how to use the Qur'ān is part of our personal journey.

However, she also noted, "My mother used to say, before you leave the house, read at least one verse of the Qur'ān." A Christian likened that to making the sign of the cross on one's body "to remind yourself that you are made in the image of God."

One Christian noted that children can pick up problematic misunderstandings of rote prayers, especially regarding judgment and eternal punishment. A question arose concerning how to teach divine justice to children without frightening them unnecessarily. The conclusion was that children should be taught, in concrete rather than abstract ways, that actions have consequences. In any case, rote prayers do provide a starting point; children do need concrete things to ponder. "We teach children a language," a Muslim added. "We don't say, 'You can wait and decide what language to speak when you grow up.' We also teach children manners; we don't say, 'You can wait until you grow up to learn how to behave among other people.' Learning one's faith is not just rote learning."

The fact that Ibrahim Mogra's paper had focused on a method of teaching young boys about Qur'ān recitation and prayer led one group to discuss issues of gender and religion at length. Their conclusion was that girls (both Muslim and Christian) should be taught that they are equal with boys by using female role models; daughters and sons should be treated the same way. One of the blessings of modernity, they noted, is that we started thinking about gender equality.

With regard to Islam's prescribed prayer (which must be said in Arabic) versus spontaneous prayer (which can be offered in any language), one Muslim noted that young people sometimes ask why they cannot perform ṣalāt in their own language. If that were allowed, they argue, they'd be more inclined to perform the ritual. The jurists say no, but some scholars have discussed this. While one Muslim was inclined to agree, feeling that it would make prayer as relationship to God more meaningful, others disagreed sharply, emphasizing that while *duʿāʾ* can be said in any language, ṣalāt must be performed in Arabic, and adding that, even though it is not easy for most Muslims to learn Arabic, they doubted whether Muslims would be more observant if they could perform ṣalāt in some other language. Encouraging this approach could be perceived as an attack by secularism. Underlying this discussion was the issue of Muslim attitudes toward the Arabic language per se.

The discussion of the necessity of Arabic in ritual prayer raised the issue of "holy envy" (a term made popular by Krister Stendahl): Muslims have a shared vocabulary, little sayings in Arabic that are as natural as breathing, while Christians don't have a shared vocabulary to such a universal degree. A corollary to this discussion is the issue of loss of a tradition—the question of how to educate people that tradition is not just the past. "For me," said another Muslim, "it is a question of striking a balance: how to keep a tradition alive; asking whether a tradition has served its purpose." With Copts, it is the same issue, one Christian noted. Many prefer the traditional language, even if it is not well understood. Similarly, some young Roman Catholics prefer the liturgy of the Mass in Latin. "They are looking for a mystique—an emotional, imaginative engagement," a Christian noted. "Latin is evocative. I can see the value in the evocative and in accessibility."

"I have always been struck by the relationship between physical purity and prayer," said one Christian—thinking of the Islamic practice of *wuḍūʾ* (ritual cleansing), which Muslim children learn to perform at an early age. "There are elements of it in some forms of Christianity. In celebrating the Eucharist, for example, the priest performs a simple hand-rinsing ceremony. But the requirement of physical washing by all worshipers in preparation for prayer is one of the main practical differences between Islam and Christianity. I wonder about what theological differences this practical difference implies."

Prayer instruction is not just for children, several noted; adults may also be taught to pray by a number of means. One Muslim commented: "I am struck by the idea of prayer as something you practice, like music or a sport." Another noted the need to avoid distraction. "Ask yourself: Are you thinking about God or are you thinking about lunch?" However, one of his discussion partners observed that one cannot really forget about everything outside. If one is distressed by a family burden, that distress won't go away because one wants to pray. Being distracted doesn't mean prayer is not heard. Only one decision is crucial: the decision to want to pray. Our judgment of the quality of our own praying can be dangerously inaccurate. Another added that there are different categories of the intention to pray. Yet another Muslim found it easier to pray in a Muslim country, harder to pray in a secular university context.

Muslims and Christians alike affirmed the value of ritual. As one put it, "Ritual prayers give people words when they run out of words." A Muslim asked whether there are Christian parallels to ṣalāt. One Christian recalled describing the Daily Office of Evening Prayer to a Muslim. "I told her that it includes recitation of set texts, time for free supplication, and a rhythm of various postures (kneeling, sitting, standing). My friend interrupted me, saying, 'I had no idea that Christians pray' (meaning, perform *ṣalāt*). She knew full well that I made supplication, so she meant that she had no idea that Christians had a schedule of prayer times or prayer rituals with postures." A Muslim noted the common misconception among Muslims that Christians and Jews are not observant. A Christian explained that keeping the monastic daily prayer practice is the choice of certain Christians, as Christian prayer itself takes a broad range of forms—Quaker or Pentecostal prayer being quite different from Catholic, for example. "It is not consistent, nor is it obligatory. It depends on which Christians we're talking about."

One group considered whether technology helps or trivializes prayer. Some mentioned having prayers on one's iPhone. "I read my prayer on the train while going to university," one Christian explained. "In New York City subways, you'll see Jews reading Torah, Christians reading Bible, and Muslims reading Qurʾān." A Christian mentioned that attending Mass by watching it on television is acceptable if one is ill. Watching worship on television is becoming more common, but it promotes individualism and pulls us away from community. Another Christian agreed, saying that technology may help when one cannot pray otherwise, by infusing empty places with prayer. It is not a substitute for personal contact, however. An email from one's priest is not the same as pastoral care in person. Another Christian wondered if the younger generations feel differently about this, noting that children form Internet play communities. A Muslim mentioned online communities that help isolated Muslims feel a part of Islamic celebrations and observances. Some even wonder if a virtual *ḥajj* might become possible.

Some Christians talked about the connection between singing and praying. "Through learning and singing hymns, religious imagination is stimulated while the intellect is being taught religious doctrines," one explained. Words are vessels that are passed down from hand to hand, but they sometimes "leak." The meaning of the words can never be exhausted, so an endless process of translation and retranslation takes place. "This imparts to Christianity a certain 'restlessness' as regards the articulation of religious doctrine," he said. "The rite of the Eucharist, however, is beyond words, and thus transcends this 'restlessness.' Being a rite essentially composed of gestures, one does not need to worry about 'getting it wrong' conceptually or verbally."

Mention of hymn-singing led another Christian to ask about the prohibition of music in Islam. In response, a Muslim mentioned the range of attitudes held by Muslims regarding singing and singing with instrumental accompaniment. The popularity of the *nashīd* tradition of instrumental music was mentioned by several groups. One Muslim mentioned a ḥadīth that validates the use of instrumental music for healthy joyousness. Another said that Qurʾān recitation is musical in a particular way, as is the *adhān* (the call to prayer). However, the music of the Sufi *tekke* (lodge) differs from the normative sounds of the mosque. In the *tekke*, listening to musical instruments may be considered a form of dhikr (remembrance of God), and dance-like movement may be associated with dhikr. A Christian likened this to charismatic forms of prayer in the Church of England: a form of popular piety, but not the norm.

A Muslim noted that Rūmī emphasizes the idea of persistence in prayer. Five-times-a-day prayer is, in a sense, knocking on God's door five times a day. Eventually someone will open the door of the house. Rūmī also says that sometimes God holds out because, if you receive, you'll go away! God has the final word, a Christian reminded the group; but we can still ask. Another Christian said that he takes great comfort in Luke 11:13, "If you then, who are evil, know how to give good gifts to your children, how much more will the heavenly Father give the Holy Spirit to those who ask him!" That is, the one thing we really need is what's on offer. What God has on offer is Godself!

Some participants raised questions about prayers of mediation or intercession. A Christian asked whether there is a difference between Sunnī and Shīʿī practice, and received affirmation that intercession is practiced in both branches of Islam. One can always make a request of God on behalf of someone else. The issue, however, is whether it is permissible to pray "to" or "through" someone—the Prophet, for example. Most supplications are addressed to God. At the level of folk Islam, however, can be found the tradition of "saint worship" at tombs, but it is still clear that this is simply a different form of praying to God.

The practice of *dhikr* also received considerable attention. Recollection of God links mind to heart, a Christian noted, suggesting that the Jesus Prayer is a Christian equivalent to dhikr. "Dhikr nurtures the practice of finding God in all things. It's a reminder of our ultimate accountability to God." One Muslim noted how Rūmī had called dhikr a pool you dive into to escape the sting of hornets. "It's immersion. Its main function is to put aside everything but God. It's a God-given means of remembering God." Remembrance is a highly charged term in Christianity, a Christian noted; it is central in the Eucharist. "In a sense, *ṣalāt* and Eucharist are parallel. We're not just recalling that something happened; we become part of it ourselves. *This now* is *that then*—a remaking present."

A Muslim explained that in Islam there are ninety-nine Names of God. "At least one name will be meaningful to you." This recalled earlier discussion of various meanings of *Raḥmān* and *Raḥīm* in the Fātiḥa. Someone noted that, in the Bible, God is called friend. In Islam, one of God's ninety-nine Names is *Walī* (friend). "We're encouraged to use God's Names in our invocations," one Muslim explained. "Particular Names are used by Sufis at certain times for dhikr and eating." One Muslim confirmed that all Muslims use the ninety-nine Names of God, but some names would be more popular than others. "In Sufism," a Muslim noted, "one finds the doctrine: the Name is the Named. In uttering the Name of God, the reality Named is rendered present."

One evening during the seminar Christians were invited to be present during a time of Muslim prayers and found it moving that the Muslim who recited the *Duʿāʾ Kumayl* wept openly as he did so. A Christian wondered whether this is more normal in a Shīʿī context. Sunnīs do likewise, several said. It is expected on some occasions. In Shīʿī practice, weeping would come in close conjunction to any mention of the family of ʿAlī. Thus, when reciting the *Duʿāʾ Kumayl,* it is customary to shed tears. One Muslim shared his impression that there is not so much weeping in the Christian tradition. A Christian countered, "Well, we do have lamentations. Some of us need to be reminded of that aspect of our tradition. Lamentations is the title of an entire book of the Old Testament. There are no lamentations per se in the New Testament, but it does mention the practice of lamenting." Conversely, another Christian pointed out, the monastic tradition includes a theology of *penthos* (mourning) that mentions the gift of tears. Another noted the wide range of practice among Christians regarding weeping. In the Pentecostal tradition, one might expect weeping as the overall intensity of the service mounted. But there may also be quiet weeping in the more staid Christian traditions, for example in response to a particularly moving congregational hymn or choral anthem.

Someone brought up the place of tears in "remembrance." The Christian tradition does have places for this; for example the Ignatian tradition speaks of the gift of tears—of sheer joy in the presence of God. A *ḥadīth qudsī* says, "I am with those whose hearts are broken." The Supplication of ʿAlī says, "The weapon of the believer is weeping." When making any supplication, Muslims are encouraged to shed a tear or two. On the last night of Ramaḍān, Muslims weep as they say goodbye to the month. A ḥadīth says, "If you can't cry, make a face [i.e., pretend to weep] and God will give the tears." Is this faking? Pretending? A Christian responded, "Well, we teach children to be polite by telling them to 'fake it' until they get it. Why not do the same in learning to pray?"

In noting the commonality between training in Islam and training in the Christian religious life, one Christian noted that it is said that there is no monasticism in Islam; "yet the closest thing Christianity has to Muslim practice is monasticism! Monasticism is a rule of life that regulates the minutest details. It assumes that there is nothing in human life so trivial that God wouldn't have an opinion about it. It is a sacralization of the whole of life. Islam seems both to resist monasticism, yet also, to a degree, to embrace it."

"But monasticism is associated with celibacy and giving up the pleasures of life," another Christian countered. A Muslim responded that the Qurʾān critiques asceticism—the detachment characteristic of the monastic life. The first Christian nodded; yet he heard great resonance between the madrassa training Ibrahim Mogra had described in his paper and novitiate-training in Christian monasteries. "There's a sense that discipline in the Christian life is educative and formative," said another Christian. "A discipline need not feel imposed. You accept it; that's not a bad thing." A Muslim agreed. "A ḥadīth says, 'The best of deeds is what you do habitually.' The critique of monasticism is about its isolation, not its rhythm of monastic life." Other Muslims noted that the Qur'ān's critique of asceticism has not prevented Sufism from a tendency toward isolation and celibacy, although, for Sufis, seclusion usually was for a specific period, after which one would return to ordinary life.

Growth in Prayer

Growth in prayer was the topic of the provocative papers by Timothy Wright and Timothy Gianotti. Timothy Wright had described a plan for reading the whole Bible in a year. A Muslim wondered whether that was a typical practice for Christians. Several answers were given. One can use a "One-Year Bible" which divides the Old Testament (minus the Psalms) into 365 portions; the New Testament likewise; and the Psalms likewise. At the end of a year, you have read the whole Bible. Some Christians use this as their personal devotional practice. Some Christian traditions use a lectionary—a calendar of readings that covers most of the Bible in a one-, two-, or three-year cycle. A lectionary encourages the discipline of attending carefully to the whole Bible, not just the parts we find most congenial. A Muslim explained that certain Qur'ānic sūras are likewise prescribed for reading at certain times or certain days. Another Muslim asked about the use of scripture commentaries as an aid to prayer. One Christian expressed a preference for premodern and patristic commentaries such as those of Augustine or Gregory of Nyssa, since they are as spiritual as they are scholarly.

Timothy Wright had mentioned spiritual writings. A Muslim asked what such writings might be. Christians offered examples, such as *The Imitation of Christ*; writings of the early church fathers; *Showings* of Julian of Norwich; *The Cloud of Unknowing*. A passage from this last work (a treatise on contemplation by an anonymous author influenced by Pseudo-Dionysius) had been included in study materials to be read before the seminar. A Muslim noticed a similarity between the *Cloud*-author's instructions and Sufi practice. One Christian mentioned that it was delightful how often the week's discussions had turned to George Herbert, the *Cloud of Unknowing*, and Julian of Norwich. "Our Muslim colleagues seemed really to like these folks—much in the way we Christians appreciate al-Ghazālī and Rūmī."

In fact, when one Christian asked about the place of al-Ghazālī in Muslim piety, a complex discussion unfolded. Some Muslims responded that al-Ghazālī is "very mystical," or "very Sufi," or "not a good fit with most simple Muslim people, and most Muslims are simple." Another Muslim countered that al-Ghazālī is loved by millions, not just intellectuals—as is Rūmī. The Muslim across the table was not swayed: "I like al-Ghazālī, but I don't understand him. I am a simple Muslim." A Christian then asked what Muslims are to do when they have a problem with prayer. The Muslim responded, "You either go to pray, or you don't go. That's the only problem. Islam is a response to the complication of Christianity. It's simple; that's of its essence. Sufism is very complicated—perhaps good for some, but not for most." But some Muslims do worry about the quality of their prayer, a Muslim countered; they are eager for a way to improve, to come closer to God. Sufism offers them a technique; and actually, its goal is simplicity and growth in virtue—as Ibn ʿArabī taught.

A Muslim mentioned that al-Ghazālī and Rūmī speak of the notion of total trust in God, in which supplication disappears. He inquired whether this notion appears in Christianity as well. It does, a Christian confirmed: "Christianity has the notion of 'union,' of seeing only God; union without absorption. The Orthodox call this *theosis*. But reaching this state would not mean that one would stop praying in community."

A Christian offered this explanation of what happens in prayer:

> We believe that when we pray, the eternal Word of God returns to the Father through us. We become part of Jesus's glorification of God. It is therefore God glorifying God. In the Eucharist we repeat the words of Jesus over our bread and wine. When we bless the bread and wine, we say his words, "This is my body . . . ; this is my blood." This is related to the doctrine of the Trinity, for in this doctrine we are on a search for words to express the ineffable mystery that God glorifies God. When we enter into the life of Jesus, we enter into God's reflection of His own glory. The doctrine of the Trinity does not assert three distinct essences; rather, the divine unity is always self-differentiating. There is one indivisible and inseparable life; but it is a life which relates to itself in different ways. The Godhead is superabundant plenitude; it is an unutterable unity. Whence the paradox: the Father, Son and Spirit contemplate one another within that unity; they each contemplate in one another that unfathomable reality that each of them is. This reciprocal contemplation is a corollary of the mutual co-inherence (*perichoresis*), and is also connected to the self-emptying (*kenosis*) of the Persons.

In reply one Muslim suggested: "This implies that 'I myself, in contemplating God, am being emptied of myself (as both cause of authentic contemplation and consequence thereof); this self-emptying through contemplation on the human plane is a reflection of the self-emptying through mutual contemplation that takes place within God.' This is an inspiring application to prayer of the *kenosis* proper to the Persons of the Trinity."

Theology and prayer are closely intertwined, a Christian asserted. "Theological elaboration is necessary, but the aim is always to return from doctrinal complexity to spiritual simplicity." The lives of the saints provide a personification of prayer. Studying the lives of the saints is a means of moving ourselves from complexity to simplicity. "Sanctification is more a process of unbecoming than becoming: we undo our ego; or rather, God undoes it for us. At the same time, we are made fully human by God through prayer. Prayer makes us aware of how God makes us what we are, in spite of ourselves."

On this theme of simplicity, a Muslim asserted that the addition of anything philosophical or mystical takes religion beyond the nature of the ordinary person into the realm of the few. "The *mutakallimūn* [theologians] and the legal scholars were responsible for making Islam complicated," he said. A Muslim colleague countered: What about the inner life? "Prayer, fasting—that's it," the first scholar replied. "If I can perform the ritual, that's enough for me." As he saw it, Islam's obligatory prayers are the whole—not just the beginning—of devotion. A third Muslim noted that the mutakallimūn were pious people—as were the classical jurists. In which case, why did they produce these complications? "It was a defensive science," another Muslim replied. "It doesn't matter what is going on in your heart and mind so long as you're coming to pray." Said a fourth Muslim, "I've never heard anyone express this view so bluntly."

During a lively discussion on suffering a Christian observed that one response to suffering may be more fervent, heartfelt prayer. God "tests" us in order that "we might reveal ourselves more fully to ourselves. We do not fully know who we are until we are put to the test by God. As we grow in our prayerful response to the test, we are brought closer to the truth of God." Spiritual struggle, with its setbacks as well as its triumphs, is a means of aligning ourselves with God's truth. God's tests are not imposed arbitrarily. "Rather, the closer one comes to his truth, the greater becomes the commitment to it, and thus the challenge to be faithful to it in all circumstances is deepened: it is here that the necessity of prayer is made manifest." Another Christian countered that God does not put stumbling blocks in our way. "There are struggles, but a loving God does not test the beloved; God trusts the beloved."

One Muslim asserted that, without challenges, there would be no improvement, no progress in soul-making. A Christian commented: "That leaves me cold. What is the purpose of these challenges?" In response, the Muslim asked: "What about tough love?" Another Christian mentioned

Julian of Norwich's notion that "sin is necessary, but all will be well. . . ." He also offered St. John of the Cross as an example of patient waiting. The Muslim continued, "Challenge leads to growth, to closeness to God." "My issue is not with challenge," said the first Christian; "it's with a notion that God is the agent in these. It makes God horrid, changeable." Conversations on prayer and struggle are tightly related to how each tradition deals with questions of evil. In fact, theodicy was the topic of several tangential discussions.

"We are impatient for the results of prayer," another Christian noted, "whereas we should understand that the spiritual life truly begins only after we have passed through the 'desert of dryness,' where we feel no consolation. Then we are given to drink from the fountain of truth. At Gethsemane, we were told to watch and pray, lest we come into temptation. One meaning of this is that, once you enter the temptation, once you engage with it, you have lost already." A Muslim referred to a saying of Ibn ʿAṭāʾillāh that made a similar point: "When the enemy attacks, remember the Friend. If you enter the arena of battle with the enemy, he has got from you what he wanted: to distract you from loving the Friend."

One group explored the notion that prayer trains the imagination, helping us to acquire new spiritual reflexes, preparing us to meet trials—not in our own power but with the power of God. This can only be done through selflessness, someone pointed out; and this selflessness in turn can only be nurtured by prayer in which the ego is absent. "The more the ego is absent in our everyday life, and not just in contemplative prayer," this participant stressed, "the less we can be subject to temptation. Where there is no ego, there is nothing to tempt; there is no need to defend oneself, as there is nothing there to defend. The adversary cannot find any ego to tempt."

The discussion continued with one of the Muslims expressing disagreement with Timothy Gianotti's premise that prayer is a struggle. A Muslim colleague asked whether he saw fasting as a struggle, a difficulty. The first Muslim retorted, "For Muslims, fasting is easy. Hardships are part of worship, but they are accepted and so it is easy." This claim sounded like "growth in prayer" to another Muslim. "It is growing," responded the first Muslim; "but not struggling."

"Muslims seem to want to talk less about growth, or the higher levels of prayer," noted one Muslim. Growth in prayer can be described as jihād, another Muslim pointed out— jihād being understood as continuous growth. So many ḥadīths speak of it, he noted, wondering whether the Christian lexicon has a similar term. Repentance, *metanoia*, and conversation were offered as possibilities. A Christian clarified the third suggestion, explaining that Benedictines take a vow to spend one's whole life "turning." *Conversatio* has a double meaning. It can mean "turning together"; it is not done alone. A Muslim noted that other Islamic terms may point to necessary reciprocity. The attention of one Christian had been caught by a point made in Timothy Gianotti's paper that prayer is never complete unless one cares for the poor in one's midst, especially when paired with the paper's further assertion that there is no difference between growing in prayer and growing as a moral person.

A Muslim wondered why Timothy Wright had called prayer a "love affair." A Christian responded, "You never get people to commit themselves unless it is out of love. Vocations dry up because of lack of love." Having asked whether Muslims are trained to pray out of fear rather than out of love or adoration, a Christian noted that fear does not necessarily mean "scared of." For example, in one of his *Devotions on Emergent Occasions*, John Donne repeats the word "fear" frequently, with its meaning alternating between "fascinated" and "frightened" by God. "'Perfect love casts out fear' (1 John 4:18)," another Christian noted; "Is this in the Islamic tradition?" A Muslim replied that both fear and love (or awe) are in the Qur'ān. The key term, *taqwā*, includes both. A participant noted that *taqwā*'s full semantic field includes "protection from what's out to get us" (i.e., the Day of Judgment). However, some scholars stress that *taqwā* means "God-consciousness," rather than the fear you'd have of a wolf. One Muslim agreed, saying that he rarely uses "fear of God" as the translation of *taqwā* now. Rather, he uses "God-consciousness" or "God-righteousness" with children because they understand that. "I'm conscious of the Englishness of my own children," he said. "We have to keep society in mind when interpreting." *Taqwā* is multivalent, another Muslim noted; we can choose to emphasize one of its aspects. On the other hand, "we have plenty of imāms who do hell-fire preaching; I leave it to them!" A Christian noted that the 2011 wedding of Prince William to Catherine Middleton used a seventeenth-century liturgy that included mention of fear of the Day of Judgment. "The scary thing about judgment in Christianity is not the hellfire, but that all secrets will be revealed; all will be laid out."

One Muslim asserted that, in Islamic theology, love for God is a requisite of faith in God and his Prophet. Another suggested that, while mystics find praying out of love more attractive, praying out of duty is the best approach for most ordinary persons. Such duty includes performance of preparatory ritual washing. One Muslim pointed out that cleanliness has a spiritual as well as a bodily dimension. Another suggested that Christians are stronger on the love dimension of prayer while Muslims are more successful at using the carrot-and-stick approach. Because God knows our nature, he offers rewards for prayer. However, deeds aren't sufficient for gaining Paradise. A

Christian pointed out that even if we don't feel God's love, it doesn't mean God doesn't love us. "My concern isn't about God's love for us," a Muslim countered, "but rather our love for God."

A point that emerged in some discussions is that prayer is both a gift from God and also something at which the believer must work. Prayer is, therefore, a means of formation and direction of the self toward God. Prayer is an art, one Muslim noted. Thus the paradox is that prayer is not something one will find by looking; but only those who look will find it. A Christian agreed, saying that even the desire to turn to prayer is evidence that divine light is already at work within.

Notes

1. Scribes for Building Bridges 2011 were Janet Soskice, Recep Şentürk, Lucinda Mosher, and Reza Shah-Kazemi.

2. M. A. S. Abdel Haleem, *Understanding the Qur'an: Themes and Styles* (London: I. B. Tauris, 1999), 15.

Afterword

ROWAN WILLIAMS

Two themes seem to pervade a great deal of the rich material gathered here. The first is the inescapable recognition in both Christian and Muslim reflection on prayer that it is not enough to think of praying as something we do. A lot of the time we may speak of prayer as if it were a matter of human action directed toward a distant God, seeking his attention. Yet as soon as we remember what kind of God we are talking about, such a model breaks down completely; for this is a God who, for the Muslim, can be described as closer to us than our jugular vein (Qur'ān 50:16), a God whose creative energy is not exercised once and then abandoned but who—to use a Christian wording this time, with strong Jewish undertones—"carries the universe along by his powerful utterance" (Heb. 1:3). God is eternally active in sustaining the world; he is always "speaking" it. And this means that when we pray we are not initiating some new development but aligning ourselves with that "utterance." It may help us to make sense of the pervasive belief common to the Abrahamic faiths that perhaps the most effective vehicle for prayer is the recitation of the divine Name or Names. We speak God's Name and so make our utterance an utterance of God's revealed identity; we pray by declaring who God is, who God has shown himself to be. We desire to say nothing but the echo of what God has said and done.

To do this requires the disciplines by which we abandon our individual preoccupations, our images of God and ourselves, our expectations of God, conditioned as all these are by both the limits of our finite imagination and the constraints created by our failures and disobediences. Prayer at its most liberated and God-directed may or may not be literally wordless, but there is agreement that on the way to this liberation a great deal in us needs to be silenced so that something may emerge that is—in the words of T. S. Eliot—"more / Than an order of words, the conscious occupation / Of the praying mind, or the sound of the voice praying" ("Little Gidding," ll. 46–48). For Christian and Muslim alike, the "point" of prayer (an odd phrase in many ways) is that God's life in us should be made manifest, and that whatever obstacles we set up to the sovereign freedom of God to act in and around us should be dissolved by the intensity of his presence.

For the Muslim, this is a particularly focused realization of our complete and unconditional dependence on the Creator, a realization of how we are suspended over nothing by the divine utterance; again and again the Qur'ān characterizes God as the one who makes what is from what is not, whose mere word can bring life. The human aspiration to self-sufficiency is at the root of disobedience, and prayer is our recall to the acknowledgement of our insufficiency. For the Christian, though, the principle of seeing prayer as God's act in us has a further dimension grounded in the doctrine of the Trinity: incorporated into Christ, the believer prays to God the Father in the name and Spirit of Jesus. The eternal prayer of the Son to the Father is now happening in us by the indwelling of the Spirit. It is a particularly intense version of the conviction that our prayer echoes God's utterance: Christians would say that this utterance is an everlasting act before creation by which God pours out his life and glory in such a way that there is an eternal answering outpouring of love, to which we give the names of "Word" and "Son." Hence, the importance to the Christian of the "Lord's Prayer" given by Jesus to his disciples, beginning "Our Father"—and hence, too, the importance of the Eucharistic sacrament as embodying the communication to us by Christ of his life in such a way that we can share his relation with the Father.

Various contributions to this book explore the tensions between Christians and Muslims on this particular subject, and there is much valuable clarification as to what the real questions are and the points at which mutual misunderstandings arise. But it is striking that the conviction that prayer is in some sense the action of God in us, the moment when our temptations to self-sufficiency are most decisively countered, is so strong in both contexts. And the mention of this "recall" to the acknowledgement of dependence points us to the second theme in common, that of "remembrance." Prayer is a moment of mindfulness: at the opening of the second sūra of the Qur'ān we are enjoined to be "mindful of God" (2:2), and this is a constant note throughout the Qur'ān. Not only is prayer not to be thought of as simply a human activity undertaken when we want to attract God's attention; it is not to be thought of in isolation from an entire and habitual mindset; prayer arises from a steady habit of seeing our environment against the background of God's ordering and sustaining of everything. Out of this comes the ideal of doing everything for the glory of God, consciously doing whatever prosaic duties confront us in the awareness that how we act will once again manifest—or fail to manifest—God's own all-pervading agency. Prayer is not and cannot be an occasional matter. It is rooted in, and it in turn nourishes, a daily commitment to proper self-awareness: not self-consciousness or the deliberate building-up of a persona—quite the opposite, in fact—but the conscious willingness to allow each moment and each action to be transparent to God.

Regular patterns for prayer—the *ṣalāt* and the Divine Office—have to be seen in this light. Prescribed times of prayer and styles of prayer do not imply that God is unable to listen unless we approach through authorized channels. God's unfailing nearness is axiomatic in this discussion. But, as suggested earlier, these ritual habits are there to remind us of what is abidingly true about God and ourselves and our relation to God. Around the skeleton of such practice many have built quite densely textured patterns of devotion of a more personal or emotionally charged kind—though, as some of the contributions here have shown, there is a strong tradition in both faiths of cleaving to the minimum structure not to avoid the personal or to reduce obligations so much as to underline the risks of elaborating practices that can make us think we are doing the work or that we need to do or say more so as to guarantee that God will hear—a point stressed in Jesus's own teaching on prayer in the Sermon on the Mount (Matt. 6:7) and echoed in Qur'ānic warnings against "heedless" praying to make an impression (107:4–7). God instructs the Prophet not to be "too loud in your prayer, or too quiet" (17:110): we should be cautious about introducing into our prayer the desire to be exceptional, to go beyond what is prescribed. Yet this is not a prohibition against any imaginable development beyond public or ritual prayer, simply a warning against busyness, anxiety, and self-serving. There is in both Christian and Muslim tradition a wealth of devotional resource that witnesses to the overflow of love and desire outside the boundaries of "prescribed" prayer; and if these are rightly seen as extensions and deepenings of remembrance rather than attempts to increase the bargaining power or spiritual status of the praying subject, they are not inconsistent with the warnings of Jesus and Muḥammad.

Ultimately prayer is, for both traditions, the place where our humanity most fully comes into focus and is regrounded, almost re-created. Whether we begin from the Christian conviction about humanity being in the divine image or the Islamic belief in the human person as God's "vicegerent" in creation, both would see the purpose of human life as consisting in becoming more and more an effective channel or vehicle of God's action in the world, and both would therefore also understand the sense in which our self-dispossession is a necessary aspect of our fulfilment. It would be completely wrong to see this as some sort of dissolution of what is created, as if created nature were not good or precious in God's sight; it is rather that our most significant human capacities are at their highest when they freely give way to their Creator; in honouring the priority of the Creator in this way, by accepting their dependence on divine gift, they radiate God's generosity and compassion. So, far from being cancelled or frustrated, they are suffused with that radiance and are themselves glorified. And it is in the paradoxes of prayer that this most clearly comes to light, when our liberty and desire and imagination reach out, in a sustained act of positive self-giving, to their limit and accept their creatureliness, so opening themselves up to the inflowing of divine presence and energy.

In sharing perspectives on prayer as Muslims and Christians, we are drawn into some very significant recognitions—remembrances—of what it is we believe about God and about humanity. We see that if God is the God we claim him to be, his action and ours can never be rivals: we cannot compete with God; God need not compete with us. We cannot sustain our human dignity by insisting on our self-sufficiency and seeking to rule God out; all we shall do is deny the source of our every moment of life and thus risk cutting ourselves off from the roots of reality. And God, who, as a famous ḥadīth says, willed to be known, has nothing to fear from his creation and wills, in making himself known, to equip human creatures to do his will and "enact" his action in the world through his grace and power. The explorations in these pages make it clear that it is in reflecting together about what our spiritual practice is and means that we best clarify the "grammar" of the God we both believe addresses us in mercy.

Personal Reflections on Prayer

BEFORE THE SEMINAR each participant was asked to write a short personal reflection in response to this request: "Imagine someone who claims not to understand prayer asking you what prayer means to you. What are your first thoughts? What do you tell this person? Feel free to draw on your own experience." This section consists of these reflections.

Muhammad Abdel Haleem

To me, prayer (*duʿāʾ*—supplication), as the Prophet Muḥammad said, is the essence of worship. In the Qurʾān God encourages us to pray and promises us he will answer (40:60). We pray in obedience to Him and trust in His wisdom, power, and care. This "essence of worship" puts us in an intimate, enriching relationship with the Merciful Lord, which adds to our faith and makes life more meaningful.

The Qurʾān gives us good examples in the prayers that proved effective in diverse situations for those who had more knowledge of God and were closer to him. Zachariah prayed, "Lord, my bones have weakened and my hair is ashen grey, but never, Lord, have I ever prayed to You in vain" (19:4). Joseph, in his supreme moment, thanks God for graces already granted and praises him before asking for more: "My Lord, you have given me authority; you have taught me how to interpret dreams; Creator of the Heavens and earth you are my protector in this world and the hereafter. Let me die in true devotion to You and join me with the righteous" (12:101).

The Ḥadīth adds a vast corpus of duʿāʾ suggested by the Prophet for all situations, powerful in meaning and language. These come readily to my mind, and I feel that by repeating a relevant prayer, my duʿāʾ stands a better chance of being accepted. Using the Prophet's prayers shows me the prophetic way of seeing a situation and knowing what prayer to say in it. My sense of language is enriched by his eloquence. *Ṣalāt* (the five times daily formal prayer) reminds me that God should be kept central in our lives: we need Him.

Asma Afsaruddin

The Arabic words *munājāt*, *duʿāʾ*, and *ṣalāt* capture the essence of prayer—prayer as private conversation with the Almighty; as glorification of His exalted status and invocation of His wisdom and mercy; and as communal supplication and adoration of God. Prayer may be considered the natural consequence of the human *fiṭra*—the inborn disposition in us to do good and worship the Creator; it is the means by which we therefore discover and nurture our fundamental nature and dignity as human beings. It is a constant reminder of the next world and of the true purpose of our worldly existence—it is the bridge between life as we now know it and the life that we can only imagine and hope for in the hereafter. Prayer eases our loneliness and anguish, provides solace in the midst of the searing grief that the loss of a loved one inevitably brings, and reminds us that we are allowed to feel weak and vulnerable, for there is One greater than all of us from Whom we can draw strength and sustenance. Prayer cleanses us of our sins and envelops us in divine love—again and again. Prayer—regardless of its outer form—is also the common bond among worshippers of God everywhere, superseding cultural, social, and even religious differences. In Qurʾān 20:14 God commands, "Worship Me and establish prayer so as to remember Me." In the adoration and remembrance of the Almighty through constant communion with Him lies our fulfillment as human beings.

Akintunde Akinade

Prayer is at the core of our constant yearning to communicate with the Ultimate Reality. It underscores the human quest for the divine. As an African theologian, I affirm that prayer is the heart and soul of the spiritual life. It entails a deep awareness of God's presence in the entire creation and evokes a profound sense of gratitude to the transcendence. Prayer as "conversations with God," to borrow a phrase from the late Church historian James Melvin Washington, connects to the innate human sense of higher morality, values, and aspirations. As a Christian theologian who is deeply interested in interreligious dialogue, I believe that prayer is fraught with resources and potentials for interreligious communication and engagement. Both the inner and outside expressions and aspects of prayer provide the opportunity to transcend the nagging problems of self-centeredness and pride and lay our concerns and vulnerability at the feet of the source of our existence. In the midst of the travails and uncertainties of life, prayer and contemplation provide succor for the weary soul. They provide the auspicious moment to stop and open our heart and soul to our Creator and to contemplate the splendor of grace that transcends all understanding.

Seyed Amir Akrami

The way in which I personally relate to prayer is reflected in what the Prophet said in a ḥadīth that prayer is like washing yourself five times a day in a river. This is perfectly in tune with the Qur'ān: surely prayer keeps away from indecency and evil (29:45). Therefore, the main purpose and function of prayer to me is to restrain from all sorts of immoral behavior. But the Qur'ān reminds us that this cannot be achieved unless one prays in humility, and it is this spirit of humility that brings about the desired results: "Seek help through patience and prayer, since it is exacting except for the humble, who assume they will meet their Lord, and that they will return to him" (2:45–46). Mawlānā Rūmī, to whom I am greatly indebted for my understanding of prayer, makes a similar point when he speaks of the winds of anger, lust, and greed sweeping away the person who does not perform the ritual prayers.[1] On a more profound level, prayer can set us free from all thoughts that hinder our spiritual perfection. Again, Rūmī illustrates the point vividly, describing a naked man jumping into water to escape from hornets, but as soon as he raises his head out of the water they sting him. The water symbolizes the remembrance of God (*dhikr*) while the hornets represent distracting thoughts during dhikr. If we hold our breath in the water of dhikr and are patient, we shall be freed from distracting thoughts and temptations.[2]

Vincent J. Cornell

For me, prayer is both communication and communion. Of the three main forms of prayer in Islam—the formal prayer (*al-ṣalāt*), the supplication (*duʿāʾ*), and the prayer of remembrance or invocation (*dhikr*)—I perform supplications the least, except to ask for God's favor for others. Although I am permitted to ask God's favor for myself, I seldom do so, partly because I feel certain that my destiny is preordained and partly because I feel that it is pretentious for me to ask favors for myself. As the great Andalusian Sufi Abū

Madyan (d. 1198) stated, when you are in the station of servanthood, you should view your actions as hypocrisy, your spiritual states as pretentiousness, and your speech as a lie.

In a famous ḥadīth, the Angel Gabriel told the Prophet Muḥammad: "Worship God as if you see Him, for even if you do not see Him, He sees you." This is how I try to approach the formal prayer, *al-ṣalāt*. For me the *ṣalāt* is both a form of communication with God and a return to Him. More precisely, it is like the return of the prodigal child, who humbly comes home to his Creator in shame and hope. I have long been moved by the admonition of Abū al-ʿAbbās al-Sabtī (d. 1204), the patron saint of Marrakesh, who said that we should come to our prayers without begrudging God anything, and that when we raise our hands at the beginning of prayer, we should empty ourselves of everything and say to God within ourselves, "I possess neither much nor little."

Prayer as communion is represented for me by *dhikr*, the remembrance or recollection of God, which is also the essence of prayer. Abū Madyan said, "Say 'Allah!' and let go of existence and all it contains if you desire to attain perfection. For everything other than God, were you to realize it, is nothing—whether in part or in whole." When we look deeply into ourselves, whether in our intellect or our heart, what do we see but our actions? Out of what do we construct the narrative of our identity? Our existence, such as it is, is fleeting and not entirely real: "between flower and song," as the Aztecs said. Our choices are found in what we do, and what we do has no real meaning unless we do it for God. If we are not God's creatures, we are nothing. So is anything better or more appropriate for our station than the remembrance of God? As the Holy Qurʾān says, "Verily prayer works against vice and sin, but *dhikr Allah* is greatest" (29:45).

Caner Dagli

For many years an argument of Ibn ʿArabī, the twelfth-century philosopher-mystic, has always affected my attitude in prayer. Briefly, he says that God is more wise and more loving than we could possibly fathom, and this love is moreover unconditional and absolute, unconditioned by anything we do. It is because of this love that the world was created and we continue to exist. But God, being infinite, could not be bound only by His unconditional and unqualified love. Ibn ʿArabī says that we cannot limit God by considering him to be only infinite and only absolute; when it comes to prayer, this means that there are also those things that only come into being when they are asked for—not because God needs to be asked as such but because the act of responding to His creature's request is another aspect of His love and creative power. To make it even more imponderable, Ibn ʿArabī tells us our very prayer itself, the act of remembrance that opens the door to then formulating a prayer, is considered itself an unasked for grace from God.

A passive attitude of, "God, you know what's best, so I leave it to you," does not get the full picture, and neither does, "God will do what He will do, so I leave it to Him." Paradoxical as it may sound, one must pray for what one wants, since to do otherwise would be to limit God. This insight has always helped me make sense of personal prayer in the face of the unwieldy concepts of omniscience, omnibenevolence, and omnipotence.

Gavin D'Costa

What is prayer for me? Sometimes it's like speaking to myself with a vague sense of despair and emptiness, wondering if this chatter is vain and deluded. In communal prayer, I feel helped by others to raise my mind, heart, and spirit to give praise to God; to examine the way my life blocks out the love of God; to bring my concerns and the community's concerns to God for guidance and direction; and to enter more deeply into a personal and communal transforming relationship with God through his Word. Through the Eucharist, especially, I feel drawn into the life of Christ, both as witness and as participant in his life through the Spirit. The Spirit is able to take me, if I am receptive, to the table of disciples who eat with Christ, to the cross of Christ, and to enter into the new life of the resurrection: some sense of hope, community, love, and mission. In community prayer, I sometimes experience alienation and contempt for what is going on; a boredom at repetition. Private prayer begins in the morning when I walk my dog around the park. If the day is beautiful I praise God naturally, and when it is pouring with rain and I'm tired I still repeat the words and sometimes find a way back into praise. I use this time to try and bring my day, in anticipation, into God's light and love. I also have to concentrate on avoiding other dog-walkers who like to talk!

Susan Eastman

The poet Gerard Manley Hopkins said faith is God in us knowing God's own truth. I think prayer is something similar.

To someone who wonders what prayer is about—to whom perhaps it seems a silly kind of talking to oneself, or a way of trying to manipulate

God—I would say that it is just the opposite: it is a practice whereby my attention gets directed away from myself, toward God, who has come close in Jesus Christ. Prayer is worship, praise of God, attention to God, and coming before God without dissembling. It reminds me that the center of gravity really is not in me or in anything else, but in God. This in turn brings a certain sort of freedom based entirely on God's goodness, power, and trustworthiness. That means prayer is an opening to the liberation that God has brought to pass through Jesus Christ—liberation from false perceptions, false loyalties, ridiculous concerns and expectations, and judgment of others and myself. Such liberation also involves self-examination in the freedom created by the sheer gift of divine mercy.

Prayer is therefore a mode of guidance not because God "tells me what to do" but because it opens up previously unimaginable possibilities in any given situation. It is a kind of corrective lens. But prayer also is asking for divine help in very specific and concrete situations and relying on God's grace and power. It involves a paradoxical combination of surrender and confidence.

David Ford

Thoughts for Someone Beginning to Pray

Prayer is wonderfully diverse—at least as interesting and varied as relations with other people and the rest of creation. The following are some key elements for me. The main way to learn it is simply to get on with praying.

- "Come, Holy Spirit!" is for me the prayer of prayers, from which all other prayer flows—St. Seraphim of Sarov is a teacher of this. The secret of prayer is that God gives his own Spirit freely.

- When I was a student I was told by an Anglican monk about the Daily Office, a regular pattern of prayer with lectionary (regular readings from Old and New Testaments), and that has been my staple diet ever since—it can combine Psalms (with thanks, praise, lament, confession, and simply crying out to God), meditating on other Bible readings, traditional prayers, spontaneous prayer "heart to heart," and silence. Try it for five years or so to see if it works.

- The great prayers for me are the Psalms; the Our Father; John 17; 2 Corinthians 13:13; Ephesians 3:14–21; the Eucharistic Prayer; the General Thanksgiving of the Book of Common Prayer; and the annual cycle of collects. If you were to get deep into a year's collects you would emerge with a rich, balanced theology for living.

- Besides the Eucharist and the Daily Office, key liturgies for me are the Methodist Covenant Service and the Triduum (Good Friday, Holy Saturday, and Easter Sunday). Take part in them.

- Never forget the core simplicity of prayer: petition—asking God in trust (Karl Barth is a good teacher of this).

- Finally, two occasional practices that have greatly helped me: praying "as long as it takes," open-endedly, for an hour or more, or perhaps all night, when gripped by a problem, a joy, a grief, or just by being with God; and studying the Bible, Tanakh, and Qur'ān "for God's sake" with prayerful Jews, Christians, and Muslims.

Lucy Gardner

Prayer can be many different things (adoring, pleading, resting, wrestling) and it can take many different forms (words, silence, movement, stillness), but it is always a response to God (be that joyful, hopeful, despairing, or angry). God's action, God's movement, God's Word (of creation, or forgiveness, or judgment, or blessing), even God's "silence" comes first; our prayer is what we offer or send back in return. Agnostics and atheists can pray.

As I speak or simply wait in prayer, I deliberately turn my attention, my whole being, to God. I try to be honest before God, about who and what I think I am, about what I think of and long for (for myself and others), about how I feel. This is *me* coming before God. But as I listen and watch in prayer, I learn the real truth (about God, the world, and myself) from God. This is me coming before *God*.

In the Psalms, we are given words to pray when we have none ourselves—words to cover anything we might want to say to God. For Christians, these words are not just tools; they are God's Word. Gradually we learn that God prays in us; empowered by the Spirit, we become united to Christ especially in his prayer to the Father. I "start" by offering my prayer and myself, but discover more and more that I am in fact always being offered and drawn by God. Christ's eternal prayer is one of thankfulness and love; as I learn to pray, I learn to be loved, and to love with God's love.

Timothy J. Gianotti

Prayer for me is, of course, always changing shape and tone and texture, all of which arise from my own fluctuating condition and spiritual state. Underlying all this, however, throbs a mystery of connectivity and reciprocal remembrance: my remembrance of God and God's remembrance of me. In one of the Divine, theopathic utterances attributed to the Prophet Muḥammad (may God's blessings and peace be ever upon him and all of the messengers), God is believed to say, "I am as My servant thinks I am. I am with him when he remembers Me. If he makes mention of Me to himself, I make mention of him to Myself; and if he makes mention of Me in an assembly, I make mention of him in an assembly better than that. If he draws near to Me an arm's length, I draw near to him a fathom's length; if he comes to Me walking, I rush to him." For me, then, prayer is the rope or cord that keeps me consciously connected to my source; remembering that the Arabic word for the Divine attribute of "mercy" derives from the word for "womb," I see prayer as the spiritual umbilical cord that is never cut, always available, always ready to nourish and sustain us.

Toby Howarth

God's call in the Bible is to love God and to love our neighbor as ourselves. Prayer is for me the deepest way I can respond to that call because love is a gift of grace. I know in myself my love for God and for those around me is inadequate. But in prayer I am aware of being loved as a child is loved by his parent, unconditionally and full of challenge. Prayer is a communal practice: it is what we as a congregation do in church on Sundays and other occasions. It is what we as a family try to be faithful to each weekday morning in reading scripture, silence, sharing about the day ahead and committing one another, the church and the world to God. It is words said before a meal, or meeting regularly with a "prayer partner." It is the daily private discipline in which I draw on the Psalms and liturgy of the church, and it is what I find myself doing when I'm worried or unexpectedly joyful. Although they don't always feel spectacular, I hold onto these ordinary communal practices as a participation in the relationship of love between God and the church established through Jesus Christ's life, death, and resurrection and celebrated in the prayer of the Eucharist. The energy of prayer is the vast, wild, and intimate energy of God's Spirit who cannot be contained in the church and who is at home in the most surprising places. So prayer is always happening, and engaging in prayer is choosing to come home to the love of God and neighbor.

Muhammad K. Khalifa

Prayer is both an individual and collective effort on the part of human beings to communicate with the Divine. It is a daily reminder of the humanity of man and the glory and magnitude of God. Prayer is a faithful expression of the total submission of man to the will of God, and of the real feeling of complete dependence on the Divine. It is a free and spontaneous pouring out of the heart before God. It may be difficult to define the place of prayer in religion, but, as noted in the history of religions, prayer is the heart of worship. It is a multifaceted daily religious activity that includes many forms and kinds of worship such as invocations, thanks, praise, dedication, supplications, petitions, confessions, repentance, benedictions, and so on. In prayer we also see the reflection of all religious and ethical values. Prayer is a daily practical lesson in the values of love, mercy, justice, equality, and the brotherhood of humanity. It is also a daily lesson in discipline, respect for time, and love of work. In sum, prayer is the rhythm of life. It gives system to life and creates in man the values of tolerance, forgiveness, social responsibility, and love of neighbor and of humanity at large. Finally, prayer is a trialogue between man, God, and the world. The dialogue between man and God as presented in prayer is reflected in the relation between man and the universe. This dialogue is the basis for the relation between human beings and between them and the world. This relation is based on the principle of the love of God and is reflected in love of humanity and the world. Prayer is a daily meeting between man and God for which man has to be pure both physically and spiritually. It is a daily testament with God and a continuous proof of His existence in our lives. Prayer is the sign of faith, a daily declaration of obedience to God, and a final positive proof of salvation and of the success of man in this world and in the world to come.

Daniel A. Madigan

"Resonating" would probably be the word that best captures what I understand by prayer, and what at the best of times I find happening to me in it. I deliberately say "happening to me" because my sense of prayer is not that it is my activity but rather that God is the active one. This resonating has various aspects. The Word through which all things came to be (John 1:3) resonates in me as in all creation, and a profound part of prayer is "coming home" to God's universe through becoming attuned to that resonance. Further, the Word's becoming flesh in Jesus means that human life has become the medium of God's self-expression, and so my own life too, as it resonates with the life of Jesus, can be at God's disposal in this way. In entering into the concreteness of the scenes of the life of Jesus, as the Ignatian tradition of contemplation teaches me to do, and even more in celebrating the Lord's Supper and the other sacraments, I find myself becoming an echo of that Word-made-flesh, even a physical echo. None of this is done alone, of course. My prayer is in community, even if at the moment I happen to be alone. There are words, actions and images, stories and songs that resonate with this diverse group of people and set up a common resonance among us. This is a not a community to be closed in on itself but turned outward in compassionate service. The compassion that brings to our lips words of petition for ourselves and the world is no more than an echo of God's own compassion for us.

Jane Dammen McAuliffe

Two phrases frame my experience of prayer. One is the classical catechism definition: "Prayer is the lifting of the mind and heart to God." The other is the famous passage from Paul's Letter to the Romans where the Spirit "makes intercession for us with groaning which cannot be uttered" (Rom. 8:26). For me, "lifting the mind and heart to God" usually involves some effort at interior quieting. Ideally, this means finding a space of solitude, taking a few deep breaths and simply trying to still, however temporarily, the chattering monkeys in my mind. I ordinarily have something from the Gospels, Psalms, or an author such as Thomas Merton at hand, and slowly scanning a few verses or paragraphs is usually enough to pull me into a deeper quiet. Alas, the monkeys always reassert themselves, often quite quickly, so I repeat the process again and again until the time that I've set aside for a prayer period is spent. Sometimes, but not always, something seems to happen in the silence, something that may echo the reassurance of Romans 8:26.

More spontaneously, prayer can erupt as a kind of interior conversation. Of course, I'm never sure whether I'm simply talking to myself or if somehow there are two parties involved. Yet I certainly hope that an unexpected insight or a sudden sense of inner tranquility reflects the promptings of the ever-present Spirit. There are also episodes of intercessory prayer, of simply begging for help with life's problems and pains, where the heart outruns the mind and sweeps aside the persistent doubt and disbelief.

I've spoken here about personal prayer rather than communal and liturgical forms. Even within the realm of personal prayer, I've focused on just a few practices. Over the years I have tried others and will probably continue to experiment, reminding myself that God reaches out to us in different forms and ways. When some practices prove uncongenial, I am guided by a final dictum: "Pray as you can, not as you can't."

Ibrahim Mogra

Prayer is not a spare wheel to be used when in trouble but it is a steering wheel that guides you to God. For me it is an opportunity to be with God five times a day, just the two of us in conversation as I try to become His friend. Every day I enjoy being in the company of my loved ones as much as possible and with every spare moment. I love God more than all these people and so yearn to be with Him more despite being busy with work and life. Five times a day, prayer gives me that opportunity. I do not have to meet Him only in prayer. He is with me all the time. Sometimes I forget and so disobey Him. I must remember that He is closer to me than my jugular vein, as the Qur'ān explains. So I turn to Him in prayer and supplication night and day. I thank Him for all His blessings and ask for more. I ask for the poor and needy, the homeless and hungry, for health and happiness, peace and prosperity, for a life of obedience to Him, a peaceful end with faith, for salvation and an eternal place with Him. I chant His many beautiful names softly to myself and sometimes with others, while waiting at red traffic lights or in a dimly lit room, before a meal and after, upon carrying out any activity seeking Him and His love. So I pray.

Dheen Mohamed

Prayer for me is *dhikr*, a reminder: a reminder of who I am and what I am meant to be. By the very fact that I am human, I forget, I falter, and how often have I found myself trespassing beyond the limits prescribed by my Lord. In the hubbub and pace of modern life, it takes very little to forget one's bearings, and I am no exception to the rule. At times I feel remorse for my excesses and at others I am just indifferent to them. It is prayer that prevents me from getting carried away by the distractions of the world and keeps reminding me of my origins and ultimate destiny. It is in prayer that I get rid of my remorse by invoking the love and mercy of my Lord, and it is also in prayer that I seek forgiveness for my indifference. In prostration, the lowest point and yet the climax of my prayer, I am reminded that nothing pleases God more than humility, and nothing invites His wrath more than arrogance. As my forehead, palms, knees, and legs (not to mention my nose—my mark of dignity) touch the ground, I know I have disarmed my Benevolent Lord and proceed to empty my heart of all my fears, worries, and complaints, absolutely sure that at that moment nobody loves me more than He does. These are the most intimate moments of my everyday life, and I can only realize them in prayer. And the deeper I go, the clearer I become about myself and the nature of my relationship to my fellow human beings and nature.

Lucinda Mosher

Lex orandi lex credendi: "praying shapes believing." First we learn to pray; belief and understanding come later. Or, if you would understand my believing, study my dialogue with God via the Book of Common Prayer—its liturgies featuring texts and postures (some prescribed, others optional), encounter with vast portions of scripture, occasions for silence—and song. The Book of Common Prayer is my prayer handbook; so is the Hymnal. "One who sings prays twice," says Augustine. Indeed, my most robust dialogue with God happens through music: playing the organ, singing hymns, leading a choir.

When Jesus said, "Pray like this," he provided a template; from it and the Psalter we may discern prayer's ingredients: praise, confession, petition, intercession, and thanksgiving—which I'd teach children by drawing an outline of my hand, each digit representing an element. Praying may name a range of activities for Christians; others may distinguish carefully between prayer and meditation or *supplication*.

"Supplication is the marrow of worship," says Muslim tradition. Indeed! Supplication—worship's core, its connective tissue—may be primal. If so, our initial contact with the divine provokes us not to praise or exclaim but to ask for something. Yet supplication's form is not usually a question but an imperative. Its intent may be "humble," but "please, would you . . . ?" is articulated rarely. Nevertheless, in supplication literature we seldom find mere lists of wants; praise and thanksgiving customarily bracket petition. But petition provides insight into the human condition: its limitations, anxieties, calamities; its recognition of Holy Mystery; its moral vision.

Michael Plekon

I grew up in a family in which attendance at Sunday services, communion, and prayers at home before bed were all a regular, essential part of life. On the walls of our home were icons and the crucifix. The great feasts were celebrated and the Lenten fast was observed. Later my parents supported me when I expressed interest in a vocation to religious life and priesthood in the Carmelite Order. I entered the order's novitiate and stayed five more years as a friar until I left. Later in life I was ordained and have served in the ministry now for almost thirty years. So since childhood communal liturgical prayer, reading the scriptures, and meditation have all been a part of my life.

However, no matter how accustomed one is to its many forms, prayer is never easy. The people in your life, their cares and concerns, other issues concerning family, friends, work, events in the country and world, books one is reading, things one is writing—all of these and much more flood in on me, whether I am in the vestments preparing the bread and wine or celebrating the liturgy in church. They flood in when I am doing daily prayers at home or on the train into New York City where I teach.

Long ago someone wise in the life of the Spirit told me that none of these ideas, persons, or events should ever be scorned as "distractions." In fact, all were coming to me from God, the Spirit breathing them and anything else good into my heart and head in prayer—as prayer. Even the darkest sadness, the most terrifying fears, and enormous joy are the material of prayer.

This is because prayer, at the root, is life—my life, all the others, all the issues and worries, everything—but also God living, breathing, thinking, mourning, worrying, rejoicing in me. Whether it is the Psalms, passages from the Hebrew Bible or the New Testament, or the words of ancient teachers or contemporaries of mine, whether it is no words at all but just watching, waiting, looking, for me, prayer has become the world in which I live, in which I find myself. To be sure, there are very different moments and dimensions, from liturgical prayer in community to gazing at a painting or becoming lost in a Chopin nocturne or, for that matter, in listening to a student, a parish member, my spouse, or one of my children.

They are all there, in prayer: God, Father, Son, and Spirit; the angels and all the saints, those gone before, those around me, and myself; and perhaps even those also yet to be.

Sajjad Rizvi

Prayer is our becoming, our emergence, our connection with what it means to be human and to be seeking the divine; ascending to our origin, or being rooted and realized in what it means to be us, finding tranquility in the self and in one's community while escaping the vicissitudes of life, our repose and refuge much like sensual pleasures and our partners who embellish us and conceal our faults. Prayer is standing before the Lord in fear and hope, bowing in praise and thanksgiving for the bounties and graces that one enjoys, prostrating to encapsulate our earthly origin and our utter helplessness and need for God. Prayer is supplication, whispering of the heart, loud and ecstatic shouting, responding to the call of the reed-pipe, laughter and dance and weeping, and intimate conversation with the beloved. Above all prayer is about finding—both the self and God—to paraphrase the grandson of the Prophet and friend of God: "O Lord, who has lost anything if he has found you, and who has gained anything if he has lost you?" Ultimately, prayer is a series of paradoxes: conversations in what seems to be a monologue (or even a rant), seeking riches (in every sense of the term) in the depths of our indigence, claiming ownership over oneself and the object of one's prayer yet realizing that even the words of our prayer do not really belong to us, hope in the presence of doubt, love and mutuality.

Philip Seddon

Prayer, for me, is the Archimedean point of the universe, my central spiritual stadium, the arena of deepest struggle and of spiritual realization. If I read scripture prayerfully, God can address me. I can return to myself and to my senses; I can seek, find, and be found by God. Praying openly with others also encourages me to deeper trust in God's open heart. Prayer is dialogue, communion, rest.

I fail as much as I succeed. I forget to pray, I lose my way, I lose heart. But prayer reminds me that God's door is always open. I can walk with confidence into the presence of God, and without fear or hesitation, talk to Jesus as Friend and Home, with tears or laughter.

I want my prayer to help my mind shape the longings of my heart. I don't want my prayers to be dominated by thinking. I want my intellect to be filled and expanded by God's love. In seeking the presence of the One who is greater—the Creator—deep within my soul, I learn who I am before God and in God. Prayer becomes a mirror that reflects back to me the face of God in Jesus Christ.

So I do not simply pray *to* God; I want the Holy Spirit to utter God's prayers in me. I pray *within* the Trinity, where I can intercede for the sins and sufferings and blessing of the world, myself included. I try not to escape from God's generous gaze on me, where there is deep love and joy.

Recep Şentürk

Prayer (in Arabic *duʿāʾ*) is an activity that sets humans apart from animals. In other words, humans alone pray. Therefore, abandoning prayer is losing a distinct human quality. One can even say that perfect humanity is achieved through prayer.

Prayer is itself an act of worship by expressing one's neediness toward one's Lord. There is no specific time for prayer because God is beyond time: His door is always open to everyone who seeks refuge and help. Thus prayer makes one ascend the conditions of the reality of this world to the highest level of existence, which is the divine.

Prayer reflects awareness about the multiple levels of existence and the interconnectivity among them, in particular the connection between divinity and humanity. Prayer connects a human being to God directly without any interference and mediation. This connection replaces the feeling of loneliness and anxiety—two common contemporary problems from which modern humans suffer—by unity with God.

Prayer is expressed in many ways, mainly by words and actions. Sometimes it goes directly from the heart of a believer to God without any need of means of expression. The most effective prayer is the one that combines heart, words, and actions.

One should not doubt whether one's prayers will be accepted by God because this would be disrespectful to God, as though He refuses to give small things His needy servants ask of Him. He never rejects a prayer offered with sincerity, but He decides how (granting the same thing or something better) and when (in this world or the next) to answer it. He is the Most Generous; thus it is not suitable for Him to refuse anything asked of Him. However, the proper etiquette of human beings with God requires them to defer to God in their prayers because their prayer is based on their limited knowledge while God has infinite knowledge and knows what is best for His servant.

Reza Shah-Kazemi

Prayer goes to the very heart of our existence as human beings; it is our raison d'être. As human beings we are uniquely endowed with a mode of awareness that is only fully intelligible in connection with the freedom of our will: we alone are free to direct our awareness to the source whence it emerged and to integrate it therein. The source of our limited awareness is not only infinite consciousness, it is also absolute reality and perfect love. Prayer, at its deepest or most contemplative, is the most direct means by which the human accident returns to the divine substance: the "drop" of human awareness returns to the "ocean" of divine reality. Prayer, at whatever level, helps to displace egocentric consciousness, granting us a taste of the spiritual joy that accompanies liberation from the ego, rendering transparent the contours defining the "drop" of individual consciousness. As the stranglehold of the false, egocentric self loosens, one senses a very real possibility of realizing one's true self in the bosom of the Real. And such self-realization, in the measure of its authenticity, overflows as the gift of self to others: what one gives to the neighbor is heartfelt love, for one has tasted the love that flows from the heart of the Real. To be human is to be capable of prayer; and to pray is to bring to fruition the blessed seeds of beatific Reality embedded within the human heart.

Samy Shehata

Prayer is a call and response; God is calling and we are responding. It is God's call as a Creator and a father. Prayer is the place where pride is abandoned, hope is lifted, and supplication is made. Prayer is the place of admitting our need, adopting humility and complete dependence upon God. Prayer is the exercise of faith and hope.

Prayer is a communication process that allows us to talk to and listen to God. God wants us to communicate with Him. Prayer is to bow our knees, confess our sin, receive God's forgiveness, and ask that the will of God be done. God is sovereign and loving, and He knows what is best for us and others, even if we don't agree.

We should pray ceaselessly, in every decision we take and in seeking guidance as the day progresses. We pray because we know that God hears us and because we desire to see results. We pray by faith, consistently, and for others, trusting God. We pray and we know that our prayers are answered.

A variety of body postures accompany prayer: standing, sitting, kneeling, prostrate on the floor. Prayer may be done privately and individually, or it may be done corporately in the presence of fellow believers. In prayer we lay before Him our complete self in confession and dependence. There is nothing to hide when in quiet supplication we are reaching into the deepest part of ourselves and admitting our needs and failures.

Philip Sheldrake

For me "prayer" means the ways that I express my relationship with God. This includes, but is not limited to, certain practices. My experience is that the regular practice of prayer, or "praying," gradually shapes a more continuous awareness of God. For me praying is both "in common" and alone. Praying together is quite structured, but it expresses my understanding that religious faith is essentially a collective matter. When I pray alone my preference is for stillness—simply being present to God without thoughts or words. But I generally find it helps to start in one of two ways. One way is to take a short passage of scripture, ruminate on it, and maybe respond personally to it, or to take a single phrase or word and repeat this rhythmically. Either way, this practice tends to lead me beyond the words into silence. The other way similarly leads to stillness but begins, depending on context, not with words but by focusing on something visually powerful—an icon, the sea, or a particular built space—that evokes divine presence. Finally, another way of personal prayer is to reflect briefly in the evening on the day that has passed—asking God to help me recall God's presence to me during the day in people, places, or events, and how I responded or failed to respond. Basically, this practice helps deepen my overall awareness of and attentiveness to God in the midst of everyday life—occasionally expressed in moments of spontaneous "conversation."

Mona Siddiqui

Prayer is man's contact with God. I cannot help but pray; it's an instinctive reaching out and for me it fulfills the yearning that lies in being human. Prayer is far more than the humbling ritual of prostration and even the stretching out of one's hands in desperation. Prayer is the hushed murmuring of God's name when I am scared or feel alone; it is the loud call of Allah when I feel God cannot have a choice; he must answer me. Knowledge of a higher being is felt most acutely through prayer. As William James said, "The humblest outcast on this earth can feel himself to be real and valid by means of this higher recognition. . . . For most of us a world with no such inner refuge when the outer social self failed and dropped from us would be the abyss of horror."

There is a difference between saying prayers and actually praying. Most of the time I am praying in gratitude for the health of my family and the safety of home. But although hope is the essence of faith, I also pray because sometimes I am so afraid that I need to feel that I can be with God; that if I turn to him, he is waiting. Prayer is a longing that can seize you anywhere and anytime, and I never pray thinking that God is not listening. In the end I think all forms of worship are dispensable except prayer.

Janet Soskice

Prayer can be different things for the same person at different times and even within the same day. There are the formal prayers that Christians pray in churches or pray privately from books, there are impatient outbursts of thanksgiving or supplication, there is quiet reflection and even casual "chat." There seems to be no "formula" for prayer except that every case is a seeking of the face of God.

I was an adult when I came to faith. I was agnostic until, in my early twenties, God touched my heart. I did not immediately become a Christian, but one thing was evident—now I was speaking with God. This is what Augustine says (to God) after his full embrace of Christianity—"now I was speaking to you." This was possible because Saint Augustine now believed God had spoken and was speaking to him—not in heard words of successive syllables from the sky but in his heart, by other people (his mother), and above all through scripture. Foundational to my understanding of the practice of prayer (prayer life) is that I am speaking to God because God has spoken to me (and to all of us if we listen).

Prayer like this is not always planned but wells up from my belief that God is not far away from each one of us but very, very close. For this reason I find it helpful to speak of a "prayer life" for it is an orientation of being and a set of practices, some of them physical.

It is important to *know* we are close to God, even if at times we do not *feel* this. Some people are aware of the presence of God almost all the time when they pray, others very rarely, but God's presence does not depend on our emotions. We can know God is with us, faithfully, always and everywhere. We can pray when we are distracted and distressed. We should not be afraid to ask God for anything.

Many Catholics and Anglicans use books of morning and evening prayer for private devotions. These bring together formal prayers, scripture reading (determined by a shared calendar of readings), psalms, and times for personal reflection, praise, and entreaty. You can say these prayers with a group or by yourself, but whenever you do you are also joining the prayers of Christians around the world.

I learned an important lesson about prayer while my husband's elderly aunt was living with us—she died in our home last year at the age of ninety-nine and a half. A lifelong and devout Anglican, in her last years with eyesight and energy failing, she very much appreciated being read the Evening Prayer. Long after she had ceased to be able to speak in a normal way, whether from weakness or other infirmity, she would join in as we reached the Lord's Prayer and other familiar prayers in the service. Her body was habituated to the prayer. Even with mind failing, her life of prayer continued—her body and spirit could still pray.

Michael Welker

Doxology, lament, petition, and thanksgiving are the basic elements of prayer. Doxology—the glorification of God—however, does not necessarily come in a jubilant and joyful tone. In prayer, doxology can, so to speak, remain latent, silent, whereas even the strongest lament in prayer includes—or rather is surrounded by—a doxology that can come in the form of counterfactual trust or desperate hope. Thus, prayer covers all the way, from faithful trust to desperate cries.

In prayer we encounter the living God in all his mystery and richness, God our Creator who wants to sustain, to rescue, to save, to elevate, and to ennoble us in our creaturely frailty, helplessness, lostness, misery, and futility. We encounter God, our redeemer, who wants to reveal to us not only his own love and glory but also our dignity, kindness, and strength. In prayer we open our hearts and souls, reach out and call not only for God but also for our own full existence and being. In prayer we get the chance to become familiar with God and with our own depths. We distinguish mere wishes and unrealistic expectations from our true life keeping up with God, following God's pace, as Dietrich Bonhoeffer put it.

In prayer we connect utter modesty and the utmost hope. The Lord's Prayer offers us a model of a prayer truly directed to God—not to a heaven of dreams and illusions. This prayer is doxological from beginning to end: "hallowed be thy name, thy kingdom come, thy will be done on earth as it is in heaven . . . thine is the kingdom, and the power and the glory." In a modest way it prays for our basic sustenance: "Give us today our daily bread." It is aware of the abyss of our endangerment, our self-endangerment, and our needs: "forgive us our trespasses . . . do not lead us into temptation, deliver us from evil." Finally, it also acknowledges our own power and dignity: to love and to forgive one another. On this level we encounter God face to face: "forgive us our trespasses as we forgive those who trespass against us." On this level we can also challenge God in the midst of creaturely suffering and in our inability to understand his ways.

Rowan Williams

The idea that the Christian praying is somehow entering into an activity already going on has for many years been crucial to me in thinking about prayer. The New Testament speaks about the Spirit giving us the kind of words, the kind of voice, that Jesus uses in his relation with God the Father.

So the task in prayer is not to take a long journey up to heaven in the hope of being heard there but to try and remove the obstacles that make me swim against the stream of self-giving that flows from Jesus to the Father. This entails stilling the body and breathing regularly, repeating a simple formula to settle the mind, and quietly but firmly refusing to follow distracting chains of images or ideas that may arise. The mediaeval classic called *The Cloud of Unknowing* tells us that in times of distress we need only to say one word that will anchor us and call us back—just as in a burning house all we need to say is "Fire!" So we call on the Holy Name of God when we are confused and heavily oppressed in prayer. And it is out of this attempt to let go of fantasies and obsessive thoughts that we gain the freedom to pray for others most fully and truly—when we are sufficiently free from ourselves to see them as they are, not to see their needs only in terms of ours.

Timothy Wright

Prayer is my ongoing love affair. In prayer I reach the depths of my being. From there I reach out to the God who loves me more than I could ever comprehend, the God who loves me so much that I am never forgotten (though I forget God frequently).

So praying is making love with the Lover who is the Maker of love. The miracle: what should be one-sided (me on my knees to the Lover) has become a dialogue; the Lover's self-revelation in inspired scriptures has taken the initiative to make that possible. Through dialogue I focus my love on issues of immediate concern—frustration at failure, triumph at the presence of love, thanksgiving for the privilege of being "me" in love, joy at being forgiven by the one whose being is mercy.

Praying, both formally and informally, reminds me to see the God who creates in the beauty of nature, reminds me to look at the God who in Jesus took the path of self-giving love to the limit, reminds me of the God who is Spirit, alive alongside and within me, offering the vision of future fulfillment beyond my wildest dreams.

Each day I pray that the Lover will never forget me, flawed lover that I am, that I will be taken into risen life, and that I will be absorbed into the one who is love.

Jihad Youssef

When I pray I'm in a relationship, in a connection, in a moment of truth where I'm received and accepted just as I am. Praying, you are loved as you are; it's a space in which you are alone with the One, the loved One, who is receiving you. Nevertheless, exactly there, after leaving everything and forgetting everyone, you discover that you are not alone and that you find and encounter them all in what is called the communion of saints. Prayer is hospitality since God is your guest and you are his. It is an annihilation, an absorption in God, prostrating to Him, worshiping Him, and asking for mercy and wisdom. Yet it is also an occasion to be yourself, to be an open book in front of the One who can write there a word of life. Moreover, it is in Him that you know yourself and keep knowing Him more and loving Him more and more. This gives sense to everything. Prayer is at the same time an attitude of intercession that even makes possible the sunrise every morning.

Notes

1. *The Mathnawi of Jalaluddin Rumi*, trans. and ed. Reynold A. Nicholson (Cambridge: Trustees of the E. J. W. Gibb Memorial, 1990), vol. 1, bk. 1, l. 3796.
2. Ibid., vol. 2, bk. 4, ll. 435–38.

Index